Robert Lowell and the sublime

Robert Lowell

Oil painting by Mary Hart, based on Houghton Library photograph,
shelf mark bMS Am 1905, by permission of the Houghton Library, Harvard University.

ROBERT LOWELL
and the sublime

Henry Hart

Foreword by Jay Parini

Syracuse University Press

First Edition 1995

95 96 97 98 99 00   6 5 4 3 2 1

The paper used in this publication meets the minimum requirements
of American National Standard for Information Sciences—Permanence
of Paper for Printed Library Materials, ANSI Z39.48-1984. ∞™

Library of Congress Cataloging-in-Publication Data
Hart, Henry, 1954–
Robert Lowell and the sublime / Henry Hart.
p. cm.
Includes bibliographical references and index.
ISBN 0-8156-2610-X (cl). — ISBN 0-8156-2658-4 (pb.)
1. Lowell, Robert, 1917–1977—Criticism and interpretation.
2. Sublime, The, in literature. I. Title.
PS3523.089Z684 1995
811'.52—dc20   94-38430

For Susannah and Maria

Henry Hart is an associate professor in the English Department at the College of William and Mary. He is the American editor of *Verse*, an international poetry journal, and has published widely on modern poetry in such journals as *The New England Review, The Southern Review, Contemporary Literature, Twentieth Century Literature*, and *Journal of Modern Literature*. He is the author of *The Poetry of Geoffrey Hill, Seamus Heaney: Poet of Contrary Progressions*, and a collection of poems, *The Ghost Ship*.

Contents

Foreword

Jay Parini

In "A Clear Midnight," a remarkable late lyric, Whitman writes:

> This is the hour O Soul, thy free flight into the wordless,
> Away from books, away from art, the day erased, the
> lesson done,
> Thee fully forth emerging, silent, gazing, pondering the
> themes thou lovest best,
> Night, sleep, death and the stars.
> . . . .

This "free flight into the wordless" epitomizes the tradition of the sublime, which is often marked by a quasi-Gnostic desire to move beyond the shackles of ordinary language, with its petty distinctions and calibrations, into an exalted state of perfect understanding.

But the state of release into wordlessness that Whitman evokes is merely the telos barely glimpsed by poets in the midst of their individual agon, their battle with powers that threaten to overtake or thwart their heroic progress toward this ecstatic end. Whitman's poem may be seen as the last stage in a dialectical dance marked by contention. The American way of poetry, which Henry Hart—a poet-scholar of considerable talent—writes about with great assurance in this important book on Robert Lowell, is agonist to a fault, rooted in a poetics of conflict. From Emerson on, our poets have felt compelled to test their imaginative strength against the heavenly powers, becoming self-elected heirs (as Lowell himself points out in an interview quoted by Hart) to Milton's Lucifer and Melville's Ahab. The only question in their mind is, Who is the stronger force?

The danger of this antithetical quest for the sublime, for "Night, sleep, death and the stars," is one of solipsism; poets all too easily sink into their own world, cut off from the daily stuff of life. What Keats calls "the egotistical sublime" is fraught with existential pitfalls; in fact, one sees too many American poets falling prey to easy sublimity and making fools of themselves on paper and in public. Although Lowell occasionally fell from the heights of sublimity to the depths of the ridiculous, he strove to anchor his poetry in history, and his ultimate reach for the sublime in his best work attains a grandeur all its own.

Hart has done some admirable digging in libraries and manuscript collections, taking us back to Lowell's beginnings—at St. Mark's, at Harvard, and at Kenyon—to find early and telling instances of an interest in the poetics of sublimity. This interest became an obsession that dominated his poetry from start to finish. "If 'one story and one story only' resonates through Lowell's work, as Randall Jarrell and more recent critics have maintained, it recapitulates an agon in which one daemonic figure struggles against another in order to attain sublime power," writes Hart. In a sense, this version of "the sublime" as a concept offers a key to understanding Lowell's seemingly disconnected and inorganic oeuvre. The Promethean struggle to beat down all figures or conventions standing in the way of enlightenment, of "Night, sleep, death and the stars," links the early religious, the autobiographical, and the political phases of Lowell's work. It is no surprise that his translation of *Prometheus Bound* became the focus of his work in the mid-1960s, when all his political and artistic struggles appear to have come to a head and he found himself longing "to break loose, like the chinook / salmon," as he writes memorably in "Waking Early Sunday Morning."

Life Studies, which must be counted among the most influential books published by an American poet since *Leaves of Grass*, was in some ways an anomaly, and Lowell returned to his at times maniacal pursuit of the sublime in *Near the Ocean* and later books, where the ground of contest becomes at once the family and "history," read as projection of the family romance. In mapping Lowell's development through the concept of the sublime, Hart clarifies the landscape of this poet's complex imagination in highly original ways, connecting Lowell firmly with the tradition of American Romanticism that looks back to English and German Romanticism and, beyond that, to Milton for inspiration.

Hart's study comes at just the right moment. Lowell's personality (and aura, which had as much to do with his family connection as with his poetic talent) was such that it tended to overshadow the poetry, and, sadly, he became as much a creature of publicity (especially during the Vietnam War, which he strongly opposed) as a man admired for his originality or depth as a writer. His poetic stock was extremely valuable at the time of his death, but the slippage began soon after. Although he is hardly obscure, Lowell has been losing ground with serious readers of American poetry, who seem to have little interest in "confessional poetry," a school that existed largely in the minds of literary journalists.

The real nature of Lowell's achievement will take many years to assess properly, but Henry Hart has begun the hard work of reading Lowell in the context of a tradition that he has both extended and modified. The tradition of the sublime is perhaps the central tradition of our literature (and politics), and Hart's sensitive reading of its permutations on American soil and its specific applications to Lowell can only enhance our understanding of this important poet in significant ways.

Preface

Although the genealogy of most scholarly books is complex, this book's is relatively simple. My two largest debts are to Ashley Brown, who informed me of John Crowe Ransom's aesthetics class at Kenyon College in which Robert Lowell studied the sublime, and to Jahan Ramazani, who first apprised me of recent scholarship on the sublime. An NEH Travel to Collections grant supported a research trip to the Houghton Library at Harvard, where I hunted through Lowell's papers for clues to his obsession with the sublime. Generous semester and summer research grants from the College of William and Mary enabled me to take time off to work on the book. My wife, Susannah Livingston, offered encouragement as well as editorial help with the final manuscript. Steven Gould Axelrod gave me sound scholarly advice for improving the manuscript. Rob Wilson, Jay Parini, and Robert Crawford also helped along the way.

Several of these chapters appeared in preliminary form in scholarly journals, and I am indebted to their editors and readers for their comments: *The New England Review*, "Robert Lowell and the Religious Sublime" (1991, 14:27–47); *Twentieth Century Literature*, "Robert Lowell and the Politics of the Sublime" (1991, 37:105–29); *Contemporary Literature*, "Robert Lowell and the Psychopathology of the Sublime" (1991, 32:496–520); *The Southern Review*, "Robert Lowell and the New Critical Sublime" (1992, 27:353–70); *The William and Mary Review*, "Robert Lowell: The Tragedy of Sublimity" (1993, 31:82–101); *ESQ: A Journal of the American Renaissance*, "Robert Lowell, Emerson, and the American Sublime" (1993, 39: 279–307).

Williamsburg, Virginia   Henry Hart
January 1994

Acknowledgments

Permission to quote from materials listed below is gratefully acknowledged.

Excerpts from uncollected material from the Robert Lowell archive reprinted by permission of the Houghton Library, Harvard University.

Excerpts from *Life Studies*, by Robert Lowell, copyright © 1959 by Robert Lowell, copyright renewed © 1987 by Harriet Lowell, Sheridan Lowell, and Caroline Lowell; *For the Union Dead*, by Robert Lowell, copyright © 1964 by Robert Lowell, copyright renewed © 1992 by Harriet Lowell, Sheridan Lowell, and Caroline Lowell; *Near the Ocean*, by Robert Lowell, copyright © 1967 by Robert Lowell; *Notebook 1967–68*, by Robert Lowell, copyright © 1967, 1968, 1969 by Robert Lowell; *Prometheus Bound*, by Robert Lowell, copyright © 1967, 1969 by Robert Lowell; *The Dolphin*, by Robert Lowell, copyright © 1973 by Robert Lowell; *For Lizzie and Harriet*, by Robert Lowell, copyright © 1973 by Robert Lowell; *History*, by Robert Lowell, copyright © 1973 by Robert Lowell; "Epilogue" from *Day by Day*, by Robert Lowell, copyright © 1977 by Robert Lowell; *Collected Prose*, by Robert Lowell, edited by Robert Giroux, copyright © 1987 by Caroline Lowell, Harriet Lowell, and Sheridan Lowell. Reprinted by permission of Farrar, Straus and Giroux, Inc.

Excerpts from *Land of Unlikeness* by Robert Lowell reprinted by permission of Cummington Press.

Excerpts from *Lord Weary's Castle* by Robert Lowell, copyright © 1946 and renewed 1974 by Robert Lowell, reprinted by permission of Harcourt Brace and Company.

Introduction

If Longinus were alive today, he would be astonished by the numerous interpretations of what he once called *hypsos*. For the Greek philosopher who may or may not have written *On the Sublime* sometime during the third century, *hypsos* or "loftiness" was achieved by deploying a highly charged rhetoric that, paradoxically, elevated the minds of listeners above rhetoric. Geniuses like Homer displayed "a consummate excellence and distinction of language . . . not to persuade the audience but to transport them out of themselves" (125). The goal of this high style was ecstasy rather than advocacy. If orators convinced and poets enchanted, Longinus argued, the speechmakers should court the muses more deliberately. "A well-timed flash of sublimity," he declared, "scatters everything before it like a bolt of lightning and reveals the full power of the speaker at a single stroke" (125). Whoever witnessed this Zeus-like rhetorical power could not help but absorb the divine afflatus. The listener, wholly mesmerized by the speaker, lost his or her sense of identity, merged with the source of power, and ultimately imagined that he or she *was* the source, that he or she produced the declaimed text. To reach the joyful altitudes of *hypsos*, one needed to be propelled by divine hubris.

Although Longinus found Plato's writings sublime, and therefore must have believed, at least during moments of enraptured reading, that he *was* Plato, the older philosopher initiated what would become a deep-seated opposition to the poetic frenzies Longinus extolled. While Longinus was hardly an inflammatory anarchist who thought *all* inspirations divine (he inveighed against the stylistic excesses that render descriptions ridiculous and characterizations implausible), he nevertheless resisted Plato's rigorous devotion to reason. He persistently trumpeted the "fine frenzy" (143) of poetic enthusiasm and the "violent upheaval of the soul [that] demands disorder" (191). For this early connoisseur of chaos, thrilling

xvii

disorder was the cause as well as the effect of the sublime's transfiguring power.

It was not until Nicolas Boileau published a French translation of *Peri Hypsos* in 1674 that the term "sublime" gained currency in Europe, and it was not until the eighteenth century that it became a topic of literary scrutiny and debate in England. Edmund Burke's *Philosophical Enquiry into the Origin of Our Ideas of the Sublime and Beautiful* (1757) gave the subject its most sustained commentary and also prompted its sundry migrations into disciplines beyond aesthetics. Longinus had provided a precedent for allegorizing the sublime by examining *hypsos* in religious, political, ethical, and rhetorical contexts. The sublimity of great writers, he contended, was comparable to the "divine power" that "impregnated" the Pythian priestess and "inspired [her] to utter oracles" (167). Sublime writers, as mythopoetic Romantics would claim centuries later, were like gods dispensing grace to dazzled audiences: "Even those who are not easily moved by the divine afflatus share the enthusiasm" (167). With regard to the politics of sublimity, Longinus stipulated that the nobility of the gods, heroes, and great writers can be fostered only by a democracy that ensures open competition.

His conception of the sublime, however, was based not on a democratic flattening of hierarchical relations between master and slave so much as on their reinforcement. It is ironic that Longinus should condemn his immediate society for its enslavement to pleasure, extravagance, insolence, disorder, and other vices, because his sublime requires the listener's sudden enslavement to a masterful rhetorical performance and ends with the listener's extravagant claim that he or she has usurped the master's position. For Longinus the sublime stimulates presumptuous self-promotion, an ascent toward illusory status, and finally a false belief in originality and mastery. It spurs megalomaniac fantasy. The newly empowered reader or listener, giddily convinced that the once oppressive hierarchical relations have been overturned, soon learns that the revolutionary act is an example of what Freud called "the omnipotence of thought" or "wish fulfillment." After the sublime moment the relation between authoritarian author and subservient witness remains.

Interpretations and critiques of the sublime have a venerable genealogy, yet few could have predicted their sudden and widespread recrudescence in contemporary criticism. By revealing the aesthetic term's relevance to many different doctrines, commentators have created a multidimensional "allegory of the sublime." "All commentary is allegorical interpretation" (*Anatomy* 84), Northrop Frye once commented. In explaining what we read, we inevitably transform it according to our favorite heuristic models. The Freudian decodes texts in terms of oedipal plots, sexual symbols, and the libidinal dynamics of the mind; the Marxist, in terms of class struggles, quests for productive power, and the multitudinous depredations of capitalism. Dante, steeped in biblical exegesis, proposed a Christian model of interpretation, encoding his great allegory, *The Divine Comedy*, so that its significance resonated in literal, typological, tropological, and anagogical contexts. Like all allegories, Dante's was ideological: a translation of pagan texts and historical experience into the hierarchical Catholic cosmos of sin and salvation. As Frye noted, "Allegory smooths out the discrepancies in a metaphorical structure by making it conform to a conceptual standard" (*Great Code* 10). Whether the "conceptual standard" belongs to Freudian, Marxist, Christian, or some other doctrine, critic and artist read and write their materials according to preordained patterns and perspectives. For the allegorist, as for Oscar Wilde, critic and artist serve similar idols. As the etymological root of allegory—the Greek *allegorein*, to "speak in other terms"—intimates, they speak in ways other than the literal way and speak for others in ways other than the ways they literally speak. They take other texts, whatever they may be, and translate them into diverse ideological contexts to legitimize their meanings.

From an early age Robert Lowell gravitated toward allegorical writing and interpretation because of his love for conceptual density, be it Freudian, Marxist, or Christian. Even as a teenager he was reading Dante's *Divine Comedy*, absorbing Charles Eliot Norton's commentary (Parker 252), and trying his hand at allegorical exegesis. An article inspired by an allegorical drawing of the desert saint, Simeon, by his school friend, Frank Parker, revealed in germinal form a hermeneutic tendency that would intensify during his twenties, when Aquinas, Dante, and their various Catholic commentators became obsessions. His youthful commentary "The True Light" culminated with a reflection on the distance between sublime ideals and mundane facts. Even when he cast off his early symbolic armor to confront the world more nakedly in *Life Studies* and successive volumes, Lowell tended to interpret and dramatize his experience as a conflict between sublimity and reality that had literary, political, psychological, and religious ramifications. Like allegorical writers of the past, Lowell depicted an ongoing *psychomachia* between clashing personae and principles. Arrayed on his phantasmal battlefield were presidents, dictators, fathers, mothers, gods, and devils in all their august and daunting splendor. Like Don Quixote tilting at windmills, Lowell engaged these illusory figures in struggles for sublime power; when more realistic perspectives prevailed, he struggled to divest himself of all such illusions.

Surveying the transition from explicit allegories written during the Middle Ages and Renaissance "to the most elusive, anti-explicit and anti-allegorical" literature of modernity, Frye speaks of "a sliding scale" of forms that exist between the two poles (*Anatomy* 91). Scholars have often pointed out that Lowell's career evolved along this "sliding scale" from poems saturated "with a large and insistent doctrinal interest" (*Anatomy* 91) to confessional and historical poems saturated with quotidian facts. Throughout his poetic transformations, however, Lowell kept returning to a central narrative that expressed his deepest compulsions. After his famous shift in *Life Studies* and *For the Union Dead*, for instance, Lowell insisted that there was as much continuity as discontinuity with his earlier style.

As if to rebuke the critics who praised him for jettisoning his dense religious symbolism and opting for a more secular one, Lowell said of his middle poems: "In many ways they seem to me more religious than the early ones. . . . I don't feel my experience changed very much. . . . It's very much the same sort of thing that went into the religious poems—the same sort of struggle, light and darkness, the flux of experience" (*CP* 250). His friend Randall Jarrell delineated this recurrent struggle in his astute review of *Lord Weary's Castle*: "Underneath all these poems 'there is one story and one story only.' . . . The poems understand the world as a sort of conflict of opposites" ("From the Kingdom" 19). Against "the Old Law, imperialism, militarism, capitalism, Calvinism, Authority, the Father," Lowell's various combatants struggle for salvation. They long for "the realm of freedom, of the grace that has replaced the Law, of the perfect liberator whom the poet calls Christ" (19–20). In the battle between opposing forces Lowell wielded such rhetorical firepower that Jarrell encouraged him to restrain it. In an essay documenting the way Jarrell shaped Lowell's early style, Bruce Michelson comments: "Oversaying leads to hot air much more often than it does to the sublime. It is a testament to Jarrell's eye as a reader that he saw in Lowell the chance for the better fate, his susceptibility to the worse one" (144).

The conflict at the heart of Lowell's "one story," as Jarrell surely knew, was oedipal. It is interesting to note that recent critics like Jonathan Veitch find the same oedipal drama implicit in later volumes as well. Veitch claims: "Despite its scope . . . each poem in *History* seems to tell the same story or, at least, the same kind of story" (458). Encoded in Lowell's idiosyncratic telling of history is "a typology, rooted in the 'unchanging fire' of the oedipal drama, that is highly resistant to Lowell's manifest desire for a world that breeds on change" (461). According to Veitch, Lowell comments on the "great men" of history as if they were part of "a monstrous 'historical' allegory. . . . Monumentalized into colossi of obscene desire, the 'heroes' of *History* are Freudian drives allegorized out of their tacitly assumed 'naturalness'" (478). In this "allegory," Veitch rightly observes, Lowell is self-reflexive; he passes judgment on his own desires for power as well as those he finds mirrored in history's famous and infamous leaders. His purpose is "to demythologize even the therapeutic Freud whose disciple he had been" (478).

In his monumental study *Allegory*, Angus Fletcher points out that allegorical narratives typically chart "daemonic agents" battling or questing for ideals whose sublime power triggers an ambivalent response. He notes that "enthusiasm"—the kind so prized by the early Protestant sects that Lowell both identified with and vilified—often accompanies devotion to sublime ideals and often has pathological consequences. As a result the "daemonic agent" compulsively engaged in the allegorical pursuit of godly ideals and of God Himself often views his enchantments critically. Sublime ideals, after all, are terrible as well as awesome. In his oedipal drive to combat, embrace, and triumph over powerful father figures and the ideals they represent, Lowell often catapulted himself toward them with the manic frenzy he called "pathological enthusiasm" (Hamilton 227). Throughout his life Lowell attempted with the aid of religious rituals, psychotherapy, antipsychotic drugs, and poetry to assuage his addiction to both enthusiasm and sublimity. "What so many find wrong with American culture is the monotony of the sublime" ("Talk" 43), he told A. Alvarez late in life.

What so many found wrong with Lowell was the monotony of *his* enthusiasms and sublimities. Although sublimity and monotony are obvious opposites, in Lowell's psyche and culture the cycle of mania and depression, enthusiastic flight and embarrassing fall, sublime boom and tragic crash was so entrenched that he could only view the sublime's appeal as tiresome. "Most of his poems are networks of interlocking ironies; they are composed of elaborate patterns of synthesis and disintegration, doubt and faith, affirmation and rejection" (18), Hugh Staples pointed out in his seminal study of Lowell. His poems are composed of paradox and ambivalence partly because of his divided attitude toward the sublime. If Lowell's goal was "the unified central vision of what Emerson termed 'the complete man,'" a vision that healed the "basic bifurcation in American literature between writers who experience primarily with the head and those who experience primarily with the blood" (Axelrod 10–11), his unities between brain and blood were truces in an ongoing war. His intellectual campaigns for the sublimity conferred by high ideals persisted, and in the end never reached a healthy resolution.

Lowell described his way of interpreting personal and historical experience as an embattled quest for the sublime most succinctly in his two interviews with Alvarez in the 1960s. In the first he refers to himself as a kind of American Everyman, an archetypal Ahab embodying the best and worst traits of his country: "I'm very conscious of belonging to the country I do, which is a very powerful country and, if I have an image of it, it would be one taken from Melville's *Moby Dick:* the fanatical idealist who brings the world down in ruins through some sort of simplicity of mind. I believe that's in our character and in my own personal character; I reflect that it's a danger for us" ("Conversation" 35). In the second interview he speaks of and for American artists who strive to attain the sublime while aware of its tragic cost. Once again he comments on his personality and country in a typological way, seeking out personae from the past whose flights and falls foreshadow the nefarious aspects of the American sublime: "We leap for the sublime. You might almost say American literature and culture begins with *Paradise Lost.* I always think there are two great symbolic figures that stand behind American ambition and culture. One is Milton's Lucifer and the other is Captain Ahab: these two sublime ambitions that are doomed and ready, for their idealism, to face any amount of violence" ("Talk" 42). The single-minded idealism of these prototypical figures compels them to overthrow the terrifying grandeurs of God and Moby Dick in order to rule in their stead. In Steven Gould Axelrod's words, by consciously aligning himself with these and other American prototypes, "Lowell made himself into the classic figure of the American poet, a Whitman for our time, though a more tragic one, as befits our time" (7).

Again and again Lowell scoured the past for precursors whose quests for sublimity were analogous to his own. "For all its dynamism, his poetic oeuvre is unified," Axelrod contends. "At its center is Lowell himself, discovering, altering, creating the conditions of his own existence" (4), and, it might be added, recruiting others who shared his penchant for the sublime. He read and wrote public history the way he read and wrote private history—as a struggle for powerful and empowering ideals. Vacillating between empathy and protest, self-aggrandizement and self-abasement, Lowell placed those responsible for the world's terrible beauties and grotesque failures at center stage. Irvin Ehrenpreis developed this theme when he wrote in "The Age of Lowell": "For an age of world wars and prison states, when the Faustian myth of science produces the grotesquerie of fall-out shelters, the decorous emotion seems a fascinated disgust" (155). When he declared, "Among living poets writing in English nobody has expressed this emotion with the force and subtlety of Robert Lowell" (155), he could have been referring to one version of the sublime. A "fascinated disgust," after all, is little different from the "sort of delightful horror" or "tranquility tinged with terror" (Carritt 43) that Edmund Burke defined as the sublime in one of Lowell's undergraduate textbooks. According to Ehrenpreis, the emotion was embedded in the typological structure of Lowell's life and art.

In *Life Studies*, for instance, "Without losing the tone of fascinated disgust, he now found it possible not only to treat himself as part of history but to treat history as part of himself. The course of his life became the analogue of the life of his era; the sufferings of the poet became a mirror of the sufferings of whole classes and nations" (174). Lowell envisioned his life allegorically until he died.

"All your poems are in a sense one poem" (Seidel 57), Lowell once said, but does this mean that Lowell's "one poem" or "one story" amounts to an allegory of the sublime? Before leaping to conclusions, it is prudent to recall Maureen Quilligan's skeptical evaluation of such critically fashionable terms as "allegories of reading" in *The Language of Allegory*. The genre of allegory that includes *The Divine Comedy*, *The Faerie Queene*, and *The Pilgrim's Progress*, as she points out, both resembles and differs from *allegoresis*, which is a method of commentary. Historically *allegoresis* came first; it was essentially an attempt to reconcile primitive texts with a society's current, prevailing ideology. If Homer's or Virgil's epics were pagan, they could be transfigured—reinterpreted or rewritten—so that they conformed to Christian concepts. The "whole conception of allegory—derived from the process of imposing it on originally nonallegorical texts—was then applied to actual allegorical narratives, that is, to those poems taking place in a specialized, often dreamlike landscape peopled by personified abstractions" (Quilligan 31) and plotted according to puns and etymologies (as in *The Faerie Queene*, where "error," which means "wandering," instigates the "errant" wandering in the story). As Quilligan reminds us, a "subtly complicated connection . . . exists between allegorical narrative and *allegoresis*. . . . The allegorical author simply does what the allegorical critic does, but he writes a commentary on his own text rather than someone else's" (51, 53). According to Quilligan, generic allegories are deeply self-reflexive; their narrative actions are struggles to figure out, to interpret properly, a text or even a single word. Typically their characters dwell on the Bible, their deeds and misdeeds amounting to a commentary on the Bible's significance.

It is tempting to construe Lowell's narratives of flights and falls as an etymological commentary on "sublime," since the word derives from Latin roots meaning both "uplifted" (*sublimis*) and "under the threshold" (*sublimen*). The enthusiasms of his historical as well as contemporary figures, like his own, are both inspiring and dispiriting. Possessed by daemonic ambitions, his personae soar above natural or moral limits and, as a result of their transgressions, plunge below those limits to their dooms. A typological view of experience, errant quests through dreamlike landscapes (usually nightmarish hells and purgatories), personifications—those quintessential denizens of allegory—and abundant worldplay, characterize at least Lowell's early poetry. The encompassing structure of his oeuvre, however, differs markedly from an allegorical narrative. Riven with paradox and skepticism, Lowell's "doctrinal interests" fluctuate to a degree that precludes the sort of stable architecture characteristic of allegory.

Although the plots of traditional allegories tend to follow the compass needle of comedy, moving through divisions and ordeals toward happy reconciliations, Lowell's plots move in the opposite direction—toward tragic fragmentation, despair, and death. And his style shifts away from allegorical symbolism toward greater realism as his career progresses. The "figure in the carpet"—Jarrell's "one story"—may stay the same, but the fibers composing it change. Discussing Lowell's early allegorical writing, where "obvious patterns or paradigms control the subject matter," Charles Altieri maintains that in *Life Studies*, Lowell adopts the more secular procedures of prose: "Now Lowell strives for syntactic and narrative casualness, a fidelity to the flux of experience that makes the poem appear spontaneous reflection and not artifact. Even when organizing patterns of repetition are perceived, they resist being formed into a general interpretative statement" (23). The patterns may resist neat interpretative conclusions because of their sundry ambiguities, but all of Lowell's poems, early and late, offer such resistance. Furthermore, a general pattern *is* discernible in poems written for *Life Studies* and following volumes, and it relates to the sublime.

No one has investigated the importance of the sublime in Lowell's work, even though the aesthetic term engaged him in impassioned debate throughout his career. The following pages explain Lowell's conception of the sublime; set it in the context of commentaries by Longinus, Edmund Burke, Immanuel Kant, Harold Bloom, Thomas Weiskel, Rob Wilson, and others; and show how his moral critique of the sublime influenced his stylistic development. My opening chapter focuses on Lowell's first forays into *allegoresis*—his commentary on his school friend's drawing of the pillar saint, his brief article on Dante's *Inferno*—and examines his early allegorical style. His interest in the sublime intensified during his college days at Harvard and Kenyon, so it should come as no surprise that his poems published in student journals and in his first book, *Land of Unlikeness*, should allegorize the sublime. I scrutinize how these poems resemble and differ from traditional allegories, and explain how Milton's Lucifer and Melville's Ahab become prototypical "daemonic agents" whose "sublime ambitions," whether political, psychological, or religious, are ultimately tragic. In a way his questers coalesce into an American Everyman with whom Lowell feels an ambivalent affinity. This ambivalence is borne out in "Waking Early Sunday Morning" and several sonnets of his late period. Because Lowell's ambivalence toward the sublime derived in part from his tangled relations with his parents, and because Lowell deemed Freud a kind of contemporary savior, I end the chapter by sketching out the fundamental oedipal drama behind Lowell's engagement with the sublime.

With her usual perspicacity, Elizabeth Bishop once remarked: "Cal (Lowell) and I in our very different ways are both descendants from the Transcendentalists" (quoted in Costello 8). In the second chapter I investigate the influence of Emerson's transcendentalist notions of the sublime on Lowell. Lowell's early poems frequently refer to Emerson, but usually in a disparaging way. Following the New Critics, who dominated the literary scene in the 1930s and 1940s, Lowell mocked Emerson's Romantic views. He was not, however, as anti-Emerson as he pretended, and later in his life admitted as much. Emerson's discussion of sublimity and enthusiasm in "The Over-Soul" and in his other writings is important to a genealogy of Lowell's views on the sublime. Transformed into a hometown Ahab or Lucifer by Lowell's overheated imagination, Emerson was another prototypical forefather with whom the poet quarreled. According to Lowell's early Catholic, conservative perspective, Emerson's sublime idealism was a recipe for all sorts of individual and political calamities. Buttressed by his Southern Fugitive mentors, Lowell claimed that the modern military and industrial wasteland was partly caused by Emerson's revolutionary Protestantism, his repudiations of tradition and history, and his transcendental approach to nature. In his later, more radical moods, however, Lowell was just as revolutionary, iconoclastic, and transcendental as Emerson.

The third chapter explains the influence of John Crowe Ransom, Allen Tate, Yvor Winters, and Wallace Stevens on the development of Lowell's attitudes toward the sublime. Ransom's class, Philosophy 25—Aesthetics, which Lowell took at Kenyon in 1939, and its textbook, *Philosophies of Beauty* by E. F. Carritt (a collection of commentaries on the sublime and beautiful from Longinus, Burke, Kant, Georg Hegel, Arthur Schopenhauer, and others), provided Lowell with lessons he never forgot. Drawing on collected and uncollected poetry and prose, I explore Lowell's early work for traces of Ransom's Kantian belief that the sublime is rational, moral, and divine. I also show how Lowell increasingly rebelled against Ransom's Kantian principles by identifying the sublime with irrational, amoral, and rebellious figures like Ahab and Lucifer. This reaction was provoked in part by his other mentor, Allen Tate, who summed up his aesthetic principles in "Longinus and the 'New Criticism,' " and by Wallace Stevens, whose meditations on the darker side of the sublime in "Esthétique du Mal" and "The American Sublime" had a lasting effect on Lowell.

After tracing his preoccupation with the sublime to Romantic as well as to neoclassical sources, I begin to map the different contexts in which the sublime resonated most noticeably for Lowell. First I concentrate on political history. Although Lowell usually identified with the "sublime ambitions" of history's great men and women, he also recoiled from them. On the one hand he followed Ezra Pound, William Butler Yeats, and other modern writers by romanticizing authoritarian political figures because they transcended the mediocrity of the status quo. On the other hand he mocked them for their grandiose pretensions and condemned them for their brutality. "I was never to understand what Lowell's politics were" (250), Alfred Kazin wrote, expressing the general incomprehension felt by his friends. Lowell's political vacillations between revolutionary and reactionary extremes were due in part to his ambivalence toward the sublime and to his conviction that in pursuing sublime ideals, nations and individuals often destroy what they should preserve. For Lowell, saint and Satan were the two faces of his Janus-like self. His friend Stanley Kunitz recounts insightfully:

> It had required a heroic endeavor to construct the strong persona of his poems: actually, he had a weak grip on his identity. In manic episodes he had confused himself with Christ, St. Paul and Hitler—particularly Hitler, whose dark spirit rose violently to possess him. Men of power had always fascinated him. Once, when I visited him at McLean's Hospital in Boston, he read "Lycidas" aloud to me, in his improved version, firmly convinced that he was the author of the original. ("Sense" 234)

All too aware of his obsessions, Lowell again and again stressed the connection between "sublime ambitions" and their monstrous or ludicrous consequences. History for Lowell was a kind of masquerade in which he appeared as a satanic Everyman constantly changing masks in order to project, expose, and evaluate his baffling personality. Typologically merging different characters from different historical periods to reflect myriad aspects of himself, his sublime drama resembled allegories of old, but in severely altered form.

Drawing on Longinus's contention that "the true sublime, by some virtue of its nature, elevates us: uplifted with a sense of proud possession, we are filled with joyful pride, as if we had ourselves produced the very thing we heard" (139), in my next chapter I explain that Lowell's uplifting identifications with famous authors and infamous authoritarian figures were partly due to his manic-depressive illness. Because Lowell declared that Freud spoke to his condition more incisively than any other thinker (according to Katherine Wallingford, "To Allen Tate he bragged in December 1953 that he had 'been reading . . . all Freud' " [5]), it makes sense that he would allegorize his sublime compulsions in terms of a psychoanalytical model. Weiskel's Freudian interpretations of the sublime are particularly relevant, and I apply them to the way Lowell depicted his "family romance."

When Lowell shrugged off his bouts of megalomania as merely "pathological enthusiasm," he was consciously drawing on a long-standing theological debate instigated by evangelical Protestant movements during the eighteenth century. This tradition, especially as it pertained to the New England divine Jonathan Edwards (the subject of several poems and of an unfinished biography by Lowell), influenced his attitudes toward the religious sublime. His early devotion to Catholic ritual and Catholic apologists attempted to curb the Protestant enthusiasms he found engrained in his culture and psyche. Catholic and Kantian rationalism, however, proved to be as much of a help as a hindrance because Lowell pursued all religious ideals with manic enthusiasm. On the religious plane of Lowell's "one story," his Lucifer, Ahab, and other related personae quest for godly ideals with a rapacity that makes a mockery of those ideals. As with other manifestations of sublimity, Lowell takes his religious alter egos to court for their odious betrayals of humane principles. His allegorical narratives move toward confession as he diagnoses his collusion in what Harold Bloom has called "the American Religion"—that loose array of Protestant sects that sanctifies enthusiasm and "the egotistical sublime."

"With the advent of postmodernism, the notion of the sublime has staged a spectacular comeback" ("Vulgar" 7), Terry Eagleton observed in a review. Much has been written on "the postmodern sublime" in an attempt to update the age-old term and make it apply to the baffling complexities, excesses, and hypnotic splendors of contemporary culture. In my last chapter I examine Lowell's stance toward the styles and themes of the postmodern sublime, especially in the sonnet sequences he wrote near the end of his career. What Fredric Jameson has called "the hysterical sublime" in avant-garde "schizophrenic writing" applies, to a certain extent, to the sort of postmodern style Lowell practiced in his sonnets. About *Notebook* (which was later transformed into *History*), Lowell said: "It is less an almanac than the story of my life" (*N* 262). His epic survey of history reveals more about Lowell's private history than about public history, and no doubt this is why he claimed his multivolume sonnet sequence reflected "the autobiographical sublime" (H 2701).

Notebook, History, and the other books of sonnets amount to a kind of postmodern *Prelude*, which, like Wordsworth's epic, focuses as much on the

"Growth of the Poet's Mind" as on the historical forces that shaped it. For Lowell-the-skeptic, the mind's compulsions and history may in the end be unknowable, unrepresentable, or at least distorted by language. The mind behind history's "sublime ambitions" and power struggles, he implies, is as quixotic and multitudinous as his own. Because Jean-François Lyotard has written interestingly on the Kantian theme of incommensurability between sublime ideals and historical facts, stressing the way postmodern literature tries to bear witness to transcendent ideals by presenting the unpresentable, I invoke his insights to better explain Lowell's later aesthetics.

In one of the most comprehensive and penetrating studies of the sublime to date, Rob Wilson in *American Sublime: The Genealogy of a Poetic Genre* addresses many of the themes addressed by Lowell and, like Lowell, essentially delivers an *allegoresis* of the sublime. His stated purpose is to "pluraliz[e] the American sublime as a poetic genre" (14). For Wilson, as for Lowell, the quest for sublimity has been endemic to American culture from the Puritans to the present. It defines the "master narrative" of American history and is embedded in our poetry from Bradstreet to Whitman, Stevens, and Lowell. It marks our national identity like a genetic code. "One beholds the American sublime, quite circularly then, by beholding 'America' as the site and subject of sublime production" (13), Wilson avers. The ethical questions that Wilson raises correspond uncannily to those that worried Lowell. "Can a cultural community distinguish itself or long survive without positing such a set of self-enabling fictions" as national grandeur and superpower status? "How does one stand to behold the American sublime, except as a function of one's historical positioning as an American who wills the ongoing grandeur (and grand poetry) of his people as collective subject? How does one stand to behold the American sublime, furthermore, without also representing the material damages and excesses of such confidently American claims to idealize power and to aggrandize the self as the source of such ends?" (13–14).

For Wilson the awesome and awful forces unleashed by the military machines of the Second World War cast a sobering pall over America's confidence in its "sublime ambitions" and "manifest destinies," just as they did for Lowell. "The American sublime came early and stayed late in the grander poems and paintings of this superpower climate: but Hiroshima marks one historical turning point, as does Auschwitz, after which the postmodern rapture-rupture of ecstatic forces in the landscape cannot help but disrupt and dismantle the American poet's comfortingly ethereal 'transports to summer' " (14–15). Such historical cataclysms threaten to transport the American poet to a nuclear winter rather than an edenic summer.

Envisioning their aesthetic terms through multicultural spectacles, both Wilson and Lowell strive to give a rigorously moral analysis of the sublime that balances its enabling powers against its disabling traumas.

In his pluralist genealogy Wilson discusses a natural sublime, a technological sublime, a nuclear sublime, a camp sublime, a postmodern sublime, as well as several other sublimes. Eagleton has posited a Marxist sublime; Jameson, a hysterical sublime; Bloom, a Gnostic and oedipal sublime; David Morris, a gothic sublime; Joanne Feit Diehl and Barbara Freeman, a feminist sublime. In fact, theorists have been pluralizing the sublime since Longinus first wrote *Peri Hypsos*. The result is an *allegoresis* of the sublime in which, as Frye would say, metaphorical structures are made to conform to the conceptual standards of commentators. Treatises on the sublime are translated so that their messages jibe with ideologies of the moment. Because the human struggle to transcend overpowering phenomena—whether they be wildernesses, hurricanes, tyrants, presidents, gods, patriarchs, superegos, or "strong" texts—is such a fundamental experience, the sublime has wide applicability. If "The sublime . . . in poststructuralist thinking becomes a fiction for transcendence, itself a fiction of absolute discourse" (2), as Mary Arensberg proposes in her introduction to *The American Sublime*, Lowell is poststructuralist in the way he exposes the fruits of sublimity as illusory. He is also prestructuralist in his compulsive quests to grasp those fruits, and sympathetic toward all those dangerous, deluded heroes who do the same.

While some critics state that the sublime has been interpreted in so many different ways that it is now a meaningless abstraction, it can be argued just as convincingly that the term's elaboration over the centuries has enriched rather than depleted its significance. In an America that seems to become more of a leviathanic "terrible beauty" every year, a critique of the sublime is particularly relevant to our contemporary situation. "At times," Arensberg writes, "the American sublime is a struggle with other poets: a strong daughter wrestling power from her father to make a clearing of her own. At other times, the sublime is a struggle with Otherness: the silence of a 'wide landscape of snow' or the ghostliness of the haunted muse. Yet the idea of the sublime is certainly not a moribund aesthetic, but, like Ishmael awash on the bark of Queequeg's coffin, the American sublime survives, alone to tell the darker thread of the story" (19). Although Lowell may have wished the sublime were "a moribund aesthetic," it survived with unusual tenacity in his life and writing.

More passionately and more ambivalently than most poets in the postwar era, Lowell played the role of America's Ishmael to tell of Ahabian hunts in which he as well as his nation indulged. His story was a dark but also an enlightening one. It was a multidimensional testimony to the sublime's terrifying yet enchanting allure, and it was descriptive as well as prescriptive. What Keats said of Shakespeare—that he "led a life of Allegory"—can be applied to Lowell. In a lecture Anthony Hecht once quoted from Keats's 1819 letter—"A Man's life of any worth is a continual allegory—and very few eyes can see the Mystery of his life—a life like the scriptures, figurative—which such people can no more make out than they can the hebrew Bible." Hecht concluded: "Through his constant moral and artistic endeavour to situate himself in the midst of our representative modern crises, both personal and political, [Robert Lowell] . . . has led, for us—as it were, in our behalf—a life of Allegory; and his works are the comments on it" (*Obbligati* 289). For Hecht as for Jarrell, Lowell was a kind of "unacknowledged legislator" or self-appointed representative of the problematic ideals of his nation and world. Interpreting and dramatizing his life as if it were figurative and universal, like a sacred text, he became exemplary. As allegorical as Christian in *Pilgrim's Progress*, he became a guide for others navigating a course among the pitfalls and peaks of the American sublime.

Robert Lowell and the sublime

I

Allegories, Tragedies, and Sublimities

Beginnings

Where is the beauty in the harsh turbulence of *Lord Weary's Castle?*
How can the themes of incest and suicide in *The Mills of the Kavanaughs*
be termed 'beautiful'?" (3), DeSales Standerwick once asked. Although he
reassures us that "beauty is there," it is not so much beauty as sublimity.
Whether they are laudatory or antagonistic, critics in general have shied
away from a rigorous examination of Lowell's interest in the sublime. If he
had never mentioned the ancient aesthetic term, the critical neglect would
be understandable. Considering his remarks to Alvarez, however, it is ob-
vious that he found the concept central to his poetry, personality, and cul-
ture. As it turns out, references to the sublime emerge in his earliest work
and continue to surface throughout his career. Papers in the Lowell archive
at Harvard's Houghton Library abound with allusions to the sublime. Exam
books and essays from Lowell's student days at St. Mark's prep school,
Harvard notes on Shakespeare and romanticism, and poems written at
Harvard as well as at Kenyon provide ample evidence of his early obsession.
Among Lowell's later papers are unpublished drafts of poems to friends
such as Bishop, Jarrell, and Berryman that document the political, psycho-
logical, and religious ramifications of the sublime. Many of his published
poems, plays, and essays also contain references to and reflections on the
sublime.

What are we to make of these many instances? One of the clues lies
in the interpretation of Frank Parker's allegorical drawing of St. Simeon
Stylites that Lowell published in *The Vindex*, St. Mark's literary journal. (It
is interesting to note that Lowell collaborated with Parker throughout his
career; Parker provided etchings for all of his books.) Although it is written
by a mere schoolboy, the *Vindex* article is uncanny in the way it predicts the

1

themes, attitudes, and narrative structures of Lowell's mature poetry. His friend's drawing depicts a "pillar saint" surrounded by types of "sublime ambition" whose misguided powers have led to ruin (Lowell fails to specify whether his saint is St. Simeon Stylites the Elder, who lived on top of a column in the fifth century, or St. Simeon Stylites the Younger, who perched on pillars for the better part of the sixth century). At the beginning of the explication he states with moralistic bravado: "The picture represents effort in the wrong direction. The idea that we wish to make clear is that tremendous labor and great intelligence, if applied toward the advancement of evil or petty ends, are of no avail. In the centre of the drawing is St. Simon [sic], the Stylite, a symbol of true knowledge. Arranged about him are fourteen types of would-be intellectuals and stagnant minds" ("True Light" 129). Lowell finishes with a quotation from Napoleon, who, after his disastrous retreat from Moscow in 1812, echoed Longinus on the sublime and the ridiculous: "St. Simon [sic] is elevated high above everyone else by comprehension of the true light. The book and the pen symbolize real intellectual attainment, while the plumb line signifies a quite natural feeling of superiority; but more important, his insecurity. From the sublime to the ridiculous is but a step' " (129). Throughout his career Lowell would compose variations on this theme, creating a multifaceted story in which different personae struggle to attain the sublime but, more often than not, topple from their pillars and suffer tragic or ridiculous ends.

An avid student of Dante and the Church Fathers in his early years, Lowell no doubt knew the medieval way of reading allegories and nonallegorical works for literal, typological, tropological, and anagogical meanings. As if revising this scheme, in his own poetry Lowell tended to imbue quests for the sublime with autobiographical, political, psychological, and religious significance. If "one story and one story only" informs his work, it recapitulates the agon in which one daemonic figure struggles against another in order to attain sublimity. On the historical or political plane this agon often takes the form of America's early struggle against British domination. Out of an idealistic war to establish a unique national identity, as Lowell told Alvarez, "American literature and culture begins." This in turn parallels the bellicose "family romance" in which Lowell, as typical oedipal son, skirmishes with his father and various other father figures to establish his own identity. The religious aspect of the story also involves a fight to create a separate identity. For Lowell it was exemplified by American Pilgrims and subsequent Protestant zealots rebelling against the Church of England to establish their own sects. Repeating this subversiveness in reverse order, Lowell himself rebelled against the Episcopalian conventions of his parents to become a Catholic, and in a later, more radical gesture imitated Lucifer's rebellion against God and all He represents. Dismissing all forms of orthodox Christianity, he plunged into an existential "dark night" and encountered what Bloom has called a "counter-sublime"—the liberating bliss and oppressive terror of the void. In trying to become an American Everyman, Lowell dramatized his quest for the sublime on different planes that tended to intersect, as they do in traditional allegories. Throughout his career he would use his various personae as masks as well as mirrors to express and reflect various aspects of the sublime. He would judge his personae's virtues and vices, elations and despairs, leaps toward heaven and dives toward hell as if they were his own.

Although Lowell's "one story" possesses neither the architectonic symmetry of a *Divine Comedy* nor the multitudinous personifications of a *Faerie Queene* or *Pilgrim's Progress*, it nevertheless shares some of the allegorical genre's basic traits. Fletcher could be commenting on Lowell when he outlines the close connection between allegory and the sublime. Like Lowell, he fastens on Lucifer and Ahab as representative "daemonic agents"—characters whose inner gods or enthusiasms (from *en-theos*, "the god within") control their actions and destinies. Possessed by a voice, a Platonic ideal, an idée fixe, "a *manie de perfection*, an impossible desire to become one with an image of unchanging purity," they pursue abstract ideals with uncompromising vigor and violence:

> If we were to meet an allegorical character in real life, we would say of him that he was obsessed with only one idea, or that he had an absolutely one-track mind, or that his life was patterned according to absolutely rigid habits from which he never allowed himself to vary. It would seem that he was driven by some hidden, private force; or, viewing him from another angle, it would appear that he did not control his own destiny, but appeared to be controlled by some foreign force, something outside the sphere of his own ego. (40–41)

It was a similar "foreign force" that drove Lowell's "sublime ambitions."

The Catholic imagery that informed Lowell's early books, *Land of Unlikeness, Lord Weary's Castle,* and *The Mills of the Kavanaughs*—harked back to the sort of hierarchical cosmos inherent in medieval and renaissance allegories. Tugged by both good and bad daemons, Lowell, however, was most interested in those like Lucifer and Ahab who transgressed established laws and limits, rejected orders and borders established on high, and consequently brought the ultimate order of the cosmos crashing down upon their heads. Although "The tendency is for allegories to resolve themselves into either of two basic forms . . . *battle* and *progress*" (151), as Fletcher avers, the symbolic action in Lowell's poetry typically merges the two because his quest for sublimity is a battle for power. The encounter with daunting figures is a mainstay of allegory, as is the moral ambivalence of the hero, who alternately craves and fears them. According to Fletcher, all of this parallels Kantian notions of the sublime. Kant's way of reading the awesome, terrifying, and mysterious "book of nature" as a power struggle culminating in the mind's triumphant awareness of its own divine, moral, and rational power to transcend nature corresponds to the traditional allegorical journey toward a constellation of ideals.

Although Lowell's preoccupation with the sublime can be traced through published and unpublished materials back to his student days at St. Mark's and Harvard, it was Ransom's aesthetics class at Kenyon that provided him with the most scholarly overview of the subject. Peter Taylor, a classmate who took the course with Lowell, confirms that Carritt's *Philosophies of Beauty* was the assigned text. Carritt's introduction dwells on the aesthetic debate initiated by Aristotle and Longinus between beauty as mimetic order and sublimity as dazzling disorder, and offers selections from nearly all the major treatises on the sublime as well as from less-known commentaries by John Dennis, Lord Shaftesbury, Joshua Reynolds, Archibald Alison, Uvedale Price, John Ruskin, George Santayana, and A. C. Bradley. Lowell's interest in the sublime received further impetus several years later (in 1948) when he attended Tate's lecture "Longinus and the 'New Criticism.'" The essay, later collected in *The Forlorn Demon*, underscored Longinus's contention that poetry's goal is *"Not to persuade, but to entrance, like a flash of lightning"* (Tate 510).

Most of the philosophers Lowell studied in Ransom's aesthetics class conceived of the sublime as a dynamic, dialectical response to the kind of grandeur that can be both terrifying and terrific, awful and awesome. Whether the sublime emanates from a daunting father or mother figure, a charismatic but odious political leader, a mysterious, cruel god, a stunning rhetorical performance, or an overwhelming scene in nature, the experience first oppresses the mind but then stimulates it to overcome the original shock. For Kant, whose aesthetic ideas had special importance for Ransom, the sublime fell into two main categories: the mathematical sublime and the dynamic sublime. Carritt highlights these two kinds of sublimity in *Philosophies of Beauty*. Of the first Kant writes:

> The [mathematical] sublime is that in comparison with which everything else is small. . . . Thus considered nothing which can be an object of the senses is to be called sublime. Our imagination strives for a progress

to infinity, but our reason demands a complete totality as an idea to be realized. So the very fact that our power of measuring sensible objects is inadequate to this idea, awakes the feeling of a power in us superior to sense. It is the use which we naturally make of certain objects to arouse this feeling, when we judge about them, that is absolutely great, though the object of sense is not; and any other use is comparatively trivial. So not the object should be called sublime, but rather the state of mind caused by an idea which excites our reflective faculty of judgement. So we can add to our previous formulas for explaining sublimity this: a thing is sublime, if the mere power of thinking it is evidence of a mental power surpassing all standards of sense. (119)

About the dynamic variety of sublimity he writes:

When we estimate nature as being dynamically sublime, our idea of it must be fearful. . . . We can, however, consider an object as fearful without fearing it, if we so estimate it that we imagine circumstances in which we might choose to resist it, and that then all resistance would be perfectly vain. . . . A man in a state of fear is as incapable of judging nature to be sublime as one possessed by longing or appetite is of judging about beauty. . . . Bold, overhanging rocks which seem to threaten us, storm-clouds piled up in heaven and moving on their way with lightnings and thunders, volcanoes with all their destructive might, hurricanes leaving a wake of devastation, the boundless ocean in its anger, a high waterfall in a mighty river:—such things reduce our power of resistance to impotence as compared with their might. But the sight of them is attractive in proportion to their fearfulness so long as we find ourselves in security, and we readily call such things sublime because they elevate the powers of our souls above their wonted level and discover in us a faculty for resistance of quite a different kind, which encourages us to measure ourselves against the apparent omnipotence of nature. . . . Nature is not aesthetically estimated to be sublime so far as it excites fear, but because it calls up in us the power, which is beyond nature, to regard all that we care for—wealth, health, life itself—as small. Thus we come to regard the might of nature, on which for all these things we are utterly dependent, as nevertheless, in relation to us and our personality, a power beneath which we need not bend if the maintenance of our highest principles were at stake. So nature is here called elevated or sublime just because she elevates the imagination to picture situations in which the mind can realize the proper sublimity of its own destiny as surpassing nature itself. (120–21)

For Lowell those prototypical heroes of doomed sublimity, Lucifer and Ahab, measure themselves against "the apparent omnipotence of nature" and achieve heroic or sublime stature by battling what ultimately defeats them.

Although Lowell's allegorical interpretation of Parker's drawing of St. Simeon applauds the sort of transcendental reason that Kant proclaimed sublime, it also points (with the symbolic plumb bob) to the sort of "daemonic agents" (such as Napoleon) who try to win sublime power in battles with overpowering foes only to lose it, or to the sort whose fanaticism makes shreds of conventional concepts of reason and morality. Demonstrating how traditional allegories generate plots by elaborating the etymological roots of words and by offering commentary on "pre-texts" as they go, Quilligan might point to Napoleon's statement, "From the sublime to the ridiculous is but a step," as the seed from which Lowell's *allegoresis* and allegory-like "one story" burgeons. "If the concept of text and commentary supplies the form of allegory" and "the concept of interpretation, of construing words, properly provides the subject of the narrative action" (Quilligan 62), one could argue that Lowell's poems refigure Napoleon's remark on the sublime by showing how relevant it is to all quests for sublimity, whether that sublimity lies above or below the threshold. Heaven and hell, for Lowell as for Blake, can be equally sublime, just as downward falls and upward falls can be equally ridiculous. In Lowell's *psychomachia*, id rebels against superego and superego rebels against id. As he demonstrated in his translation of *Prometheus Bound*, that traditional text for *allegoresis*, *nous* or mind grapples with *nomos* or law; Prometheus and Zeus both scramble for a sublimity that ultimately eludes them. For Lowell they are two more antithetical personae who enact the contrary meanings of "sublime."

Although Lowell's early, densely symbolic poems stray from the genre of allegory, like classic allegories they reenact and comment on biblical "pre-texts," often with the satirical intention of condemning secular existence while underscoring the Judeo-Christian ideals from which the contemporary world has fallen. In *Land of Unlikeness* there is a profound split between humanity and divinity, whether God above or God within. Like Dante, Spenser, and Bunyan, whom he studied as a young man, Lowell intends to depict the hellish chasm in all its horrors but also to bridge it with a language weighted with sacred meanings. Quilligan remarks: "Allegory is a genre for the fallen world, but is a genre self-conscious of its own fallenness. In a prelapsarian world at one with God, there is no 'other' for language to work back to, for there has been no fatal division" (182). To construct a linguistic bridge between hell and heaven, Lowell repeatedly fashions typological dramas that link him to biblical characters and events. As for Dante and Bunyan, his *psychomachia* is both individual and universal. Satan and Christ battle for his soul just as they battle for the soul of America and the soul of the world. Unlike their more saintly precursors, Lowell's satanic figures, in trying to usurp divine power, fall prey to enthusiasm, go mad, wreak horrible damage on themselves and others, and finally fall into perdition. His poems subvert the typical "divine comedy" or "pilgrim's progress" in which the hero's quest for communion with God is eventually fulfilled. Violent disunion and disillusionment characterize his ends.

Lowell's beginnings, on the other hand, are more typical; they often initiate narrative action by fleshing out the semantic possibilities of polysemous words and puns. For example, "The Drunken Fisherman," which appeared in *Land of Unlikeness* and *Lord Weary's Castle*, begins by punning on "sty": "Wallowing in this bloody sty, / I cast for fish that pleased my eye" (*LU* 33). On a literal level Lowell is fishing in a river for trout. "Sty," which refers to an enclosure for pigs as well as an inflammation in the eye, indicates that the external fishing is also internal, visionary, something done in the mind's eye, which in this case is bloodshot from drunkenness. The bloody river is a trope for his corrupt body and the world at war, and he also wittily suggests he is fishing "in a pig's eye." Christ—the fisher of men's souls—wallows in the poet's blood alongside Satan, who also fishes for men's souls. "Bloody sty" by the end of the poem metamorphoses by means of a pun into a "Stygian" bloodstream. By this Lowell means that he not only is *in* hell, he *is* hell (he echoes Lucifer's similar Miltonic contention, just as he would years later in "Skunk Hour," when he declares "I myself am hell" [*LS* 90]). Christ, however, is also in him, and he imitates Christ by harrowing his hellish blood to purge it. The poem ends with a flurry of puns and paradoxes:

> The Fisher's sons must cast about
> When shallow waters peter out.
> I will catch Christ with a greased worm,
> And when the Prince of Darkness stalks
> My bloodstream to its Stygian term . . .
> On water the Man-Fisher walks. (*LU* 34)

The "Fisher" is Christ, his "sons" the Apostles, who were also fishermen "casting about" with literal nets as well as with figurative ones to "catch" men's souls. Unfortunately, the baptismal waters in Lowell's wasteland have nearly dried up; they've "petered out" because Peter, the founder of the Roman Catholic Church, has been cast into the limbo of "the land of unlikeness." Lowell brags drunkenly that he will catch Christ, whose symbol was the fish, with a worm. The "worm" may be Satan, but Satan is stalking the symbolic stream as well, and promises to do so, as the book of Revelation predicts, for a millennial "term." Satan may catch Christ or he may catch Lowell, even though the "Man-Fisher"—Lowell the fisherman as well as Satan and Christ—is above water rather than in it like a fish. In this linguistic labyrinth all the personae clash and fuse, and all seem to be drunk on spirits of one kind or another.

Although there is an intimation of transcendence and resolution at the end of "The Drunken Fisherman," it is undermined by what has come before. In the first stanza Lowell declares: "Truly, Jehovah's bow suspends / No pots of gold to weight its ends" (*LU* 34). Jehovah's rainbow, which in Genesis symbolized an end to earthly destruction, in Lowell's poem promises nothing more than the perpetuation of bloody conflicts. In "the land of unlikeness" no covenant, no connection, no contractual agreement binds God and humanity; there are no happy ends. Like the Fisher King in Eliot's *Waste Land*, Lowell's drunken fisherman is an old man who can't catch what might redeem him. He "drinks like a fish" and tells fish stories to those naive enough to believe him. He says: "Children, the raging memory drools / Over the glory of past pools" (*LU* 34). Despite his grandiose fantasies, his canvas creel has been "corrupted" by moths; he sits on his couch with a whiskey bottle and raves like a bibulous Dylan Thomas (most of his grandiose imagery in the poem derives from Thomas).

Although he seems blasphemous or simply farcical, Lowell's drunken, Luciferian Jesus is also his American Everyman, typologically conflated with biblical figures as well as Melville's Ahab. Chasing Moby Dick's spirit-spout ("Life danced a jig on the sperm-whale's spout" [*LU* 34], the fisherman says), he entertains "sublime ambitions." When he exclaims, "Tantrums thrash to a whale's rage" (*LU* 34), he signals that he is possessed by the monstrous powers he hunts. Once again Lowell is at pains to suggest that his psyche mirrors America. Both are Hobbesian leviathans full of brutish hubris and violence. In "The Drunken Fisherman" Lowell connects microcosm and macrocosm when he claims: "A grain of sand inside my shoe / Mimics the moon that might undo / Man and Creation too" (*LU* 34). Embodying the sort of lunacy behind Ahabian or American obsessions with power, the moon (like the white whale) could strike the earth and destroy everything. Originating from a simple pun on "sty," the poem's symbolic net radiates outward and gathers together the apocalyptic figures representing the many factions in Lowell's "Stygian" psyche.

Although Lowell's early skill with allegory and *allegoresis* was awkward and idiosyncratic, his interest in the ancient mode is everywhere attested. In his last year at St. Mark's he ambitiously tackled Dante's *Divine Comedy*. An article entitled "Dante's Inferno" rather jejunely collapses the traditional four-fold method of interpretation that Dante spelled out in his famous letter to Can Grande della Scala into his own threefold method, asserting: "The *Inferno* has three sides—the physical, the ethical, and the artistic" (130). Physically, "When Satan was cast out of Heaven, he hit the earth and sank half-way through. The hole he made is called the Inferno, or Hell. . . . Ethically, the Inferno is for all those who are not in harmony with God" (130). Praising Dante for his perfect artistic balancing of the physical with the ethical, he takes particular delight in the way "every circle contains a monster who is a symbol of the crime represented by that particular circle" (131). Dante's allegorical form with its grotesque depictions of unethical conduct appealed to a young Lowell whose conscience was possessed by similar daemons.

A poem like "A Suicidal Fantasy," published early in 1939 in the Kenyon journal *Hika*, again shows Lowell, however clumsily, allegorizing his morally dubious behavior so that it becomes a satanic "leap for the sublime" followed by a tragic plunge into hell. Written three years after he had knocked his father to the ground for interfering with his marriage plans with Anne Dick, and only weeks after he borrowed his parents' car and crashed it, along with his fiancée, Jean Stafford, into a Cambridge cul-de-sac, Lowell has legitimate grounds for placing himself among Lucifer's progeny. Imitating Dante's great allegory, Lowell draws on Virgil's *Aeneid* as well as pagan mythology, but in a typically ironic way. He recalls Dante's depiction of the suicide, Piero delle Vigne, who suffers in the form of a bleeding thorn tree afflicted by harpies (in Canto 13 of the *Inferno*), which in turn recalls the third book of the *Aeneid*, where Aeneas tears at a metamorphosed Polydorus ("Dark crimson blood ran out of the ripped bark" 3:37–39). Lowell weaves these allusions as well as others into an allegorical account of his violent conflicts with his father, his lovers, and his own conscience:

> Slouching on an elm overhead
> the solemn and outraged cat spied
> The maimed man stooping with his bag;
> Then the apprehensive whiskers bled,
> And the foul harpy prophesied
> Of Hades and the water bog. (19)

Lowell turns Dante's biblical cats—his lustful leopard and prideful lion—into an "outraged cat" to symbolize a conscience scathingly aware of his violence against himself and others (his imagery comes from Dante's descriptions of the seventh circle of hell, where the violent are punished).

Like traditional allegories, Lowell's "Suicidal Fantasy" begins with wordplay; the whole poem rings the changes on the hackneyed phrase "To let the cat out of the bag." Lowell's "bagged" secret is his hidden violence, his Satan within (according to medieval superstition, Satan's favorite avatar was a black cat); his sin is that he lets it out of the bag. Lowell also implies that his parents let a satanic cat out of the bag when they gave birth to him.

In the infernal "water bog" of his unconscious—"memory's pregnant bag," as he calls this womblike tomb—he confronts them. When he remembers the car crash in which Stafford's face was permanently disfigured, his catlike violence metamorphoses into sharp-clawed guilt:

> And as I spun the borrowed car
> From the trestles of my road
> Into the deathful water bog
> The catapulting sodden fur
> In avalanched emotion sprawled
> On the memory's pregnant bag. (19)

By the end of this overly compressed, lurching poem Lowell demonstrates in clear terms the irony of his allegorical method. He turns "the maimed man," the Christ-like "Maimed King" of Arthurian legend whose wound requires the healing powers of a younger knight like Perceval (Lowell no doubt picked this up from Eliot's *Waste Land*), into the image of his father. But instead of healing his father, whom he has maimed, he maims himself with suicidal guilt. Rather than try to put his satanic son back in the bag, or at least put him in an asylum for the criminally insane, his father fills his cat bag with pine cones and absent-mindedly skips stones on the hellish bog. As in later poems, he appears abstracted and unable to cope with his tempestuous son:

> But the maimed man skipped abstruse stones
> On the concentric turbulence
> Of the confounding water bog,
> And gathered some solemn pine cones
> About the yawning brown entrance
> Of his travailing cat-bag. (19)

Lowell's allegorical *psychomachia* ends in a truce between the patriarchal cat catcher and his feline son.

The reworked version, "A Suicidal Nightmare," which appeared in *Land of Unlikeness*, filters Lowell's literal experiences through other literary "pretexts" so that the cat, "crouching in your jungle-bed, / O tiger of the gutless heart," recalls Eliot's "Gerontian," where "In the juvescence of the year / Came Christ the tiger" (*Selected Poems* 31). Playing with words as before, Lowell deems his heart a paradoxical web of catgut and gutlessness, of feistiness and cowardice (perhaps because after hurting both father and Stafford, he fled the scene). The word "cat" generates the allegorical personae and plot. For a poet full of oedipal anger, the sphinx is a likely incarnation of the cat, but Lowell also puns on his nickname Cal to get cat and Cain: "Cat, you saw red, / And like a grinning sphinx, you prophesied / Cain's nine and outcast lives are in the bag" (*LU* 6). In *Oedipus Rex* the sphinx creates a wasteland, devouring those who cannot solve his riddle. Oedipus answers the riddle, destroys the sphinx, but then unwittingly creates another wasteland by marrying his mother and killing his father. Lowell's juvenile acts engender another nightmarish wasteland where he wallows like Dante's violent sinners who use their force against God, themselves, and others. Lowell's sphinx makes Tiresias-like prophesies that have an obviously biblical slant: for his crimes Lowell will be outcast like both Oedipus and Cain. Although his penitential journey parallels Dante's in hell, it also parallels Perceval and Galahad's quest for the Holy Grail and a cure for the Maimed King. For Lowell it is suicidal to the extent that he, or rather his catlike passions, are let out of the bag once again. Like Gerontian's tigers and leopards, his frenetic cat threatens to devour him with guilt. Driving into the lower circles of his psychological hell, this modern-day Dante encounters monsters of his own making:

> Watching the man, I spun my borrowed car
> Into the bog. I'd left the traveled road
> And crashed into a lower bog;
> And that was why the catapulting fur,
> A wooly lava of abstractions, flowed
> Over my memory's inflated bag. (*LU* 6)

The "wooly lava" is his infernal, catlike conscience pouring fire and brimstone on his guilty soul. His conscience's "abstractions" are his moral principles, perhaps woolly-headed but nevertheless sharply toothed. Punningly, they "*cat*apult" in an attack on his psyche like incendiary brands from ancient war machines.

As usual, by the end of this early poem Lowell's metaphors are hopelessly entangled. His sundry antithetical personae are yoked by violence. If he is the maimer, he is also the maimed, Aeneas as well as his father carried from Troy on his back. "The maimed man stooped and slung me on his back," he says. While Lowell's car "foundered in the lowest bog," he engages an imaginary double, both father and brother, in a bit of Dantesque dialogue: "Man, why was it your rotten fabric broke? / 'Brother, I fattened a caged beast on blood / And knowledge had let the cat out of the bag'" (*LU* 6). The fall into the inferno's bog parallels the fall from Eden (a kind of cage for innocent beasts). At the end Lowell combines Freudian and Christian explanations of sinful conduct by tracing his own delinquency back to his parents. Like Adam and Eve, his parents "knew" each other sexually before letting the cat (their son, Cal / Cain) out of the "pregnant bag." If Lowell's allegorical drama has expressed the polysemous possibilities of one hackneyed phrase through wordplay and mythplay, it has given teeth to another: "Curiosity (for carnal knowledge) killed the cat."

Most allegorical journeys progress through some sort of hell and purgatory and end with a vision of heaven; Lowell's collapses at a dead end, just as his actual drive with Stafford down the cul-de-sac (literally meaning "bottom of the sack or bag") ended in a terrible crash. With one eye still trained on heavenly ideals, his satanic cat plunges, like so many of his personae, into hell. As a poet he founders in a stylistic bog as well. In his "land of unlikeness," just as in Eliot's *Waste Land,* there is little or no sign of redemption. Spiritual as well as stylistic grace is beyond his grasp. In another poem, "Scenes from a Historic Comedy," Lowell again undermines the traditional plot of allegorical comedies in favor of tragedy. His first section, "The Slough of Despond," alludes to that moment early in Bunyan's *Pilgrim's Progress* when Christian, burdened by his sense of sin, sinks with Pliable into despair. Bunyan's narrator comments: "Now I saw in my dream . . . they drew near to a very miry Slough that was in the midst of the plain, and they, being heedless, did both fall suddenly into the bog. The name of the Slough was Despond. Here therefore they wallowed for a time, being grievously bedaubed with the dirt, and Christian, because of the burden that was on his back, began to sink in the mire" (45). Christian's wallowing is transitory; he soon picks himself up and continues on his pilgrimage toward salvation. Lowell's ordeal in the bog is long-lasting, relieved only by catlike leaps that land him in the bog again.

Lowell's allegorical journey in "Scenes from a Historic Comedy" begins, as usual, with wordplay: "At sunset only swamp / Afforded pursey tufts of grass. . . . these gave, / I sank" (*LU* 18). The purselike hummocks of swamp grass (Lowell plays with the notion of bag again—the etymological root of purse) can "afford" little, and when they "give," they give way, propelling the poet's dreamlike fall into a narcissistic mire where

> Each humus-sallowed pool
> Rattled its cynic's lamp
> And croaked: "We lay Apollo in his grave;
> Narcissus is our fool." (*LU* 18)

Diogenes, the famous Cynic who searched with a lamp for an honest man, will find few virtuous men here. Whatever virtues once bolstered Europe's enlightened, Apollonian culture have sunk in the hell created by the Second World War.

Once again Lowell follows Dante and reenacts a Christ-like harrowing of hell, only to find Christ Himself stuck in hell, in the form of a dead, sterile thorn tree.

> My God, it was a slow
> And brutal push! At last I struck the tree
> Whose dead and purple arms, entwined
> With sterile thorns, said: "Go!
> Pluck me up by the roots and shoulder me;
> The watchman's eyes are blind." (*LU* 18)

Again Lowell's dreaming persona shoulders a mythical maimed man. His ironic mission is to save a savior, to resurrect Christ's bodily tree—His cross—from hell, and plant it in the world so it can flourish. He enjoys the Christ-like ability to walk on water, but his overriding conviction is that he lumbers through a flood or dunghill of corruption. The cross, which Lowell associates typologically with the Tower of Babel, the tree of knowledge, and the tree of life, has fallen into a warring underworld's "dead sea" of blood. Lowell declares:

> I walk upon the Flood:
> My way is midden; there is no way out;
> Now how the Dead Sea waters swell,—
> The tree is down in blood!
> All of the bats of Babel flap about
> The rising sun of Hell. (*LU* 18)

The second section, "The Fall of Babylon," is both prophecy ("Harlot, your day is done") and prayer ("O Jesus, set my people free"), but in the end Satan triumphs and rules the contemporary world—"This is the gala day / When girdled Satan runs the Golden Gate" (*LU* 19)—presumably allowing all sinners to cross from hell into the world via California.

The third section, "From Palestine," offers little hope for an end to the "blood-dimmed tide" of bellicose ghouls that overrun the world. If the poet has tried to resurrect Christ from hell and failed, his political peers have succeeded all too well in rousing Lucifer from his pit of burning ice. Once again Lowell "apes" Dante's allegory and all other divine comedies:

> O apes of Lucifer
> Who thawed his hands with borrowed Charity,
> You split our Cross for stovewood. Fire
> Is all that you can stir

> For love or money out of Galilee;
> The *Lignum Vitae* is your pyre. (*LU* 20)

Europe (in the form of Europa the bull) and Britain are being stripped and burned as if in some modern version of a Mithraic bull sacrifice. A personified Love devoted to misguided ideals immolates the whole world in a holocaust or "whole burning." Charity, like Christ Himself, is dead. The sun is setting on the British empire and all of Western civilization as well:

> Love is the final fire,
> And makes the King of Kings his servant's slave;
> Deep deep in Mithra's sweating pit
> Europa strips for hire;
> "I am," I said, "my foot is in the grave:
> The sunset of the West is lit." (*LU* 20)

Although traditional allegories follow the Bible's apocalyptic scenario, depicting a happy end or spiritual marriage between heaven and earth, Lowell's allegorical "historic comedy" in the end offers little more than a pastiche or ragbag of apocalyptic expectations that have ended in disaster. In his typological fervor he connects saviors and sinners from pagan or biblical mythology, and then suggests they are all facets of his own psyche. In his modern *psychomachia* the "sublime ambitions" of Christian idealists, heroic anti-Christs, and those like himself who combine the two, lead to a common end: they threaten to "undo / Man and Creation too."

In the battle between Christ and Lucifer, Lowell is Miltonic and rather boorish in consistently portraying Lucifer as the tragic hero. "Satan's Confession" sketches the situation in bold outline:

> He [Christ] drains His poisoned cup;
> Thorns, nails and spearhead comb
>   The Scapegoat till His blood
>   Becomes a flood . . .
> The Game is up,
> Old Batwings circles home. (*LU* 24)

The "game," instigated and officiated by Satan, is war. In pursuing its ideals with blind ferocity (as America did, to Lowell's moral horror, by bombing German cities near the end of World War II), it ends up scapegoating the innocents and "combing" or tearing them apart in Dionysian frenzy, as if reenacting the crucifixion. This is the final result of Satan's "sublime ambition." In the end the world drowns in the redeemer's blood. Because Christ and His innocents are so brutally sacrificed (in holocausts committed by both sides in the war), their blood has no power to redeem. Christ and Satan go down together. In a little over a decade, Lowell would be appropriating Satan's mask to confess with greater candor his own role in these tragic leaps for sublimity.

When Lowell abandoned his Catholic faith for the more existential confessionalism of *Life Studies* and *For the Union Dead*, he also abandoned much of the overt machinery of allegory that had attracted him in his first volumes. "Allegory calls attention to the 'other'—in a word, to God, or to some sort of possible sacredness" (152), Quilligan tells us. It needs a Bible or *Aeneid* or *Divine Comedy* from which it can exfoliate. Lowell's early allegories normally subvert their "pre-texts," thwart conventional *allegoresis* by confusing the referents of essential characters (Christ and Lucifer, for example, can refer to America *or* to any of its enemies in the Second World War), and thereby reduce the generic form to parody or satire. His later poems reduce the form even further, leveling its personifications, symbols, and mythical characters in an attempt to fashion a more demotic style. Nevertheless, the fundamental allegorical narrative in these early poems— the embattled quest for sublime power—remains. Ahab, Lucifer, Christ, and their typological kin continue to play the roles of virtuous *as well as* vicious "daemonic agents" in the later work. Although he is dressed in less symbolic garb, Lowell still portrays himself as the American Everyman. Engaged in private and public power struggles, he continues to allegorize his hell-bent drive for the sublime.

Waking Early and Late to the Sublime

While Lowell was a student at Harvard in the mid-1930s, his thoughts on the tragic structure of sublime experience gained impetus from literature and art classes. One of his notebooks contains a hodgepodge of fragmentary poems, remarks about pre-Impressionist landscape painters, and notes on Shakespearean tragedies that keep referring to the sublime. One epigrammatic poem reflects:

> Sometimes our serious thoughts
> Are lovelier far
> When cloaked and leveled off by wine
> Like an ugly angular church
> Which in the dark . . .
> Becomes sublime. (H 2044)

The "dark," the "cloaked" thoughts, and the "wine" transfigure the "ugly" Church and make it sublime. Lowell had already learned that the enlightened and divine Kantian reason needed a dark Dionysian background to highlight it.

His notes listed under "Functions of Art" and "Four Shakespeare Tragedies" read like a gloss on Nietzsche's belief that Apollonian and Dionysian antinomies mingle dialectically in tragedy. According to one of Lowell's Harvard teachers, art should contain: "1. Loftiness of *conception*, beneficent subject; 2. skillfull, scientific and sublime *composition;* 3. . . . surprise—bewilderment." It should "Fill us with mirth . . . ; exaltation . . . ; awe" (H 2044). He underscores the need for "sublime composition" twice more before moving to a consideration of Shakespeare, who in his later works "transcends all limits [and reaches] the sublime" (H 2044). The five characteristics that Lowell lists in his definition of Shakespeare's tragic hero foreshadow the comments he made thirty years later to Alvarez about the "sublime ambitions" of American artists. He could be analyzing Lucifer and Ahab as well as Lear and Macbeth when he notes that these "daemonic agents" possess the following:

1. *Genius*—tremendous passions and desires
2. Fatal one-sidedness—carried away in some direction—self-blinding
3. Tragic trait, greatness brings ruin
4. Not always good but always gigantic
5. Perishing of power and intelligence. (H 2044)

In this 1935 notebook lay the seeds for Lowell's concept of tragic sublimity—of heroic genius transcending all limits with single-minded passion only to perish from the very impulses that led to the original transcendence. The narrative of ordeals that ended, as in *Oedipus Rex*, in "self-blinding" would effloresce again and again into the "one story" of Lowell's oeuvre.

In the mid-1960s, around the time he was translating *Prometheus Bound*, Lowell scored many of his earlier preoccupations with embattled flights and tragic falls into "Waking Early Sunday Morning," a poem that typified his ambivalent, multidimensional view of the sublime. "A poem needs to include a man's contradictions," he told Stanley Kunitz ("Talk" 54), and in "Waking Early Sunday Morning" he showed that he had repudiated neither his earlier style nor his earlier enchantment with sublimity. Before writing the poem, he complained to Alvarez of "the monotony of the sublime" in America, where major artists leap for sublimity with obsessive and disastrous frequency. The poem offers the classic features of allegory—battle and progress—as risky leaps toward political, psychological, and religious goals.

In each case Lowell records his ambivalence toward the process of attainment. Although Patrick Cosgrave contends that "there is no ambiguity of intent" (193) in the first and last stanzas and that a "stoic sense of tragedy... informs the whole" (202), Lowell's stoicism constantly breaks down under the pressure of ambiguities. More persuasively, Alan Williamson finds Lowell trapped by antinomies. Motivated by a Dionysian desire for sexual as well as mystical release, his transcendental urge "contains the seeds of its necessary cooling and rigidifying.... The last line of the poem seems a final abnegation of the possibility of a visionary release: 'our' sublime, the infinities of our scientific philosophy, the grandeurs our poetry envisions, are merely monotonous" (*Pity* 128, 127). The ends of "visionary release"—the sublime ideals—may be enchanting; the means and final results are destructive. Lowell's principal example of this paradox is John Kennedy and Lyndon Johnson's high-minded idealism that threatened to turn the world into "a ghost / orbiting forever lost / in our monotonous sublime" (*NO* 24) during the nuclear arms buildup, Cuban missile crisis, and Vietnam War.

Lowell wakes early on Sunday morning, as his poem recounts, with the urge "to break loose" from all the problems afflicting his life and nation. At first he projects his desire for transcendence onto a "daemonic agent" who, like Ahab and Lucifer, will heroically assault all opposing forces. Lowell uses one of his favorite symbols, the fish (traditionally associated with Christ and Christians), and a ladder (traditionally associated with a hierarchical, Christian cosmos) to embody his allegorical quest for the sublime. In his classical view of nature and culture, those who transgress the hierarchical order of things are punished with terrible falls. Yet the Romantic side of his personality yearns to kick free of all ladders and all obstacles, and leap for the sublime. He begins his Sunday morning meditation with a cry for transcendence:

> O to break loose, like the chinook
> salmon jumping and falling back,
> nosing up to the impossible
> stone and bone-crushing waterfall—
> raw-jawed, weak-fleshed there, stopped by ten
> steps of the roaring ladder, and then
> to clear the top on the last try,
> alive enough to spawn and die. (*NO* 15)

If the imagination ascends toward otherworldly ideals of perfection, as in Eliot's "figure of the ten stairs" ("Burnt Norton" 175), which derives from St. John of the Cross's description of the mystical way in *The Dark Night*, or if it simply grows oblivious to the deadening day-to-day routine, the symbolic action of the stanza intimates that worldly exigencies like the biological cycle of the salmon's birth and death predominate in the end. The salmon, as the poem indicates later on, resembles Lucifer and Ahab. Axelrod proposes that fish (both salmon and trout) are typologically related to Ahabian and Luciferian figures in Lowell's other major poems: "Like the drowned sailor [in "The Quaker Graveyard in Nantucket"] with his 'hurdling muscles,' the fish exude a seeming vitality but they in fact perish; like Colonel Shaw [in "For the Union Dead"] awaiting the 'blessed break,' they 'break loose' only to die" (183–184). Because their sublime leaps end in tragic falls and because, unlike their human analogues, they accept their fate without much fuss, Lowell "envies their unconsciousness" even while lamenting what they represent.

The "daemonic agent's" ambivalence toward sublime ideals surfaces in the second stanza, where Lowell, like Lucifer after his fall, tries to convince himself that it is better to reign freely in hell than to serve in heaven. Dragons and criminals, as well as adolescent boys, enjoy a kind of countersublimity by transgressing the ordinary rules of good and evil legislated by gods and superegos. Reconsidering his early reverence for the sort of "impossible" sublime that Christian personae like St. Simeon attained in their otherworldly exercises, Lowell tries to discover paradise in the imperfections and ruins that surround him. He enjoins:

> Stop, back off. The salmon breaks
> water, and now my body wakes
> to feel the unpolluted joy
> and criminal leisure of a boy—
> no rainbow smashing a dry fly
> in the white run is free as I,
> here squatting like a dragon on
> time's hoard before the day's begun. (NO 16)

Lowell's attempt to renounce Christianity's transcendental ideals as illusory and to embrace worldly limits, however, succumbs to his vacillating moods.

Later in the poem the allure of transcendental idealism returns. Although he counsels himself to "Sing softer," as if sublime conduct and rhetoric are now repugnant, he counters:

> But what if a new
> diminuendo brings no true
> tenderness, only restlessness,
> excess, the hunger for success,
> sanity of self-deception
> fixed and kicked by reckless caution,
> while we listen to the bells—
> anywhere, but somewhere else! (NO 20)

Paradoxes abound in the diction here and point to the larger paradox in Lowell's personality. His classical, conservative side advocates restraint in poetic style and personal behavior; his radical side yearns to break free of all such straitjackets. When his libidinal energies are imprisoned ("fixed and kicked"), they clamber for sublimity with even fiercer determination. The next stanza begins with a recapitulation of the original cry, "O to break loose."

The sublime attracts and repels Lowell like a magnet as he evaluates its political, psychological, and religious connotations. Doubling back on himself, he chastises his old addiction to the sublime's inspiration and rhetoric. Because he realizes he is drawing on the same sort of Longinian thunder and lightning that distinguished *Lord Weary's Castle,* and that he supposedly renounced in *Life Studies* and *For the Union Dead,* he tries to shake them off, decides he cannot, then identifies with the religious and political figures he knows are doomed by their lust for a similar rhetorical sublimity. It is as if Lowell admits that Robert Bly's famous denunciation of the melodramatic rhetoric in his poetry is partly justified. Bly indicted Lowell for "counterfeiting intellectual energy, pretending to be saying passionate things about tyrants and hangings" but in fact only spouting "a series of violent words." Bly grumbled: "He is pretending to have *poetic* excitement, when all he has to offer is *nervous* excitement. . . . It is the air of grandeur he puts on when he writes this empty rhetoric that is so offensive" (76, 75). Oddly, the much friendlier critic Ehrenpreis complained of the same gaseous oratory in earlier volumes: "The defect of *Lord Weary's Castle* is the same as that of *Land of Unlikeness.* In Whitman, Tate and Hart Crane [and Lowell], one cannot help noticing a habit of substituting rhetoric, in the form of self-conscious sublimity, for poetry" (165). As if debating his detractors, Lowell concedes that the sublime has led his rhetoric astray. Yet he also concedes that it is responsible for some of his most powerful effects.

One of the first drafts of "Waking Early" opens confessionally: "the dreams of power (what else now?) break, / and suddenly I lie awake, / and feel the unpolluted joy / and criminal leisure of a boy." Although the boy's dreams of Jehovah-like pronouncements and policies may be innocent, Lowell's daemonic pleasures in all such powers are "polluted" by an adult conscience. Therefore he rants against the allegorical forms of sublimity that once enchanted him: "I cannot take it. One grows sick / of stretching for this rhetoric, / this hammering allegoric splendor, / top-heavy Goliath in full armor / . . . bull-throated bombast stuffed with chaff" (Williamson, "Reshaping" 60, 62). Sick of his early ironclad style, he finds his situation all the more agonizing because he knows it still clings to him. The emotional impulses behind its appeal still afflict him. Engaged in a losing battle with himself, as Vereen Bell points out, Lowell declines into "nihilistic fatigue" (*Nihilist* 107).

The awareness of his propensity for sublime "dreams of power" and the rhetoric that armors them leads to Lowell's identifications with America's quests for military power and with presidential quests for political power. But the powerful in his allegorical scenario—America in Vietnam or Goliath in ancient Palestine—suffer defeat. In the "Hammering military splendor, / top-heavy Goliath in full armor," there is "little redemption in the mass / liquidation of their brass" (*NO* 20). When Lowell surveys current events, he finds only "chance / assassinations, no advance. / . . . the blind / swipe of the pruner and his knife / busy about the tree of life" (*NO* 23). Although he is an outspoken opponent of Johnson's military policies, Lowell paradoxically welcomes the president as an alter ego. Both seem incapable of implementing what they know is right, yet they share a conviction that traditional sublimities have become monotonous and reprehensible. They search for more mundane substitutes and find them in iconoclastic rebuffs to conventional propriety:

> All life's grandeur
> is something with a girl in summer . . .
> elated as the President
> girdled by his establishment
> this Sunday morning, free to chaff
> his own thoughts with his bear-cuffed staff,
> swimming nude, unbuttoned, sick
> of his ghost-written rhetoric! (*NO* 23)

President and poet unite in their jaded, sardonic ambivalence toward allegoric splendor and sublime rhetoric, but also mock their more humble substitutes—affairs and skinny-dipping.

On one level "Waking Early" is a confessional portrait of an artist divided against himself; it provides a psychopathology of Lowell's "dreams of power." Identifying with the compulsive leaping of the salmon in the first stanza, he later identifies with those "creatures of the night / obsessive, casual, sure of foot, / [who] go on grinding, while the sun's / daily remorseful blackout dawns" (*NO* 16). The nocturnal creatures who seem blissfully unaware of the daytime responsibilities of the house's human inhabitants also seem driven by Lowell's "pathological enthusiasms," those manic forces that, like the mice and termites "grinding" away in the dark, stir in his unconscious and in the end grind down his psyche. To Fletcher's assertion that "The sublime poem . . . suggests ideal Shelleyan worlds—the enthusiasm for the ideal" (247), Lowell would add Kant's stern qualification: "If enthusiasm is comparable to *delirium*, fanaticism may be comparable to *mania*. Of these the latter is least of all compatible with the sublime, for it is *profoundly* ridiculous" (128). Athough Lowell's enthusiasms resemble the sublime, they also resemble those manic bouts of fanaticism that he tried, without great success, to control throughout his life.

One purpose of "Waking Early" is to diagnose the sublime quest in terms of Lowell's manic-depressive illness. His "Fierce, fireless mind, running downhill" is bound to a cycle that, Prometheus-like, oscillates between the high of daemonic possession and the low of disillusionment, punishment, and guilt. Like Fletcher's compulsive allegorical hero, Lowell finds his psychological problems contained or represented by various "cosmic images," some conventional, others idiosyncratic. Lowell's quest, on one level, is for God and mental order. As in most modern allegories, however, God and His traditional emblems have virtually disappeared. Lowell asks:

> When will we see Him face to face?
> Each day, He shines through darker glass.
> In this small town where everything
> is known, I see His vanishing
> emblems, His white spire and flag-
> pole sticking out above the fog,
> like old white china doorknobs, sad,
> slight, useless things to calm the mad. (*NO* 19)

Deranged by "pathological enthusiasm," Lowell seeks consolation in religious, political, and poetic symbols. Unfortunately, those symbols have lost their former capacity to command his allegiance.

The religious dimension of Lowell's allegorical quest for meaning and stability is, predictably, fraught with disappointment. Lowell approaches the church hoping it will control his manic enthusiasms and sublime yearnings rather than rekindle them. In his Catholic days, according to his friend Robert Fitzgerald, the "manic or paranoiac or schizophrenic tendencies in Cal" were "awakened [by the church] and are to be struggled against" (Hamilton 151). When Lowell contemplates the church, its rituals and symbols impress him with their archaic status rather than their vital, contemporary significance. He is relieved as well as saddened that they depress rather than excite. Confronting its dead language and dead rituals, he concludes sarcastically that he might as well "put old clothes on, and explore / the corners of the woodshed for / its dregs and dreck" (*NO* 19), just as Philip Larkin's "ruin-bibber, randy for antique" (29) in "Church Going" explores the church as if it were an old barn or musty antiques shop. His cry for sanctuary in the church is typically paradoxical. Like Stevens's contemplative women in "Sunday Morning," a poem with similar anti-Christian sentiments, Lowell stays at home on his Sunday morning, evaluating the church from a distance:

> O Bible chopped and crucified
> in hymns we hear but do not read,
> none of the milder subtleties
> of grace or art will sweeten these
> · stiff quatrains shovelled out four-square—
> they sing of peace, and preach despair;
> yet they gave darkness some control,
> and left a loophole for the soul. (*NO* 20)

The Christian Word, ironically, has been crucified into a cliché. Its power to redeem, at least for Lowell, is nil.

For Lowell's quester, the sublime ideals of poetry, politics, and religion are now "a heap of broken images." The sublime ambition to commune with God has led to repeated Luciferian attempts *to be* God. Stephen Yenser draws our attention to a similar propensity that Lowell found in Sylvia Plath. In his introduction to *Ariel*, written at approximately the same time as "Waking Early," Lowell may have been thinking of Plath's imaginary, suicidal ascent into the sun's "red // Eye, the cauldron of morning" as yet another example of a satanic assault on the sublime. He declares: "In her lines, I often hear the serpent whisper, 'Come, if only you had the courage, you too could have my rightness, audacity and ease of inspiration.' But most of us will turn back" (*Ariel* 26–27, viii). According to Yenser, in "Waking," "What the speaker backs off from is death" (251). What he also backs off from is the sort of Luciferian sublimity that both Plath and Lowell found nearly impossible to control, so closely infused was it with their manic inspirations. Having managed at least to dismount from his Ariel-like muse, Lowell avoids Plath's fate, which was to rise like "the arrow // The dew that flies / Suicidal" (27) into the all-consuming sun. Nevertheless, he is still tempted by the serpent's promise of Faustian power, by Plath's hectic flight toward the sublime. Resisting this temptation, at least for now, he is foiled and fallen. He lapses into a wasteland of his own making. Rather than utter a prophetic attack, however, he grieves over vanished powers and past enchantments. Just as he would elegize Plath several years later in a sonnet, he now elegizes the sublime:

> Pity the planet, all joy gone
> from this sweet volcanic cone;
> peace to our children when they fall
> in small war on the heels of small
> war—until the end of time
> to police the earth, a ghost
> orbiting forever lost
> in our monotonous sublime. (*NO* 24)

In an earlier version Lowell identifies more overtly with the Ahabian quest for sublime ideals and the tragedy it provokes:

> No, say we fought and trusted in
> ourselves to free the earth from sin,
> were glad like Ahab to go down
> in pride of righteousness, and drown,
> that we were faithful to this boast,
> our appetite for which we lost
> the world, though free of other crime,
> in the monotonous sublime. (Williamson, "Reshaping" 62)

In "The Quaker Graveyard in Nantucket" he compared America's involvement in the Second World War to Ahab's violent assault on the white whale; now he deploys a similar analogy between Ahab and America's involvement in Vietnam to demonstrate, in Yenser's words, "that history is a succession of victors become victims" (257). What is most startling is that Lowell and America are one.

Early and late, Lowell's poetry charts quests and wars in which he identifies guiltily with the misguided idealism behind American aggression, whether the violence is directed against Native America, Britain, its own states (in the Civil War), Europe, or Vietnam. His political views vacillate widely and wildly between revolutionary and reactionary extremes primarily because he sees himself as both friend and foe, American idealist and foreign predator, rebel and dictator, son and father, heretic and God. All factions parade through his psyche and clatter their "top-heavy . . . armor" on the battlefields of his poems.

Oedipal Sublimities

Lowell's oedipal revolts against sundry "fathers"—Commander Lowell (whom he verbally and physically assaulted), President Franklin Roosevelt (whom he rebuked for his Second World War policies), President Johnson (whom he denounced for his involvement in Vietnam), and Jehovah-like ministers such as Calvin, Cotton Mather, and Jonathan Edwards—all seem inspired by a desire for totalitarian authority and rhetoric as much as by a conscientious objection to their abuses. His identifications with Caligula, Hitler, Stalin, Mussolini, and other political monsters in the middle and later poems were partly pathological, induced by chemical imbalances in his brain, and partly the result of his "sublime ambition" to fight power with the even more monstrous power that such figures represented. Stealing fire from adversaries and turning it against them, out-Heroding his various Herods, to borrow the Shakespearean phrase he uses in "Holy Innocents" (*LWC* 10), was a tactic he employed with consummate skill in the literary realm as well. Not to be outdone by poetic "fathers," he took on precursors from Homer and Virgil to Milton and Baudelaire and, in *Imitations* and other translations, imprinted them with his unmistakable stamp.

For his struggles against patriarchal powers, real and mythic, both Milton and Melville served as Lowell's early guides; both Lucifer and Ahab were his exemplary rebels. While manic affiliation with such *hommes terribles* promised an ecstatic transport from the burdens of everyday propriety and boredom, Lowell usually wrote as if he were an anxiety-ridden Satan gazing at paradise from a distance and questioning his desire to spoil it. Satan's joyous iconoclasm was Lowell's, but so was his agonizing guilt, as "For Anne Adden 4" in *History* attests:

> The universe moves beneath me when I move,
> a stream of heady, terrified poured stone. . . .
> On my great days of sickness, I was God—
> cry of blood for high blood that gives both tyrant
> and tyrannized their short half-holiday. (*H* 139)

The Heraclitean stream is here the volcanic lava or brimstone of a psychological hell, and like Earth's "sweet volcanic cone" in "Waking Early Sunday Morning," it dispenses sublimities that are both terrifying and terrific. Manic Lowell is both God and Satan, victorious tyrant and tyrannized victim, chivalric lover and callous lout. (In 1958 he had an affair with Adden, a "psychiatric fieldworker" at Boston Psychopathic, then summarily dumped her.) His psyche is split. He begins "For Anne Adden 4" sardonically: "I want you to see me when I have one head / again, not many, like a bunch of grapes" (*H* 139). In this *psychomachia*, low blood pressure is crazily calling for the high blood pressure of mania because it delivers a sublime stimulus. On a political level, Lowell's low, democratic blood is crying for the murder of the high, aristocratic "blue blood" of his Boston Brahmin heritage, which he feels is responsible for his disease. While manic he vents his bad blood, pursues women like Adden as if they were Beatrices about to initiate his *vita nuova*, and, sublimely oblivious to ethical considerations, he feels like a god on holiday. The enthusiastic god within is obviously no rational Platonist or Kantian moralist, but more like Edwards's angry God, Milton's rebellious Satan, or Ahab's inner daemon.

"Words," appearing shortly before the sonnet to Adden in *History*, spells out in more frightening detail the sort of God that possessed Lowell during his moments of "pathological enthusiasm." He declares: "In our time, God is an entirely lost person— / there were two: Benito Mussolini and Hitler, / blind mouths shouting people into things" (*H* 132). Milton applied the mixed metonymy "blind mouths" to the corrupt clergy in "Lycidas." Lowell denounces oracular wordmongers, too, but also empathizes with them, just as he earlier empathizes with the hollow, volcanic earth "orbiting forever lost / in our monotonous sublime," and the "lost" Johnson responsible for its devastation. Mussolini and Hitler are lost to the world because of their moral blindness. For Lowell, however, their captivating rhetorical power and military might make them enviable. In an earlier poem, "Beyond the Alps," his envy of Mussolini turns into a frank avowal of comradeship: "He was one of us / only pure prose" (*LS* 3). These abusive masters of the word and sword are horrific as well as ridiculous, and Lowell mocks "their Chicago deaths with girls and Lugers" (*H* 132). He exposes them as typical gangsters, their emperor's clothes stitched entirely from megalomaniac delusions.

To understand the way Lowell self-reflexively narrates, analyzes, and impugns his quest for the sublime, traditional models offered by Longinus, Burke, Kant, and other eighteenth-century apologists must be supplemented by Freudian ones. Discussing the sublime with Alvarez, Lowell ironically hailed the atheist Freud as the "religious teacher" who appealed to him most after he abandoned Protestantism and Catholicism: "He's a prophet. I think somehow he continues both the Jewish and Christian tradition, and puts it . . . in a much more rational position. . . . What I find about Freud is that he provides the conditions that one must think in" ("Talk" 40–41). Freud makes Judeo-Christianity more rational by dismantling it and then recasting it in more cogent terms. In *The Romantic Sublime*, Weiskel provides the most perceptive reconciliation of classical, Romantic, and Freudian interpretations of the sublime; and although his provenance is nineteenth-century poetry, his insights apply equally well to Lowell's. One of his aims is to bridge the gap between Kant's aesthetics and Freud's psychoanalysis: "To Freud, it was clear that 'the categorical imperative of Kant is thus a direct inheritance from the Oedipus-complex.' Hence the importance of the sublime, for this is the very moment in which the mind turns within and performs its identification with reason. The sublime moment recapitulates and thereby re-establishes the oedipus complex, whose positive resolution is the basis of culture itself" (94).

Kant's divine, moralistic reason with its categorical imperatives is the internalized image of the father-god, the Freudian superego. For Weiskel, the sublime arises from an oedipal power struggle in which the poetic son identifies with the father only to outdo him. Quoting Freud's "The Ego and the Id" on how the superego is formed through identification and sublimation—through a repression of sexuality that culminates in the "harshness and cruelty exhibited by the ideal—its dictatorial 'Thou Shalt' " (95)—Weiskel locates the sublime in the son's access to a power greater and more terrible than the father's. "The psychological fact that may be isolated here," he declares, "is the overweening strength of the superego, for its power greatly exceeds the objective occasion or ideal that has been internalized" (95). This is precisely the case with the fabulous patriarchs that served as Lowell's models; the moral and amoral ferocity that he found reflected in his band of tyrants superseded the military strength of his actual father by a long shot. Although Lowell's manic-depressive illness was induced by chemical imbalances, it was also caused by oedipal tensions that turned his "family romance" into a combat zone. Weiskel concludes that "the sublime moment releases the ego from guilt through an identification with the power by which (in melancholy) it had formerly been punished," and associates this with "mystic ecstasy" (97). For Lowell, union with one of his patriarchal gods allowed for a blissful "half-holiday." His obsessional neurosis, however, was such that depression, guilt, and contrition would follow the sublimities of mania. Having renounced his satanic god, he would submit to the god of conscience and its harrowing judgments.

Weiskel's Freudian gloss on "the egotistical sublime" reveals much about Lowell's complicated regressions and progressions. Although Kant's "dynamic sublime" and "mathematical sublime" refer to the patriarchal reason's ability to recuperate after being checked by seemingly insuperable or inscrutable phenomena (thunderous volcanoes, infinite spaces), "the father is the very member of the family romance who is missing in the egotistical sublime" (164). Keats originally applied the term "egotistical sublime" pejoratively to Wordsworth because of the latter's obsessive communing with Mother Nature and his solitary ego. The ideal poet, Keats argued, should be "the most unpoetical of any thing in existence; because he has no Identity—he is continually in for—and filling some other Body" (419). Negative capability, among other things, allowed the poet to abandon narcissistic securities and plunge imaginatively into the uncertainties and mysteries of others. For Keats, Wordsworth was too self-centered. Gravitating toward the maternal womb of nature and self, he refused the risk of dramatic engagement with others.

In social and political moods Lowell certainly felt compelled to counter his backsliding toward maternal and narcissistic sanctuaries with commitments to others. Nevertheless, the egotistical sublime was often a temptation too strong to resist. As Weiskel remarks, the Romantic ego withdraws when its desires go unfulfilled: "the regression intends the state of primary narcissism but necessarily results in the secondary narcissism we so often find in the egotistical sublime" (139). Freud elaborates on this condition in his essay "The Theory of the Libido: Narcissism": "According to our analytic conception, the delusion of grandeur is the direct consequence of the inflation of the ego by the libido withdrawn from the investment of objects, a secondary narcissism ensuing as a return of the original early infantile form" (*General Introduction* 431). The attempted return to the preconscious, infantile state in which self and other, child and mother, have not differentiated into separate identities is the theme of Lowell's numerous uncollected drafts of "The Cloister," which he wrote at Kenyon. Here a "platonic child" (H 2050), once "out of an effete womb" and still "Bright with the foreknowledge, profound / From sipping his sublimest origin" (H 2048), yearns for his ideal preexistence with "Milksop Narcissus' curdling stare" (H 2050).

Freud speculated that one side of this "narcissistic identification" is manic self-love. The narcissist "has set up the object within the ego itself, projected it on to the ego," but his sublime unities collapse into melancholic divisions: "The ego itself is then treated as though it were the abandoned object; it suffers all the revengeful and aggressive treatment which is designed for the object" (*General Introduction* 434). The sublime egotist is wracked with ambivalence because the motherly lover is gone, unattainable, yet still desired. Unrequited and withdrawn, "The libido that has . . . become narcissistic can no longer find its way back to its objects, and the obstruction in the way of the free movement of the libido certainly does prove pathogenic" (428). To revise Auden, we must love one another or get sick.

Lowell's sonnet "1930's 9," which appears in *History* right before the sequence recollecting his oedipal battles with his parents, adds another facet to the debate in which he both craves and criticizes the sublime. Lowell begins playfully with the image of the moon as a circular saw cutting through an "oak-grove," as if to stress the need to cut away dead myths associated with sacred groves. He is no doubt thinking of the golden oak bough inhabited by the moon goddess, Diana, in Frazer's *The Golden Bough*, and Graves's White Goddess, the lunar muse that drives poets into sublime frenzies. The moon might represent Lowell's cyclical lunacy or, as in Yeats's mythology, his enlightened consciousness—reason intensified to the point of madness:

> The circular moon saw-wheels through the oak-grove;
> below it clouds . . . permanence of the clouds,
> many as have drowned in the Atlantic.
> It makes one larger to sleep with the sublime;
> the Great Mother shivers under the dead oak—
> such cures the bygone Reichian prophets swore to. (*H* 112)

The beginning recalls the destroyed oaks and doomed Atlantic sailors in "The Quaker Graveyard in Nantucket" and the experiences from that "period of enthusiasm" (Hamilton 226), as Lowell called his summer in 1934 on Nantucket with Frank Parker, which informed his famous elegy.

Two sonnets before "1930's 9," Lowell commemorates his early raptures on Nantucket in the poem "For Frank Parker 2." What is particularly interesting about the latter poem is the sexual ambiguity of the sea. In "The Quaker Graveyard," the contending forces are predominantly male. The sea is Poseidon, the Homeric "earth-shaker." By the end of the poem, when the predatory whale hunters have been reduced to prey by Moby Dick, the whole sea becomes a graveyard in which the dead (Warren Winslow, the Quaker sailors, Ahab, Christ) form a composite, masculine *genius loci* that represents Lowell's inner conflicts, especially those with his father, the naval commander he understandably associates with the sea. The only female presence is "Our Lady of Walsingham," a conspicuously lifeless, "expressionless" statue that "expresses God" by expressing nothing. Her divine transcendence of the cycle of death and birth ("She knows . . . / Not Calvary's Cross nor crib at Bethlehem" [*LWC* 19]), according to Hugh Staples, puts her in touch with God's wisdom. "The anthropomorphism of this world" as well as "the poet's career . . . , the sailor's death, and the extinction of individual consciousness for which that death is a generic symbol, are not necessarily relevant to the larger purpose of God," Staples speculates. The Virgin, "who stands opposed to the context of decay and corruption, natural, spiritual and physical," looks down at this world because she has attained "the Divine Revelation of the next" (47).

Lowell, however, is not as metaphysically sanguine as Staples suggests. According to his sardonic view, the lifeless statue of the Virgin may actually express the absence of divinity, or at least the death of a *merciful* God who has the power to grapple with and rectify the world's brutal injustices. The

God who exists in the poem attacks his foes as rampantly as His secular avatars on earth. While the Virgin may appear to take a stand opposing the real world's atrocities, she also appears totally isolated and incapable of doing anything about them. If Lowell has "achieved the harmony of mystical union," an "escape from time into salvation and immortality" (42), as Jerome Mazzaro attests, he implies the timeless moment is fleeting and illusory.

In "1930's 9," by contrast, the Great Mother dominates the scene. Lowell has supplemented the sea's destructive masculine identity with a creative, watery, maternal identity. The Great Mother shivering orgasmically under the dead oak is an earth mother shaken by the sea—the masculine "earth-shaker" (as in Hemingway, the earth shakes during lovemaking). In an earlier draft, "Nature," Lowell makes the gender-neutral pronoun "one" more specific: "It makes men nobler to sleep with the sublime, / the Great Mother had, shivering under the oak, moon and cloud" (H 2690). In the final version he is less gender-specific; the moon pulling the tidal ocean and penetrating the womblike oak grove, like the unspecified "one," could be either masculine Lowell or feminine Diana. At this liminal place where water and land cross, genders cross, too.

The confusions of gender correspond to Lowell's divided attitudes toward the sublime. To "sleep with the sublime" refers to his sexual enthusiasms for various maternal lovers (they make him "large" in a phallic sense); they also instigate narcissistic regressions to the mythical Great Mother and his biological mother. As Freud observed in his *General Introduction to Psychoanalysis*: "In the sleeper the primal state of the libido-distribution is again reproduced, that of absolute narcissism, in which libido and ego-interests dwell together still, united and indistinguishable in the self-sufficient self" (424). Unions with the feminine, whether lover, mother, or earth, whether through sex, sleep, or death, are sublime for Lowell. Nevertheless, when he alludes to Theodor Reich's womblike orgone boxes, he sardonically implies that the cure is the disease. The Reichian gospel is flawed, because "two elements were truants: man and nature" (*H* 112). Human nature, according to Lowell, always rebels against those confining ideals meant to cure it.

At the end of "1930's 9" Lowell chooses as his alter ego a "Chinese draftsman" who makes his seascape eternal in a painting. Since Lowell is as ambivalent toward the sublime as he was toward his parents, he seems almost glad when the Chinaman's picture fades: "His brushwork wears; the hand decayed. A hand does—/ we can have faith, at least, the hand decayed" (*H* 112). When he addresses another painter and poet, his friend Elizabeth Bishop, in "The Two Weeks' Vacation" (H 2199), his observation that she resists the "roaring sublime" is a compliment as much as a description of weakness. It is curious that Lowell would frame Bishop's inability to settle and marry in terms of the Atlantic and the sublime. If the sublime represented the violent passions of unresolved oedipal struggles that Lowell perpetuated in his affairs with women, he must have looked upon Bishop's relative serenity with envy. He is quietly rebuking her, too, as he does in another draft titled "Soliloquy" when he speaks for and against Bishop. In this later dramatic monologue, Bishop resembles Wordsworth (she once told Lowell, "I'm really a minor female Wordsworth" [quoted in Costello 8]), and Lowell resembles Keats attacking Wordsworth for regressing into "the egotistical sublime." As so often in Lowell's poems, however, the identities of the different characters clash and fuse and get confused. "Poor Wordsworth's sorry / Lightning-rod figure and sublimity / Say little after forty," Lowell has Bishop say, primarily because Wordsworth, like Bishop and Lowell in their different ways, "tried to live / . . . [the] egotistical sublime" (H 2238). Keats's rebuke of his contemporary comes back, boomerang fashion, at both Bishop and Lowell. If Bishop was a "female Wordsworth," she was also a female Keats and a female Lowell deeply skeptical of the solitary bliss that accompanied "the egotistical sublime."

In a letter to Carley Dawson about the turbulent weeks the two women spent with Lowell in Stonington, Maine, in the summer of 1948, Bishop complained: "I couldn't take any more of that ego-maniacy, or whatever it is. . . . I do want to remain friends but I think it is going to require great care & fortitude & a rhinoceros-skin into the bargain" (quoted in Kalstone 143). Lowell's mania had been triggered both by Dawson, with whom he had curtailed a recent affair, and by Bishop, whom he now halfheartedly considered marrying. In his soliloquy, as David Kalstone writes, Bishop appears "more as a locus for Lowell's feelings than as her historical self. . . . He made Bishop a counterpart to the figure he cut for himself in his own autobiographical pieces" (183). Emphasizing their similarities in temperament rather than their differences, Lowell let all the clashing voices in "Soliloquy" coalesce into one. According to Kalstone, Lowell later realized this was a mistake (as did Bishop, who reprimanded him for distorting the facts of her biography). "It is easy to see why this particular poetic tack [in "Soliloquy"] was abandoned," Kalstone remarks; "The identifications are too confused" (183).

Identifications become even further confused when Lowell casts Bishop in the role of Dorothy Wordsworth, who in turn mirrors the wild enthusiasms and sublimities of her brother William: "The marvelous boy / Still (thirty) guides his sister to the sylvan Wye, / Mirrors the shooting lights in her wild eyes!" (H 2238). These lines, Kalstone notes, "also reveal an entangling feeling of rivalry, a quickly suppressed attempt to imagine Bishop less as an equal and more as an adoring companion" (183). They also reveal the sexist, competitive, Luciferian nature of Lowell's bids for poetic supremacy and sublimity. Bloom could be speaking of Lowell's satanic enthusiasms when he contends, in "Freud and the Sublime": "To estimate the magnitude of such excitation is to ask the classical, agonistic question that *is* the Sublime, because the Sublime is always a comparison of two forces or beings, in which the *agon* turns on the answer to three queries: more? equal to? or less than? Satan confronting hell, the abyss, the new world, is still seeking to answer the questions that he sets for himself in heaven, all of which turn upon comparing God's force and his own" (*Agon* 113). Lowell would agree with Bloom when the latter defines the sublime as "freedom in the shape of that wildness that Freud dubbed 'the omnipotence of thought,' the greatest of all narcissistic illusions" (*Agon* 101). As he ruthlessly anatomizes the sublime's capacity for tragic destruction from political, psychological, and religious perspectives, however, Lowell's judgment of romanticism is harsher than Bloom's. It finds support in Keats's attack on Wordsworth and turns it, albeit in rather convoluted fashion, against Bishop and himself in "Soliloquy."

The styles with which Lowell documents and interrogates his sublime agons obviously change over the years. The early poems tend to embody oedipal conflicts and rapprochements in a formal way reminiscent of traditional allegories, with the expected trappings of personifications, mythical allusions, rituals, symbols, paradoxes, progresses, and battles. During the "confessional" period initiated by *Life Studies*, he dispenses with the magisterial rhetoric of *Lord Weary's Castle* and adopts the candid, colloquial style he had been perfecting in sections of his autobiography like "Near the Unbalanced Aquarium" and "91 Revere Street." The final phase synthesizes the preceding antitheses by framing the same preoccupations with personal and historical "family romance" in free-form sonnets. Even the plays translated in the 1960s and 1970s—*Phaedra, Prometheus Bound*, and *The Oresteia*—bristle with tragic, family power struggles.

Although his mother usually appears in his poetry as a more daunting figure than his father, a Phaedra or Clytemnestra whose perverse schemes wreak havoc on other family members, Lowell gravitates toward the traditional Freudian scenario. Mothers represent the "bag of waters or the lake of the grave" (*D* 18)—the undifferentiated, blissful, but deathlike state to which the Romantic narcissist regresses; the father represents the differentiating, judgmental conscience that the son must somehow appropriate in order to mature. The former is linked to the Wordsworthian "egotistical sublime"; the latter, to the Kantian "dynamic sublime." In a late sonnet, "Mother, 1972," Lowell admits he is "now more than before fearing everything I do / is only (only) a mix of mother and father" (*H* 115). From the start Lowell's embattled quest to achieve the sublime takes place on family turf. By dramatizing his struggle on so many other planes, he imbues his tragedy of the sublime with an allegorical richness even while scaling back and at times overtly rejecting the tropes and narrative designs that define the allegorical genre. Even in his later poems, as Williamson asserts, "Lowell becomes a kind of Everyman" bent on expressing "his peculiar fate as a mere variant of the generic tragedy, and pleasure, of being human and an individual" ("Reminiscence" 272, 271).

2

Forefathers

Emerson and the American Sublime

Lucifer's Enthusiasms

In his bid to embody the contradictions of the sublime and to become a quintessentially American poet in the process, Lowell had to grapple with that familiar hometown ghost, Ralph Waldo Emerson, whose essays gave to traditional European conceptions of the sublime a local habitation and inflection. To this forefather of American sublimity Lowell expressed the oedipal combativeness that characterized his relations with all fathers. His guns loaded with neoclassic ammunition provided by Eliot and New Critics such as Tate, Ransom, Winters, and Robert Penn Warren, Lowell fired the customary salvo: Emerson was so blinded by transcendentalist ideals that he knew nothing about their nefarious consequences in the real world. If Emerson's celebration of sentiment, solitude, self-reliance, and a personal over-soul amounted to yet another Romantic regression to the egotistical sublime, for Lowell and his cohorts it also amounted to another endorsement or at least an encouragement of ravenous free-enterprise capitalism and all sorts of other modern ills. To a classicist steeped in Catholicism and Calvinism, Emerson's cheerful Unitarianism was dangerous in its naïveté. Human nature, endowed with original sin and constantly lapsing into moral turpitude, needed to be bridled with conventional rituals and rules. As one spokesman for the anti-Romantic modernist charge, T. E. Hulme, put it: "Man is an extraordinarily fixed and limited animal whose nature is absolutely constant. It is only by tradition and organisation that anything decent can be got out of him" (116). In his New Critical phase Lowell agreed.

Those Southern and British mentors who guided Lowell's thought as a young man revered tradition, whereas Emerson often blithely dismissed it. To them Emerson was too democratic, too radical, too Protestant, too American. Emerson blasted aristocratic hierarchies and authoritarian ways;

Lowell's neoclassicist teachers sought to resurrect them. "The root of all romanticism," Hulme maintained in his attack, is "that man, the individual, is an infinite reservoir of possibilities; and if you can so rearrange society by the destruction of oppressive order then these possibilities will have a chance and you will have Progress" (116). To the jaundiced eye of the neoclassicist, Emerson represented revolutionary progress, a repudiation of past orders and all their hallowed rules, and a mindless plunge into the future. For Pound, Eliot, Tate, and their followers, authoritarian regimes were necessary to prevent the masses from descending into anarchy.

For at least two of Lowell's peers, Tate and Winters, Emerson was an avatar of Lucifer determined, albeit unwittingly, to lead America to the madhouse. Lowell's view of Emerson and his brand of sublimity was shaped by these New Critical biases. Like his attitude toward Lucifer, however, his attitude toward Emerson fluctuated. Although he often expressed a Southern or British contempt for Emerson's revolutionary idealism, he just as often confessed to an enchantment with the sort of revolutionary zest Emerson espoused. In many ways he was as antiauthoritarian as Emerson. If Lucifer symbolized the iconoclastic energy required to wrestle sublimity from traditional powers, Lowell and Emerson, like Blake's Milton, were of the devil's company without always admitting it. As Boston Brahmins, however, they never lost their ambiguous respect for tradition, no matter how much they pilloried it. If contemporary scholars such as Bloom dismiss Lowell because of his supposed antipathy toward Emersonian romanticism and sublimity, they do so out of a misconception. Lowell and Emerson, in fact, share many of the same paradoxical attitudes toward the sublime. Emerson's transcendental idealism attracted Lowell; "he was in his way as much a transcendentalist as Emerson" (265), Richard Tillinghast declared. But because of his manic-depressive illness and his tragic sense of history, Lowell obsessively exposed the inflammatory side of that idealism. A new look at Lowell's Emersonian roots is needed to clarify the complex relationship between these two elusive New England writers.

When Lowell explained to Alvarez that his love affair with sublime power was embarrassingly American and that it was typologically related to Lucifer's battle for godhood in *Paradise Lost* and Ahab's pursuit of the white whale in *Moby Dick*, he could have been acknowledging an affinity for Emerson's ideals as well. In Lowell's view, Emerson was also a "daemonic agent." If he kept his passions in check and avoided personal tragedy, he nevertheless encouraged "sublime ambitions" and tragedies in others. For Lowell, Emerson was akin to the early Puritan settlers and their pioneering heirs who ruined the American paradise the way Lucifer ruined Eden. If America's wars with tyrannical father figures, from King George to Mussolini, Hirohito, and Hitler are comparable to Lucifer's apocalyptic battles with God or Ahab's with Moby Dick, then Emerson is an unwitting member of the satanic group whose "sublime ambitions . . . are doomed and ready, for their idealism, to face any amount of violence" (Alvarez, "Talk" 42). For Lowell, the lofty idealism that propelled America in its early quest for political and cultural independence and its later quest for superpower status found an articulate champion in Emerson. Although Lowell's allegorical analogies are far-fetched when logically extended (America is not always Luciferian or Ahabian, its enemies are not always gods or angels, it has not suffered tragic defeat in most of its wars), Lowell is repeating in coded form what Eliot and his Southern apostles said about Emersonian idealism (and by extension about American sublimity): that the enchantment with ideals of self-reliant and self-aggrandizing power is ultimately self-destructive.

When Emerson remarks with mischievous gusto at the end of "History" that "The idiot, the Indian, the child, and unschooled farmer's boy stand nearer to the light by which nature is to be read than the dissector or the antiquary" (*Collected Works* 2:23), he sets himself up for the sort of rebuke Lowell and his mentors leveled against him. Why should the idiot and child be closer to the over-soul and nature's lessons of self-reliance and self-worth than the scientist and historian? Lowell would undoubtedly laugh at such unguarded romanticism. When Emerson asserts that any and every person should "know that he is greater than all the geography and all the government of the world" (*CW* 2:6), Lowell would be correct in echoing Winters's caveat: This sort of self-aggrandizement is akin to madness. Lowell regularly suffered from just such delusions of grandeur. To say Emerson is wholly oblivious to the psychological repercussions or corollaries of his grandiose ideas, however, would be false. One of his brothers, Edward, suffered from manic-depressive delusions similar to Lowell's and in fact was treated in the same hospital (McLean's, in Boston). In other contexts Emerson refers to these delusions as products of "enthusiasm," the term that he, like Lowell, associates with Protestant fanaticism and feelings of sublimity. Emerson could hardly help being aware of the long-standing theological controversy over enthusiasm and the sublime; his father named one of his sons after Harvard's most vociferous antienthusiast, Charles Chauncey, the scourge of Jonathan Edwards and all those who espoused the latter's brand of charismatic evangelism.

Like theorists of the sublime from Longinus to Burke and Kant, both Emerson and Lowell describe enthusiasm as a highly charged form of sublimity, but also a dangerous one. Both realize its potential for personal and mass hysteria, and value a religion based on reason rather than on unbridled emotion. Still, they find a place for enthusiasm in their worldviews. Their private debates with enthusiasm and sublimity take much of their impetus from Kant, whose aesthetics Emerson echoes in his essays and Lowell revises in his poems. Although Emerson may not have studied Kant's doctrines in the original, he certainly absorbed them from Coleridge and Kantian friends like James Elliot Cabot. Kant, of course, was at pains to differentiate the sublime's rational, moral, and divine attributes from religious frenzy. He does not, however, completely censor enthusiasm: "The idea of the good to which affection is superadded is *enthusiasm*. This state of mind appears to be sublime: so much so that there is a common saying that nothing great can be achieved without it. . . . From an aesthetic point of view, enthusiasm is sublime, because it is an effort of one's powers called forth by ideas which give to the mind an impetus of far stronger and more enduring efficacy than the stimulus afforded by sensible representations" (124).

In a passage from his essay "Circles" that Lowell must have read, Emerson repeats Kant's claim that "Nothing great was ever achieved without enthusiasm," but then adds with his characteristic high spirits: "The way of life is wonderful: it is by abandonment. The great moments of history are the facilities of performance through the strength of ideas, as the works of genius and religion" (*CW* 2:190). Because the strength of ideas could propel even the healthiest mind toward delusion and frenzy, Kant feels obligated to stipulate that enthusiasm is sublimity gone berserk. It is the germ that makes the fanatic froth: "In enthusiasm, as an affection, the imagination is unbridled; in fanaticism [the mind is afflicted by] . . . an undermining disease" (128).

In Emerson, Lowell found a transcendental enthusiast disguised as a Kantian rationalist, a homespun philosopher who because of his cool, well-mannered temperament could endorse sublimity and even flirt with fanaticism while remaining sober and sane. To Lowell's overheated psyche, Emerson's sublimity and enthusiasm, as Winters insisted, were always potentially pathological. Reading in "The Over-Soul" that "The simplest person, who in his integrity worships God, becomes God; yet forever and ever the influx of this better and universal self is new and unsearchable. It inspires awe and astonishment" (*CW* 2:173), Lowell could have discovered a description of the "fanatical idealist" whose "simplicity of mind" mirrored his own. Indeed, his diagnosis of the American psyche to which he felt so attached may have derived from Emerson's discussion of enthusiasm and sublimity in "The Over-Soul." Out of the heart of nature, Emerson avers, God's spirit pulses to inspire and unify all in democratic harmony:

> We distinguish the announcements of the soul, its manifestations of
> its own nature, by the term *Revelation*. These are always attended by the
> emotion of the sublime. For this communication is an influx of the Divine
> mind into our mind.... By the necessity of our constitution, a certain
> enthusiasm attends the individual's consciousness of that divine presence.
> The character and duration of this enthusiasm varies with the state of the
> individual, from an extasy and trance and prophetic inspiration . . . to the
> faintest glow of virtuous emotion.... A certain tendency to insanity has
> always attended the opening of the religious sense in men, as if they had
> been "blasted with excess of light." (*CW* 2:166–67)

Lowell knew all too well what it was like to be "blasted with excess of light,"
and to have the light of Lucifer (his name means "light-bringer") and his
various historical avatars illuminating his mind rather than the civilizing
glow of a benign divinity.

What is important to recognize is that Lowell's ambivalence toward the
American sublime and its often unsavory cousin, enthusiasm, is found in
germinal form in Emerson. Although Emerson seems to have condoned or
encouraged enthusiastic responses to the sublime, his attitude was divided.
His debate with himself paralleled his debate with his father's sister, the
eccentric, well-informed, and very devout Aunt Mary who influenced many
of his ideas. "She was an enthusiast" (36), one of Emerson's biographers,
Evelyn Barish, points out. What Emerson's brother William said about her
would be said about Emerson by detractors years later: "She was full of
vagaries and misshapen by religious enthusiasm, capable of producing 'sub-
lime' epistles, but too 'elevated' above mortal concerns to appreciate the
just and simple truths of existence" (Barish 42). In his mocking "Homage
to Emerson, on Night Flight to New York," Robert Penn Warren criticizes
Emerson for the same reason. Having been literally elevated above the
ground at night, Warren's imaginary Emerson has lost touch with the world's
hard facts. Out of his blindness he entertains the delusion that "There is /
No sin. Not even error." Therefore, Warren satirically comments, "At 38,000
feet Emerson // Is dead right" (153). At lower altitudes, according to this
former Southern Fugitive, his sublime perceptions are dead wrong.

Lowell questions and counters this charge in an essay on Emerson
written near the end of his life: "Can we honestly accuse him of ignoring
Original Sin? He was unable to do so" (*CP* 186). As it turns out, Emerson
was not as ingenuous as his critics imagined. He actually expressed some of
the same reservations about sublime attitudes and altitudes as Warren.
Although he liked to quote his aunt's aphorisms—"Sublimity of motive
must precede sublimity of style" and "Sublimity of character must proceed
from sublimity of motive" (Barish 109, 165)—in the end he could not agree

wholeheartedly with his aunt's high-flying sentiments. Commenting on a journal entry for 1828, Evelyn Barish reveals: "already... he had understood that enthusiasm was not enough, that inner conviction of the light was not all-sufficient, that the great multitude of the best men who have left a name [were] what the enthusiast calls 'cold and prudent Christians'" (209). With this in mind, Emerson's Aunt Mary accused him of "Kantism." Emerson *was* a cool Kantian rationalist and sober Christian, but only in those moods when he believed the sublime originated in reason's divine and moral powers. In other moods he posed as a guileless Romantic, enthusiastically advocating religious and political assaults on the establishment and its sacred traditions. To say he was blind to American evils and worldly realities, so focused was he on the sort of lofty atmosphere traversed by jet airplanes, is a simplification. Incensed by the Fugitive Slave Law, passed a decade before the Civil War to appease disgruntled Southerners, he made plain his ambiguous position: "My own quarrel with America, of course, was that the geography is sublime, but the men are not" (Allen 545). Jejune idealist and hard-nosed realist competed in Emerson's psyche, just as they did in Lowell's.

Mystical Voids and American Wastelands

It took Lowell a long time to recognize that the complexity of Emerson's attitudes toward America, religious enthusiasm, and sublime idealism reflected his own. In his early poetry Lowell generally expressed the same sort of sardonic contempt for his precursor found in Warren's poem, which is understandable because Warren was one of his early teachers. Another like-minded teacher, Tate, was even more contemptuous of Emerson. His harsh appraisal no doubt appealed to a young Lowell determined to blast his Boston heritage with scathing jeremiads. In a discussion of the breakup of Puritanism in New England (he implicitly compares the Puritan period to heaven), Tate lambastes Emerson as a befuddled, starry-eyed devil: "At this juncture Emerson came upon the scene: the Lucifer of Concord, he had better be called hereafter, for he was the light-bearer who could see nothing but light, and was fearfully blind. He looked around and saw the uniformity of life, and called it the routine of tradition, the tyranny of the theological idea" (284). Rapidly switching epic analogies, Tate compares Emerson to a Greek destroying Troy (Northerners were usually Greeks in his imagination, the South another Troy for them to burn). By rebutting Puritan theology and tradition, "Emerson unwittingly became the prophet of a piratical individualism, a consequence of his own transcendental individualism that he could not foresee" (284). It is interesting to note that Lowell in his reminiscence "Visiting the Tates" casts himself in the role of a piratical Lucifer full of the sort of hubris he would later criticize. "My head was full of Miltonic, vaguely piratical ambitions" ("Tates" 557), he says. On his way to study with his mentor in 1937, he "crashed the civilization of the South" (557) by smashing Tate's mailbox. He might as well have said his head was full of piratical Emersonian ambitions, and that like one of his Northern Civil War heroes, he planned once again to invade, overthrow, and ransack the aristocratic citadel of the South.

Two years after his Southern venture, Lowell went to Kenyon to study under Ransom. Ransom's preference for Kant's sublime—a contemplative elation kindled by the mind's perception of its own power to subdue the natural world to manageable concepts, and distinguished from religious and political enthusiasm by its moral orderliness—must have spurred Lowell's skepticism of Emerson's more mystical and high-spirited version of the sublime. Eliot's anti-Emersonian bias, reinforced by his Harvard teacher Irving Babbitt, and Winters's similar stance drew Lowell even further from his New England forebear. While at Kenyon he reviewed Winters's *Maule's Curse,* a book that excoriated Emerson with a ferocity almost equal to Tate's. Although Winters sympathized with some of Emerson's moral pronouncements, he despised his trust in human spontaneity. He argued in a statement that Lowell quoted: "his central doctrine is that of submission to emotion" (19). According to Winters, the curmudgeonly rationalist and moralist, this Romantic sentiment invalidated Emerson's moral claims; in fact it precluded the possibility of moral claims. Therefore, he concluded with Tate, Emerson was a "limb of the Devil" (131), another piratical Lucifer, a rabid enthusiast whose sublime pursuits would bring the world down in ruins.

Although, according to Winters, Emerson was protected from madness by his ethical training, he incited madness in others with his transcendentalist proposals. The poet Jones Very, in Winters's laudatory explication of his work, was just one tragic victim of Emerson's inflammatory idealism. Winters declared in *Maule's Curse:* "It is worthy of repetition in this connection, that had Emerson accomplished the particular surrender which as a pantheist, he directly or indirectly recommended, he would have been mad, that is, an automaton guided by instinct" (133). Winters in an earlier chapter on Melville compared the epic ambitions documented in *Paradise Lost* and *Moby Dick,* just as Lowell would do several decades later. Although the latter work contained "a sublimity and terror probably never surpassed in literature," its main character was also an automaton whose submission to passion led to madness: "Ahab . . . obeys the traditional law of tragedy, and destroys himself through allowing himself to be dominated by an heroic vice" (74–75). According to Winters, Emerson, Lucifer, and Ahab were a triumvirate bound by their enslavement to instinctual passion. He would continue to harangue all writers he suspected of Emersonian vices for the rest of his career. Lowell echoed his harangue early on but later qualified it as he grew more aware that Emersonian romanticism fueled his own Luciferian and Ahabian quests for the sublime.

Lowell incorporates what Winters says about Ahab, Lucifer, and Emerson in his interviews with Alvarez as well as in his short essay on Emerson contained in "New England and Further." Ahab, Winters attests, "is Promethean, in that he defies the gods; but he goes beyond Prometheus in his fury, for he seeks to destroy a god. He represents, essentially, the ultimate distillation of the Calvinistic temperament" (68). He is an inverted Lucifer; he wants to kill the God of evil represented by Moby Dick rather than the God of virtue. Lowell views Emerson similarly; he calls him "our fire-bringer Prometheus without the menace of Zeus" (CP 187), which implies that he lacks Zeus's oratorical thunderbolts (his "sublime crash of fireworks" [PB 54], as Lowell calls them in his translation of Prometheus Bound) and also that he is not menaced or tortured by Zeus or any other angry, jealous god. He is not a tormented Calvinist fire-breather like Edwards. As if to answer the question: What sort of fire did he steal from the European gods to kindle a native American sublime? Lowell states rather cryptically and generally: "A new mythical or imaginary America harmoniously comes into being with Emerson. It arrived during Europe's high age of function, power, and every variety of intellectual and artistic genius . . . the blindness that still lights our days. It was then that inquiring minds first clearly saw our heritage as something to exploit and evade" (CP 186). This is obviously a reworking of Tate's remark that Emerson was so dazzled by mystical lights and illusory ideals that he was blind to their social and economic consequences.

Lowell, however, is no parrot of Tate's and Winters's prejudices. In his review of Maule's Curse he points out that Winters's rigorous moralizing is an offshoot of the Protestant ideology he seeks to uproot: "For he is himself a late beneficiary and victim of the Calvinism whose manifestations in literature [he] has so well analyzed" ("Maule's Curse" 21). To Tate's contention that Emerson believed "man . . . being the Over-Soul, is innately perfect" (284–85), thus precluding the possibility of tragedy and much Southern literature, Lowell responds that Emerson may have wanted to ignore evil but in the end could not. Although Lowell agreed with his mentors in viewing Emerson as an exemplary proponent of America's revolutionary idealism, and one who could be blind to the adverse social and psychological effects of transcendentalism, he disagreed with their way of stereotyping Emerson as a blissfully insouciant bard. Like most of the powerful historical figures Lowell contemplates and dramatizes, Emerson becomes an alter ego onto which he projects his most pressing compulsions. To his sympathetic imagination Emerson is both ally and enemy. Like Lucifer and Ahab, whose iconoclastic ideals resemble Emerson's, he is another of Lowell's multifaceted personae exemplifying the vices and virtues of the American sublime.

Although for Emerson the sublime had multifarious significance, Emerson scholars tend to cite as the quintessential instance of sublimity the famous passage at the beginning of "Nature"—"I become a transparent eyeball. I am nothing. I see all. The currents of the Universal Being circulate through me; I am part or particle of God" (*CW* 1:10). The lines resonate with Wordsworth's similar description in "Tintern Abbey" of "a sense sublime"—"A motion and a spirit, that impels / All thinking things, all objects of all thought, / And rolls through all things" (95). For Emerson the sublime influx depends on a contemplative *ascesis*, a sensory deprivation common to most mystical exercises that prepares the way for communion with the divine. Claiming that "The mind of Emerson is the mind of America" (*Agon* 145), Harold Bloom interprets Emerson's experience while crossing the bare common as a confrontation between the self-reliant ego and the fertile abyss:

> Emersonian transparency is . . . a sublime crossing of the gulf of so-lipsism, but *not* into a communion with others . . . A second-century Gnostic would have understood Emerson's "I am nothing; I see all" as the mode of negation through which the knower again could stand in the Abyss, the place of original fullness, *before* the Creation. . . . A transparent eyeball is the emblem of the Primal Abyss regarding itself. (*Agon* 158)

Joseph Kronick in his essay "On the Border of History: Whitman and the American Sublime" is more convincing when he traces Emerson's use of the term "abyss" to Jacob Boehme, and quotes from a journal entry for November 1845 in which Emerson explains its importance: "There must be the Abyss, Nox, & Chaos out of which all come, & they must never be far off. Cut off the connexion between any of our works & this dread origin & the work is shallow & unsatisfying" (54). The abyss is an original emptiness preceding any creation or communion; the transparent eyeball, a consequence of the mystic's contemplative *ascesis*. For Emerson there is a correspondence between mental abyss and cosmic abyss, and the point of his meditation is to align the two so that he can witness the Creation as if for the first time, or so that he can actually partake in the Creation. The mysterious abyss before the Creation confers a traditional "sense sublime," a commingling of fear and awe, as does the experience of divine influx culminating in the mind's conviction that it is partly divine, an incarnation of the over-soul, a host to the Universal Being, a creator in its own right.

Although in discussing this passage some scholars differentiate it from Kant's notion of the sublime, it bears many similarities to Kant's transcendentalism as expounded in *The Critique of Judgement*. Kant's experience of the sublime, like Emerson's, involved a number of stages; it began with an overwhelming natural phenomenon that checked and voided human powers of understanding and imagination, and ended with reason, which was "part or particle of God," producing a transcendent concept to explain it. Sublimity resided not in nature per se but in the calm, reflective mind that contemplated it, reduced it to concepts and words, and proved reason's superiority over it. For Kant, nature was the cause or mediator of sublimity; human reason, its ultimate provenance. He explains:

> Everything that provokes this feeling in us, including the *might* of nature which challenges our strength, is then, though improperly, called sublime, and it is only under presupposition of this idea within us, and in relation to it, that we are capable of attaining to the idea of the sublimity of that Being which inspires deep respect in us, not by the mere display of its might in nature, but more by the faculty which is planted in us of estimating that might without fear, and of regarding our estate as exalted above it. (114)

Although he picked up much of his Kantian philosophy secondhand, Emerson had great respect for Kant, and this passage shows why. Both thinkers regarded nature's infinite spaces, mysterious origins, and awesome grandeurs as the text of a supreme being whose greatest creation was the mind that could interpret the "book of nature" with sublime serenity rather than superstitious terror. Both shrugged off Calvinist bogeys and aspired to a higher reason.

Emerson's determination to shed his culture's Puritan past, and indeed to shed history and tradition altogether, had obvious political ramifications that were the subjects of angry debate among Lowell's cronies. In his provocative study of American Renaissance writers, *Visionary Compacts*, Donald Pease illuminates the paradox inherent in Emerson's political program: "Cultural legitimation becomes a problem when citizens base their personal identity as well as their nation's identity on a refusal to acknowledge the authority of institutions inherited from the nation's past. Without a past to inform their present lives, individuals have no basis for present history" (7). At the beginning of "Nature," when Emerson declaims, "Our age is retrospective. It builds the sepulchres of the fathers," and then asks, "Why should we grope among the dry bones of the past, or put the living generation into masquerade out of its faded wardrobe?" (*CW* 1:7), he himself is groping retrospectively. He is returning, albeit in camouflage, to the revolutionary moment of the Founding Fathers in a history he supposedly wants to abolish.

According to Pease, "At a time in which politicians compromised on founding principles for the sake of expediency, Emerson . . . returned to the scene of the nation's founding to recover integrity for the principles of liberty and equality and make them available as motives for the actions of all Americans" (47). Emerson's "visionary compact" envisioned an America where all citizens gathered together in a spiritual democracy, where self-reliance assured freedom from the hierarchical burdens of Europe. "Cast the hoary scales of tradition from your eyes; experience the transcendental sublimity of your minds in unmediated communion with nature and God," he seemed to exhort. "The foregoing generations beheld God and nature face to face; we, through their eyes. Why should not we also enjoy an original relation to the universe?" (*CW* 1:7) Emerson asks. But Emerson is obviously romanticizing the past, populating it with noble savages and mystical naturalists dressed in his own "faded wardrobe," even while he supposedly is consigning all such obsolescent garments to the dump.

Emerson's belief in a divine light that nature dispenses like grace to every human without the intermediary help of priest, ritual, symbol, or tradition, and that convinces each soul of its transcendent origin prior to and superior to nature, has precedents in Protestant ideology. For Bloom the exhortation to get beyond tradition and nature derives from a compulsion to repress everything that Emerson called "the NOT ME" (*CW* 1:8). Such an all-encompassing repression recuperates the primordial abyss in the self. "The glory of repression," Bloom remarks, "is that memory and desire, driven down, have no place to go *in language* except up onto the heights of sublimity, the ego's exultation in its own operations" (*Map* 59). Emerson's solitary ego exults because it has managed to repress its precursors and, through its revolutionary iconoclasm, to hollow out an abyss in which it can entertain the illusion of originality. The rebellious son has abandoned "the sepulchres of the fathers" and in oedipal fashion has usurped the fathers' engendering powers to become, in turn, a new father—the author of a countersublime founded on democratic as opposed to aristocratic principles.

In his essay "Sublime Politics," Pease reveals the social impact of the transcendentalists' repression of nature and culture in American history, and offers a critique of Emersonian self-reliance surprisingly close to that of Lowell and his neoclassical cohorts. Like Tate and Winters, Pease argues that "Emerson does not corroborate or condone these ideological uses of the sublime" (47) to justify ecological despoliation and cultural provincialism; nevertheless, he underwrites them willy-nilly. Emerson's belief that the soul should fly beyond nature and enjoy a sublime sense of transcendence, when mistranslated into a doctrine of human superiority over nature, encourages a repudiation of nature and finally a self-righteous violation of nature for industrial gain. Western expansionism and the simultaneous destruction of indigenous cultures and their natural habitats are the unintended political consequences of Emerson's highfalutin ideals: "Through the subtle turns of the American sublime, the liberal in taking axe and hammer to the virgin land could, with childlike innocence, proclaim that only through destruction of Nature's bounty could he feel . . . [he was] doing what nature commanded as if he were truly in touch with nature's will. Put simply, the sublime enabled the nineteenth-century American to create a second scene, a veritable world elsewhere where he could rewrite and reread national policies of commercialism and expansionism in quite ideal terms" (Pease 46). As if to clear a space in the wilderness for the over-soul, self-reliant entrepreneurs cut and plowed and mined until nature withered. They bulldozed the American continent into Emerson's primordial abyss. Sublimating American resources into capitalist gold, they left a wasteland of dross—a grotesque parody of Emerson's mystical "bare ground" (*CW* 1:10). When men were allowed "dominion over the fishes of the sea and the fowls of the air and the beasts and the whole earth, and every creeping creature that moveth upon the earth," as Lowell made clear in "The Quaker Graveyard in Nantucket" (*LWC* 14), the results were disastrous.

An Ambivalent Emersonian

Although it is unfair to place the blame for America's ecological depredations on Emerson, this is the gist of Lowell's critique of Emersonian and American sublimity. American history for Lowell is a testament to the tragic results of revolutionary onslaughts on tradition and nature, a map exposing the ruin instigated by the individualist's will to dominate. Many of his early poems grapple with Emerson specifically and the tragic consequences of his idealism generally, in order to scrutinize his own sublime ideals. The early poem "Concord," collected in *Land of Unlikeness,* for example, recalls Emerson's title "Concord Hymn" in a diatribe against Emersonian sublimities, even though Lowell implies that he is deeply implicated in the American ideology he attacks. He would no doubt agree with Stevens's "The American Sublime":

> the sublime comes down
> To the spirit itself,
>
> The spirit and space,
> The empty spirit
> In vacant space. (*CP* 130)

According to Lowell, in the sociopolitical domain the sublime produces hollow men who can only gaze in rapt bewilderment at "bare grounds" and "vacant spaces" of their own making.

Lowell begins "Concord" with a favorite trope—his Boston home ground as hell—and implies that Emersonian Lucifers working side by side with avaricious capitalists are responsible for transforming what was once a natural paradise into an industrial pandemonium. Mammon the gold-grubber in Milton's Pandemonium could be another Henry Ford stockpiling gold from his inventions (the later version in *Lord Weary's Castle* begins: "Ten thousand Fords are idle here in search / of a tradition" [*LWC* 33]) while proclaiming (with Emerson) that "History is bunk." Among the ruins of Revolutionary battles and transcendentalist experiments, Lowell's search for history becomes a search for the crucified Christ. It parallels Eliot's anthropological quest for "the Hanged Man" in *The Waste Land,* and promises to redeem paradise lost by offering an explanatory emblem ("the Hanging Jesus") for the way sublime idealism is misunderstood and crucified in the real world.

The poem begins with stasis, with machines (perhaps gold-colored cars) idling, and with idle capitalist gold usuriously accumulating wealth (*contra naturam,* as Lowell-the-Catholic would stipulate):

> Gold idles here in its inventor's search
> For history, for over city ricks,
> The Minute Man, the Irish Catholics,
> The ruined Bridge and Walden's fished-out perch,
> The belfry of the Unitarian Church
> Rings out the Hanging Jesus. (*LU* 17)

With his Calvinist and Catholic perspectives twinned, Lowell punningly attacks Unitarian bell-ringers for "wringing out" the flesh-and-blood Jesus, for making Him otherworldly, overly spiritual, all over-soul and no body. His last five lines reaffirm his earlier animadversions:

> This church is Concord, where the Emersons
> Washed out the blood-clots on my Master's robe
> And then forgot the fathers' flintlock gun,
> And the renown of that embattled scream
> Whose echo girdled the imperfect globe. (*LU* 16)

Scrutinizing the Second Church where both Emerson and his father preached, Lowell repeats his charge that these high-minded Unitarians washed out the bloodiness and bodiliness of Christianity and history, and thereby rendered them impotent. (Emerson actually preached a sermon in 1832 against the ritual of Communion in the Second Church, and later resigned because church officials would not accede to his request to abolish the sacrament that commemorated Christ's blood and body.)

According to Lowell, Emerson's Christ is a powerless, disembodied spirit, who in his transcendentalist preoccupations creates the vacuum or abyss for powerful capitalists to fill with their destructive gadgets and usurious practices. He may be inside the Second Church when he asks rhetorically: "Crucifix / How can your whited spindling arms transfix / Mammon's unbridled industry, the lurch / For forms to harness Heraclitus' stream" (*LU* 16). Lowell's complaint combines Catholic and Marxist injunctions against rampant industrialism with a Nietzschean reverence for authoritarian masters. A strongman (perhaps a pope or Stalin or Mussolini; Lowell hankered after all three at one time or another) is needed rather than a wrung-out Jesus if modern ills are to be purged. Lowell implies that he himself is one of the devil's company primarily because Emerson's Jesus offers such a useless model for coping with the real world's problems. Throughout *Land of Unlikeness,* Christ arouses little sympathy. As Axelrod perceives: "Lowell's Christ occasionally puts in a brief appearance at the end of poems, walking on water or peering through the trellis, but he is as estranged as all the other characters in the book. An intellectual abstraction only, he evokes no emotions" (47). A powerfully emotional and at times anarchic formalist, Lowell is close kin to Christ's opposite—unbridled Mammon lurching for forms to channel his mind's Heraclitean stream. He struggles to find ritualistic patterns to contain and civilize his furious energies, and Christ offers little tutelary help.

Although Lowell shuns Emerson, he tacitly shares his paradoxical view of history. Attempting to repress history, Emerson bears witness to its uncanny way of returning. History's never-ending oedipal rebellions against "the sepulchres of the fathers" do not vanish, as both writers might hope; they haunt their careers from beginning to end. Lowell would also like to forget "the fathers' flintlock gun" because he was periodically tempted to turn it against his actual father and all other father figures. His poem "Rebellion" illustrates his strategic way of resurrecting revolutionary fathers in order to use their weapons against them. He seeks to limit the pain of guilty rebellion while glorying in the subliminal power it confers. He acknowledges at the end:

> And I have sealed
> An everlasting pact
> With Dives to contract
> The world that spreads in pain;
> But the world spread
> When the clubbed flintlock broke my father's brain. (*LWC* 35)

Dives, the rich man in the parable of Lazarus, is another Mammon. Lowell has signed a contract with this devil to stop devilish energies from spreading through the world. But revolutionary energies have been released in his country, family, and self, and like Emerson he is as much their radical instigator as their conservative suppressor.

Although their iconoclastic rebellions appeared in different forms and intensities, Emerson and Lowell could play American Lucifers bent on wresting power from traditional authorities just as easily as they could play the authorities bent on bridling those Lucifers. They were radical and conservative by turn. With one hand they erected monuments to the past; with the other hand they defiled them. In "Concord Hymn, Sung at the Completion of the Battle Monument, July 4, 1837," for instance, Emerson advocates traditional ways of paying homage to the "sepulchres of the fathers" that at other times he renounces. The poem is dedicated to monuments that preserve the past. Emerson surveys time's ruins ("the ruined bridge has swept / Down the dark stream"), but now he prays for historical longevity in a style that hardly could be more traditional: "Bid Time and Nature gently spare / The shaft we raise to them and thee." In "Nature" he scoffed at this sort of genuflection to the dead. Now he praises the very ground the dead walked and fought on: "Here once the embattled farmers stood / And fired the shot heard round the world" (*Complete Works* 9:139). Both Lowell and Emerson, in the end, vacillate dialectically in their celebrations and renunciations of tradition. Both stand up for revolutionary iconoclasts, and at the same time pay homage to the traditional forms they seek to demolish. As Lowell's career progressed, his attacks on Emerson subsided, no doubt because he realized that his attitude toward the past was just as mercurial as his precursor's.

Tradition for Emerson and for Lowell, as for most writers, was a hair shirt that goaded them into clever attempts to wriggle free. They realized the necessity of history but spent much of their time damning and sublimating it. In their antagonistic stances toward the hallowed past, they ritually repeated its revolutionary or modernist moments of transformation. Wilson's *American Sublime: The Genealogy of a Poetic Genre* provides an incisive analysis of Emerson's contradictory quest for revolutionary origins of power as well as Lowell's despairing critique of that quest's by-products. With regard to Emerson's peculiarly American obsessions with self-reliance and its various abysses, Wilson argues:

> the will to American sublimity is read as the ego-quest to inaugurate origins of sublime power, which is to say to evacuate some self-authenticating ground out of which the wildness/newness of power can emerge. Such a struggle for strong selfhood must take place, as the Emersonian scenario mandates, whether this I-threatening "abyss" is imagined to comprise some ahistorical vacancy or gnostic nothingness; some natural immensity in which the entrepreneurial ego can lose and find itself as in an ocean or prairie; or, nowadays, the vast intertextuality of language which codes any lyric of self-intuition with traces of otherness. (8)

If an influx of sublime power depends on a mystical or pathological breakdown of the ego, a purgatorial clearing away of natural impediments to industrial progress, or a radical sloughing off of burdensome intertextual influences and historical forefathers, Emerson differs from Lowell in mood rather than in maneuver. Both are generically American in their endorsements of iconoclastic power, although Emerson tends to assault the gods of tradition with a blithe indifference to the consequences, so confident is he of the moral underpinnings of those self-reliant Americans who will fill the void with their new creations. Lowell, coming later, is more wary. He knows that America's addiction to grandeur and novelty, like his own self-aggrandizing tendencies, is ultimately destructive. Emerson, however, could also be wary and downright contemptuous of America, as his many protests against politicians responsible for Indian atrocities, slavery, secession, and the Civil War attest.

According to Wilson's argument that the "will to the *American* sublime becomes a way of doing battle in the nineteenth century with the hegemonic British tradition [and] . . . an attempt to wrest a cultural and social priority corresponding to the transformations of the American Revolution" (30),

Emerson would seem more blissfully revolutionary than Lowell and Lowell more agonizingly divided between American free-spiritedness and English traditionalism. Another poem collected in *Land of Unlikeness*, "Concord Cemetery After the Tornado," again suggests that the crux of Lowell's argument with Emersonian sublimity centers on the issue of the abyss that revolutions engender. Such power vacuums, as any student of revolutions knows, attract all sorts of terrors. Once again, Lowell's depiction of Emerson *as* an abyss, a grave, or a void that lacks the strength or intelligence to combat the destructive storms that it incites, is also a caustic self-portrait, an attack on his own pacifist idealism that caused him to become a conscientious objector during the Second World War. Pacifism and appeasement, as history proved, merely provided an abyss for Hitler to invade and occupy. Lowell may be recounting the lessons of world wars and his own culpability in his depiction of a storm-tossed Emerson:

> Buzzard's Bay had spun
> Back the tidal wave
> In its almighty tide;
> But Concord, by the grave
> Of Waldo Emerson,
> Rumbles from side to side
> Taunting the typhoon's groan
> And then turns down her thumb;
> There like Drake's drum,
> Wind's wings beat on stone. (*LU* 13)

In Lowell's meteorological allegory, natural sublimities—tidal waves, mighty tides, typhoons—are analogous to political sublimities, and he interprets them as Darwin might: as struggles for survival in which the powerful triumph. If nature, like politics, abhors a vacuum, Concord and Emerson's grave provide a vacuum for the tempestuous powers to fill.

"The Quaker Graveyard in Nantucket" would develop these notions on a larger scale (the echoes of the earlier poem are unmistakable in lines like "The winds' wings beat upon the stones, / Cousin, and scream for you and the claws rush / At the sea's throat and wring it in the slush / Of this old Quaker graveyard" [*LWC* 15]). In this elegy occasioned by the death of his cousin, Warren Winslow, in a freak torpedo accident on his naval ship, Lowell allegorically aligns numerous forms of military, religious, and ecological violence. Here Ahab is a kind of Emersonian transcendentalist gone mad. His revolutionary combativeness *contra naturam* has paradoxically created the vacuum that the violently breaking sea (that represents, in part, the violence of the Second World War) rushes in to fill. In this grand argument with himself and his country, Lowell intimates that Quaker idealism and Emersonian transcendentalism beget their opposites—very real, bloody conflicts. "The heel-headed dogfish barks its nose / On Ahab's void," he writes, and the drowned Quaker sailors "are powerless / To sand-bag this Atlantic bulwark, faced / By the earth-shaker" (*LWC* 14) of the war. When Ahab loses his battle with the white whale, the sea (the Homeric "earth-shaker") unleashes its Poseidon-like fury. The balance of power collapses. Any intimation of a sublime triumph disappears; a Darwinian or Hobbesian state of brutal conflict resumes. In this complex dialectic, the quest for the American sublime by the supposedly pacifist Quakers begets violence and when abolished, allows even greater violence to prevail.

In "Concord Cemetery After the Tornado," Emerson's grave becomes a synecdoche for the vacuum at the heart of Concord as well as at the heart of America (and implicitly at the heart of Lowell)—a vacuum that makes way for turbulence. According to Lowell, Emerson's sublime produces revolutionary energies only to be destroyed by them, creating another abyss that then "taunts" other combatants (as Henry Newbolt's propagandistic poem "Drake's Drum" taunted Englishmen to fight in the First World War). Out of the void created by the First World War, the Second World War mushrooms. To Lowell's jaded eye, America's Emersonian idealism is responsible not so much for an ahistorical transcendentalism as for a history of escalating violence and ever more powerful ways of dispensing that violence. In this Emersonian wasteland Lowell echoes Eliot:

> What does this rubble say,
> O Woman out in the rain?
> "Concord, you loved the heart
> Without a body." (*LU* 13)

Lowell's clairvoyant woman, close cousin to Eliot's Madame Sosostris, diagnoses current debacles as arising from Emersonian sentiment, a religion of the heart that repudiates or represses the body and therefore cannot cope with the all-too-bodily world when it must. The world's sins of commission burgeon from its sins of omission. Lowell's attack on Emerson's otherworldly idealism, however, is also an attack on himself. His leaps for the sublime, as much as Emerson's, are implicated in the oppressive realities they seek to transcend.

Lowell airs this traditional criticism of Emerson only to partially retract it at the end of his poem. Here Emerson appears as the Lucifer of Concord again, the Promethean light-bringer, more lionhearted than angel-hearted, more fearsome revolutionary scaring off traditional spirits than otherworldly Christian unable to repel the real world's evils. In fact he resembles the young apocalyptic Lowell himself, conducting a last judgment of his dead Bostonian townspeople with Jehovah-like ferocity:

> In the dry winds of noon,
> Ralph Waldo Emerson,
> Judging the peaceful dead
> Of Concord, takes the sun
> From every gravestone. Soon
> Angels will fear to tread
> On that dead Lion's bones,
> In their huge, unhewn hide. (*LU* 14)

Presumably the dead lion is Emerson (the stone that marked his grave was "unhewn"); the angels, Emerson's admirers who fear to tread on his grave out of sanctimonious respect. Or they could be those squeamish traditionalists whom Emerson—and Lowell, too, in his anarchistic moods—scared off like a lion.

Lowell's ambivalence toward Emerson jibed with his ambivalence toward himself, America, and the sublime. During his last decade he again condemned the American sublime for threatening to pitch not just consciousness and continent but the entire world into the void. The obsessive grasping for more and more powerful forms of domination, in politics as well as other fields, provoked Lowell's complaint about the monotony of the American sublime. His trope of the earth as a hollow volcanic cone in "Waking Early Sunday Morning" transforms a stock image of sublimity (the volcano) into something even more frightening. As the environmental and cultural devastation of Vietnam by America reminds Lowell of the more harrowing devastation of nuclear Armageddon, he envisions a future planet reduced to a ghost cycling through space. Much of the pathos in the poem's final stanza derives from his recognition that he *is* the self-reliant and self-righteous volcano (he "trusted in / [himself] . . . to free the earth from sin," as one draft phrases it [quoted in Williamson, "Reshaping" 62]). His manic, fire-breathing energies, while dormant for the moment, unite him with figures like Ahab and Emerson, both in his volcanic outbursts and in his hollow victories.

One of Lowell's last confrontations with Emerson comes in *History*, his long poem in which "the autobiographical sublime" (H 2701), as he called it in the draft of one sonnet, resembles his precursor's projection of the self onto the world's stage. He may have recalled Emerson's adjuration in *his*

"History": "all public facts are to be individualized, all private facts are to be generalized. Then at once History becomes fluid and true, and Biography deep and sublime" (*CW* 2:12). According to Emerson's logic, history is essentially autobiographical and, when universalized, sublime. Lowell conceived of history in a similar way—as a multifaceted reflection of his personal quest for power. Emerson begins his essay with the Neoplatonic apothegm "There is one mind common to all individual men," and adds, "Of the works of this mind history is the record" (*CW* 2:3). If "the whole of history is in one man, it is all to be explained from individual experience" (*CW* 2:3), he writes, as if forecasting Lowell's method of projecting his personal experience onto a large cast of historical characters. Mulling over history's eminent men and women, Lowell consistently punctures their affectations and wittily juxtaposes their sublime with their ridiculous acts. In his own way he is as dismissive of grandiosity as Emerson was. Just as Emerson democratized history—contending, for instance, that "All that Shakespeare says of the king, yonder slip of a boy that reads in the corner feels to be true of himself" (*CW* 2:5), and that every person "must sit solidly at home, and not suffer himself to be bullied by kings or empires, but know that he is greater than all . . . the world" (*CW* 2:6)—Lowell satirizes history, deconstructing the hierarchical values that prop it up.

Lowell's brief sketch of Emerson in *History* deploys Emersonian strategies of deflation against him in an attempt to prick his charismatic bubble. Inside the great rebel is the ordinary Puritan (the same might be said of Lowell). Lowell organizes his life-study around images of coldness, winter, ice, and poison to show that Emerson's flights toward sublimity depend on a wearisome rejection of common pleasures. Lowell asserts:

> Emerson is New England's Montaigne or Goethe,
> cold ginger, poison to Don Giovanni—
> see him on winter lecture-tours with Thoreau,
> red flannels, one bowl of broken ice for shaving;
> few lives contained such humdrum renunciations. (*H* 85)

The image of Emerson shaving in his red flannel underwear is a bathetic riposte to the first line, in which he appears among European luminaries. It is the sort of double exposure or superimposition of absurdity upon sublimity that Lowell practiced most noticeably in *Life Studies* but in all his other volumes as well.

For Lowell, Emerson's psyche was as divided as his own. He could be a cold, prudent, prudish Christian and also a Promethean or Luciferian revolutionary stealing fire from European gods to kindle a native, American sublime. Like Prometheus bound to his crag, he suffered for his zealotry. Although he attacked Emerson as his mentors did, Lowell also identified with his divisions. That Lowell's vacillations intensified into manic-depressive outbursts proves a difference in personalities rather than in positions. As Bostonians at odds with their Puritan pasts, both understood the virtues and vices of revolutionary upheavals. Political breakups and psychological breakdowns attracted as well as repelled them. If nature led them to contemplate a primordial abyss and over-soul from which the Creation mysteriously burgeoned, they found the transcendence of nature both a boon and a danger. Both summoned reason to suppress revolutionary enthusiasms; both recognized the destructiveness of personal and social mania; both could be adamantly traditional in their poetic and political tastes. In their onslaughts on tradition, they could also be radical enthusiasts. They embraced Romantic ideals of free-spirited individualism as well as classical ideals of social restraint.

While the extremism of Lowell's bifurcated commitments to traditional rituals and symbols and the insurrectionary energies that demolish them distanced him from Emerson, the significance of the two writers in American literature is due in part to the way they both embodied and questioned the American sublime. Their contradictory responses to the sublime parallel a contradiction in America's Revolutionary past that arises, as Pease remarked, when citizens base their identity on a historical act like the Revolution that attempts to deny history and begin afresh. Eliot pointed out long ago in "Tradition and the Individual Talent" that such a crisis confronts all artists who want to be really new. Absorbing tradition in order to overhaul it, new artists appear to reject their forefathers and foremothers when actually they incorporate and extend them. In their iconoclastic forays against tradition and their transcendental flights from nature, Emerson and Lowell resuscitate and criticize those "sublime ambitions" with which, as Lowell said, "American literature and culture begins."

3

Ransom, Tate, Stevens, and the New Critical Sublime

The New Critics on Longinus and Kant

In his essay "From the Sublime to the Political," Gary Shapiro points out a current bias in aesthetics when he declares: "Today there is a widely held impression that only criticism oriented toward the sublime is really interesting" (217). Arguing that the "strain of modernist poetics and aesthetics which exalts the sublime at the expense of the beautiful" (213) now dominates the critical scene, he explains how advocates of sublimity such as Heidegger and Bloom have promoted this tendency and how their epigones and colleagues, waving various post-Romantic banners, have ousted the New Critics. As aristocratic aesthetes pining for the medieval beauties of the antebellum South, New Critics are now considered aesthetically as well as politically incorrect. Shapiro declares:

> In contrast to such theories of the sublime (Bloom's, Heidegger's), the beautiful also makes its appearance in modern poetics in the form of a criticism which emphasizes the coherence, autonomy, and organic unity of the poem. The American New Criticism was a consistent effort to read all poetry in terms of such criteria. The New Criticism has often been accused of taking a fundamentally conservative social stance insofar as it identifies the qualities of the good society and the good poem; nostalgia for an organic past is seen as the motive behind the valorization of the organic poem. (207)

Suspected of a New Critical antipathy toward the sublime, Lowell draws fire from some critics and provokes others, such as Helen Vendler, to respond: "The lack of demonic images—or celestial ones [at least in the poetry written in the last decade of Lowell's life] is the stumbling block for those who want their poets religious, and consider the quest for the sublime a necessary and constitutive condition for the creation of lyric" (157). Of Lowell's plethora of sonnets, Vendler remarks: "The literary equivalent of sublimity of feeling is momentum, yearning, journey, climax, epiphany, vision. Lowell refuses them all" (157).

Lowell's alleged repudiation of sublimity, however, was never so categorical. Lowell was certainly wary of the sublime at the end of his career because he had come to associate it with his manic delusions of power, but he was wary of it at the beginning of his career as well. Just as Yeats wavered painfully when he contemplated the martyrs of the Easter Rebellion, unsure whether to praise them as heroes or mock them as fools, Lowell agonized over those who sacrificed themselves at the altar of sublimity. For Lowell as for Yeats, the sublime was a "terrible beauty," a femme fatale that entranced, bewildered, blinded, and killed. It drove Ahab to death, Lucifer to hell, and Lowell to the madhouse. Vendler's claim that Lowell simply refused to entertain the sublime in his later work is wishful thinking. Lowell certainly felt morally and at times stylistically compelled to "back off" and "sing softer"; he also felt compelled to follow the sublime wherever it led.

While contemporary critics like Shapiro and Bloom tend to disparage New Critics as supplicants of beauty rather than of sublimity, it was actually under the New Critical aegis of Ransom and Tate that Lowell whetted his appetite for the sublime. Later he would merge their neoclassical notions of sublimity with the more daemonic aspects of sublimity he discovered in Stevens and the Romantic tradition Stevens perpetuated. A former Kenyon student, Ashley Brown, who took Ransom's aesthetics course several years after Lowell, recalls that Kant's *The Critique of Judgement* was a very important book for Ransom" (l). In the selection Carritt includes in *Philosophies of Beauty*, Kant explains how mind and nature grapple, and how the physically weaker force triumphs over the stronger as the mind plays David against nature's Goliath. Kant speaks of the "violence to our imagination" inflicted by the "omnipotence of nature" (Carritt 120, 121) and implies that the mind's violence has to be even greater than nature's in order to counter and surpass it. The gothic trial of strength given philosophical sanction by Kant must have appealed to the fiercely competitive and often curmudgeonly Lowell.

But does this mean Kant would have agreed with Lowell and deemed Ahab's contest with Moby Dick, Lucifer's mutinous war with God, or colonial America's revolutionary war with England, sublime? And what did Ransom, who for years subscribed to the anti-transcendentalist policies of the Southern Agrarians, make of Kant's transcendentalism? Although Kant in *The Critique of Judgement* confesses to "a special reverence for the soldier," he stipulates that all conflicts must be moral and reasonable if they are to be sublime: "War itself, provided it is conducted with order and a sacred respect for the rights of civilians, has something sublime about it" (112–113). For Kant, Ahab and Lucifer would surely fall into the category of immoral, irrational, disrespectful warriors and enthusiasts. As if to address Lowell's desire to confer sublimity on such ambiguous heroes, Kant dismisses enthusiasm as the sublime's illegitimate cousin, as reason's immoral impostor. For Kant, "rational raving" (128) by those Stevens would call "logical lunatics" (CP 324) in his poem on the sublime, "Esthétique du Mal," is anathema. By contrast, Lowell identified with all those fanatics attempting to wrest sublimity from Kant's "logocentric" citadel of reason, morality, and divinity.

Lowell's subversive swerve from Kant's conception of the sublime was actually given a philosophical boost by Ransom, although Lowell went much further than his teacher in assaulting Kant's transcendental beliefs. At first glance, Ransom might appear to be the quintessential Kantian. He certainly liked to think of himself as embodying Kantian virtues. "Balance, serenity, gentleness—they were words you associate with him" (CP 21), Lowell once noted; he could have added to his list reason, morality, and religion. Ironically, Ransom sympathized with the Platonic "logocentric" prejudice against poetry that characterizes so much Western philosophy, and that recently has come under attack by deconstructionists. For Plato and Ransom, poetry was prone to feed on irrational frenzy and breed enthusiasm. Lowell recalls in his memorial essay on Ransom that "He liked to be a poet, but not to be seen as one; he preferred the manner of a provincial minister or classics professor. . . . His unruffled rhetoric and arguments against blur and enthusiasm that once seemed perverse now seem like medicine" (CP 26). Ransom's Kantian prescriptions against excess must have been especially appealing when Lowell wrote the essay in 1974, since at the time he was trying, without great success, to curb further recurrences of his "pathological enthusiasms" with lithium.

Ransom's gentlemanly demeanor, however, could be deceptive; he had been an enthusiast of sorts, at least during his Agrarian phase. Devoted to the medieval traditions of the antebellum South, he and his fellow Fugitives in a sense resembled the Lucifers and Ahabs they fulminated against. Their godly monster was the North, and they attacked it (as if they were refighting the Civil War by other means) with enthusiasm that was at times decorous and at other times vociferous. Although Ransom gave up supporting the Southern cause and gave up writing poetry, too, tempering his youthful ardors with philosophy and criticism, he continued to fight his old battles in prose. His essays obsessively (although usually covertly) return to old Agrarian battlegrounds to pummel those progressive forces he associated with the North—transcendentalism, science, industry, free-market capitalism, radical Protestantism. To his Southern point of view, they formed an alliance that perpetually threatened to uproot and defeat not only the South but the entire modern world.

If for Ransom and his Agrarian cohorts Emerson was the quintessential Northerner—a proponent of transcendentalist abstractions about the South rather than historical facts, and therefore *the* enemy—Kant was another transcendentalist with whom Ransom skirmished. In "An Address to Kenneth Burke" (1942), published shortly after Lowell took his aesthetics course, Ransom summarized that section of *The Critique of Judgement* included in *Philosophies of Beauty*. Then he critiqued the *Critique*, as he must have done in Lowell's class, disagreeing with Kant's withdrawal into ethereal cerebration. His tone became gently sarcastic when he recalled Kant's auspicious resolutions to agonistic encounters: "At first the disproportion between the cognitive faculties feels painful, but presently we are supposed to be comforted by the following reflection: the mind must have a supersensible destination; and we should be glad to abandon weak sense in honor of the rationality in store for us" (*Beating* 65). Kant's renunciation of the sensible world, for Ransom, was the great sin. Kant, Ransom suggested, unknowingly abetted the enemy, whether he be the withdrawn religious fanatic quaking with "inner light" (the *en-theos* of Protestant enthusiasm) or his capitalist brother ravaging the sensible world, turning it into that abstract quantity—money. The sacrifice of sense and image to the abstract god of reason or capital was dangerous; it propelled the sublime quester toward solipsistic nonsense, greed, mania, and brutality. "Religions on the cosmic side are perfectly familiar with the crisis," Ransom warned, "and Kant himself declared, 'A concept without a percept is empty'" (66). In a tactical move, Ransom used Kant against Kant in order to reject abstractions. Implicit in this maneuver is the Southerner's attack of the ideals purveyed by the Emersonian North.

As a healthy alternative Ransom proposed a revised version of Kant's sublime. Whereas the German idealist advocated transcendence, the Southern Agrarian took his stand for worldliness. He explained:

I am interested in thinking of a possible reversal of the [Kantian] situation, and a "qualitative" or "substantival" sort of sublime. Sense has a fabulous realm to retire to beyond the reach of reason, if it wants to be so bold, a realm in which a chaotic qualitative density obtains. Matter would be its name. But if Form is empty, Matter is blind. . . . Artists have sometimes tried, not exactly to "purify" their art, which might imply the opposite intention, but to "densify" it, to the point where it may achieve emancipation from the bondage of any determinate form. The art feels wonderfully rich and strange to us then, and we strain ever so painfully to receive it; an adventure with boundless materiality. There is no passionate lover of his art who has not attempted it. But it eludes us. It is clear that imagination and reason ought to learn from the failures of each other's tours de force, and agree to inhabit their common and actual world. (66)

In this rather dense passage Ransom provided a justification for the formal densities that New Critics revered, densities so splendidly rich that they eclipsed their formal bounds and became sublime. His notion of sublimity, in this case, derived from the rhetorical power of a poem that has reached "critical mass," that embodies the density of matter rather than the transcendence of ideas. He stood Kant on his head. According to his final statement, however, he also believed that this wonderful density was ultimately unattainable. Skeptical and afraid of the sublime's power, whether it emanated from transcendentalist abstractions or "boundless [linguistic] materiality," he advocated a poetry more devoted to "the common and actual world."

It was the sublime density of word and world, which Ransom normally called the poem's "texture" and the "world's body," that Lowell tried to incorporate in his early poetry with a fury that must have shocked his teacher. Although he shared Ransom's devotion to a formal, restrained, ritualistic way of handling passionate experience, Lowell's passion was often so strong that it threatened to explode the formal bounds meant to contain it. His weighty formalism in poems like "Satan's Confession" and "The Quaker Graveyard in Nantucket" was influenced by Ransom's reflections on sublimity and enthusiasm, even though Lowell failed to heed his teacher's advice. One can hear Ransom agreeing with Aristotle, as he agreed with Kant (at least in his pronouncements on enthusiasm), when he said in his essay "The Cathartic Principle":

> I have mentioned what Aristotle thought of enthusiasm, or religious frenzy, or, I think it may be called, mysticism. He detested it. . . . Yet he found it natural, in the simple sense that the Greeks, much nearer to the Oriental than any modern Europeans, were powerfully given to it. He was therefore in the position of many doctors today who have to deal with ungovernable propensities. Enthusiasm was too strong and too common to be suppressed; therefore let it be authorized, and let the Greeks have their orgiastic rites periodically, in order to work it off and pass at least the interval periods in decency. (*World's Body* 184)

Ransom later compared enthusiasm with religious passion and with the pity and terror that tragedy was designed to purge. When he remarked disapprovingly, "Greeks had another weakness: they were addicted to pity and terror" (185), he could have been speaking of Lowell's tragic joys. Temperamentally prone to enthusiasm, Lowell struggled to purge it formally and, later in his career, chemically. Although he took his directives from Ransom's aesthetic counseling, and tried to anesthetize his manic energies with the New Critics' pharmacopoeia of symbols and rituals, he pitted form against frenzy to such an extent that he and his forms were always on the verge of breaking down.

Ransom's conception of the sublime stems from Longinus as much as from Kant, since for the ancient Greek philosopher style or rhetoric was the central component of sublimity. In the passage from *On the Sublime* in *Philosophies of Beauty,* Longinus argues:

> The soul seems to be naturally uplifted by true sublimity and, rising on loftier pinions, to be filled with joy and pride, as having itself brought forth what it has heard. . . .
>
> This I know, that nothing is so eloquent in due season as real passion, for it seems to be the prophetic utterance of some possessing spirit, and to inspire every word. . . .
>
> What then could have been in the minds of those inspired writers who aimed at perfection of style, and yet thought little of minute correctness. Surely this, among other things, that nature has set our human family apart from the humble herd of brutes, and has bidden us to the pageant of life and of the whole universe, that we might both be spectators of the mighty drama and acquit ourselves as worthy actors there. And she has breathed into our souls an unquenchable love of whatever is great and more divine than we. Wherefore not even the whole universe can suffice the reaches of man's thought and contemplation, but oftentimes his imagination oversteps the bounds of space, so that if we survey our life on every side, how greatness and beauty and eminence have everywhere the prerogative, we shall straightway perceive the end for which we were created. (37–38)

Near the end he asks the rhetorical question, "And shall we, then, deny that style, being a harmony not of mere sounds but of words, which are natural to man and touch his soul more nearly than his sense, can rain influence upon us, and, moreover, by completely subduing our minds, can always dispose us to honourable, lofty, and sublime feelings and to any others that itself contains?" (39). His answer of course is "no." To a twentieth-century audience it seems naïve for Longinus to express no anxiety about the negative side effects of influence. To him aesthetics and ethics are one; lofty stylists have a lofty, benevolent influence. Accustomed as we are to the abhorrent political rhetoric of "great" writers, the duplicities of "great" politicians, and the horrors that their charismatic words can cause, we can only smile at Longinus's innocence.

In the 1948 symposium at Johns Hopkins attended by Ransom and Lowell, their friend Tate delivered a lecture that corroborated their New Critical interpretation of sublimity. Tate's "Longinus and the 'New Criticism'" reads like an elaboration of Ransom's aesthetics, and even pays homage to him by discussing "Mr. Ransom's theory of a 'texture' within a 'structure'" (512). Longinus should be resurrected as the patron saint of New Critics, Tate argues, because his stylistic preoccupations resemble theirs: "His considerable originality consists in shifting the center of critical interest, without rejecting it as an 'interest,' from the genetic and moral judgment to the aesthetic, from the subject matter and the psychology of the author to the language of the work" (522). Tate praises Longinus for his belief that literature's purpose is to transport an audience through dazzling rhetorical displays rather than simply to convince it with logic. As Longinus says at the end of the passage in *Philosophies of Beauty:* "Style can bring into play the most varying forms of words, of thoughts, of deeds, of beauty, of melody, all which things are our natural birthright; and at the same time, by the contrast and blending of its mere sounds, can insinuate the speaker's passion to his hearers' souls and put them in communion with himself, building out of words an edifice of sublime proportions" (39). With the additional support of modernists like Joyce and Eliot, Tate envisions the author as a Daedalus figure: impersonal, godlike, engineering "an edifice of sublime proportions" yet ultimately flying above it. "The sublime is often found where there is no emotion" (521), he quotes Longinus approvingly, and then proceeds to analyze Aristotelian definitions of tragedy just as Ransom did.

Although Longinus once declared, "Inspired by [the words of great writers] . . . even those who are not easily moved by the divine afflatus share the enthusiasm of these others' grandeur" (Longinus 167), Tate follows Ransom's example by turning both Longinus and Aristotle into antienthusiasts. He quotes Ransom on authorial dispassionateness in the same paragraph where he claims: "Strong and inspired emotion is one source of, but it is not the same as, style. Pity, grief, and fear, he says, are humble . . . and without the note of the Sublime—as if in 'pity' and 'fear' he had a critical eye to Aristotle, whose doctrine of *katharsis* was practical and even 'sociological'" (522–23). Enthusiasm is base and should be purged; the sublime arises from linguistic felicity rather than emotional pyrotechnics. When Tate refers to Longinus's central tenet, that sublimity depends on "composition and distribution of words and phrases into a dignified and exalted unity," he fails to specify exactly what constitutes the sublime other than "the total work" (523). In stressing a rhetorical New Critical interpretation of literature at the expense of psychological and bio-graphical ones, he supports Ransom's platform without going very far in explaining it.

In Lowell's notebooks from his Kenyon days, which contain philosophy notes and drafts of poems (some of which appeared in *Land of Unlikeness*), there are indications of the young poet's attitudes toward his mentors' aes-thetics. Drafts of "The Cloister" offer the most revealing clues. In them Lowell satirizes the sort of rhetorical sublime that Ransom and Tate cel-ebrated, even while acknowledging its fascination for him. If his first teach-ers subscribed to a classical sublime inherent in formalist writing, Lowell was bent on probing the political, psychological, and religious dynamics of Romantic as well as classical sublimities, on confessing his ambivalence toward them with shocking candor, and on creating a richly symbolic, ritu-alistic poetry in which different planes of meaning interacted. "The Clois-ter" is one of Lowell's earliest attempts to offer a multiperspective view of the sublime. On one level he is writing autobiographically. He traces his interest in athletics (he was a brawny but clumsy football player), oratory (he studied speech as a senior and won a Kenyon oratory contest), and metaphysical poetry (he was already imitating the dense metaphysical wit sanctioned by New Critics). One version of "The Cloister" begins:

> Magnificent the man of brawn,
> Magnificent the man,
> Selfeducated and selfmade,
> Twirling on his tongue-strings the hurrahing crowd;
> But more sublime the rhyming man
> Crafty to span
> Passion and wit
> Which Manichean incest mates
> For our perverted pleasure. . . . (H 2051)

Holding up a mirror to his muscular, self-reliant self, Lowell also reflects on the political and psychological dimensions of the sublime. Rhetoric and poetry are not different, he suggests in opposition to Yeats. Their sublimi-ties are equally captivating and equally perverse in manipulating crowds like puppets. Politicians and poets—the acknowledged and unacknowledged legislators of the world—both strive for sublimity out of a desire for the sort of self-aggrandizement that comes from dominating others.

Another version of the poem reveals the political poet "Ruling by his own wit the fascinated crowd, / Self-elevated, raised, and stayed." Armed with Freud's theories of narcissistic and incestuous regression to the mother, Lowell condemns the sublime poet as a Platonic and Wordsworthian child hooked on delusions of prenatal immortality. Lowell's mockery intensifies in other drafts of the poem, so that the supposedly innocent "blest philosopher" of Wordsworth's "Ode: Intimations of Immortality" is an oedipal tyro bent on incestuously plunging into the "honeyed cist" of his mother's "whorepool." As for the crossing from sublime bliss in the womb to harsh realities: "Then the platonic child, / Bright with foreknowledge, wild / With contemplation, steps forth crowned / With sea-weeds of the immaterial ocean." The poem concludes: "Man barters natural health / For some factitious and fictitious wealth, / Milksop Narcissus' curdling stare" (H 2050). Soon Lowell would be equating this Wordsworthian child, breast-fed on the egotistical sublime, with Hitler, and later with Lucifer, Ahab, and a host of other villains and heroes pursuing will-o'-the-wisps of immortal (and immoral) power.

Stevens's "Esthétique du Mal"

Although Lowell would adopt his teachers' preferences for the splendid densities enshrined by New Critics, and struggle to contain his enthusiasms in strict forms, he would also submit those forms to apocalyptic scrutiny. Less prone to displays of fanaticism than Lowell, Tate and Ransom managed to keep their passions reasonably checked. In contradistinction, Lowell frequently erupted, and sometimes his iconoclastic energies were aimed at the eloquence and propriety at the forefront of his mentors' Southern agenda. As Lowell admitted in "Visiting the Tates," he was a rebel determined to pilfer what he could from his tutelary hosts after he "crashed the civilization of the South" (557). The aesthetics of another Northerner would help him in his piratical endeavors. Stevens's "Esthétique du Mal," in particular, would guide him away from the ideological and aesthetic principles of his Southern teachers and toward a perspective that focused more intensely on pain, evil, terror, and combative power.

Oddly enough, "Esthétique du Mal" was inspired by a correspondence Stevens conducted with Ransom. A letter dated June 17, 1944, reveals that Stevens began the poem after reading an article by Ransom, "Artists, Soldiers, Positivists," which included a letter from a soldier, in the spring issue of The Kenyon Review. Stevens wrote to Ransom: "What particularly interested me was the letter from one of your correspondents [the soldier] about the relation between poetry and what he called pain. Whatever he may mean, it might be interesting to try to do an esthétique du mal. It is the kind of idea that it is difficult to shake off" (*Letters* 468). In "Artists, Soldiers, Positivists," Ransom had quoted a soldier's articulate yet scathing critique of *The Kenyon Review* and then tried to shake it off. The soldier had scolded the editors for wallowing reverentially in Eliot's poetry and criticism and chided the "charming distemper of Wallace Stevens." He called for a poetry that faced the worst experience had to offer, that discovered its subjects through a "baptism by fire" (his call was prophetic—the confessional poets would appear in fifteen years). He wrote: "I find the poetry in *Kenyon Review* lamentable in many ways because it is cut off from pain. It is intellectual and it is fine, but it never reveals muscle and nerve" ("Artists" 276–77). Perhaps aware that this was the sort of attack he would attract with increasing frequency during the postwar era, Ransom returned to his obsessive argument about science and art: that art, unlike science, need not be utilitarian, that aesthetic experience need not be socially accountable or politically engaged, that artists need not approach nature flushed with passion, and, finally, that courtly manners should prevail.

Stevens's "Esthétique du Mal" in many respects is a rebuttal of Ransom's formalist aesthetics and an apology for the soldier's existentialist position. To a certain extent the poem repudiates the classicist's attempt to restrain strong emotion through traditional rituals and symbols, and embraces the Romantic's attempt to unfetter it. As if recalling Kant, Stevens makes the soldier exemplify the heroic power struggle for sublimity. Stevens may have Burke in mind as well when he deems pain and terror central to the sublime experience, and Nietzsche too when he castigates Christianity for weakening the pain of human destiny through pity and redemption. "Terror is in all cases whatsoever . . . the ruling principle of the sublime" (58), Burke declared, and Stevens backs him up by suggesting that the soldier becomes conscious of his own terrible and terrific strengths only by plunging into painful combat. Burke's emphasis on gothic agonies and "delightful horror[s]" (Carritt 93) also appealed to Lowell. The opening paragraphs of Carritt's selection from Burke's *Philosophical Enquiry into the Origin of Our Ideas on the Sublime and Beautiful* no doubt reinforced Lowell's propensity for the melodramatic aspects of the sublime. Burke claims:

> Whatever is fitted in any sort to excite the ideas of pain, and danger, that is to say, whatever is in any sort terrible, or is conversant about terrible objects, or operates in a manner analogous to terror, is a source of the *sublime* . . . ; it is productive of the strongest emotion, which the

mind is capable of feeling. I say the strongest emotion, because I am satisfied the ideas of pain are much more powerful than those which enter on the part of pleasure. . . .

When danger or pain press too nearly, they are incapable of giving any delight, and are simply terrible; but at certain distances and with certain modifications they may be, and they are delightful, as we every day experience. . . .

The passion caused by the great and sublime in *nature*, when those causes operate most powerfully, is astonishment or that state of the soul, in which all its motions are suspended with some degree of horror. In this case the mind is so entirely filled with its object, that it cannot entertain any other. . . .

Whatever therefore is terrible, with regard to sight, is sublime. . . . (88–89)

While Ransom and Tate lean toward Longinus's rhetorical sublime, Stevens and Lowell move toward a Burkean alternative. Although Stevens employs that stock image of the sublime—the volcano—he turns it into an emblem of existential extremity, of human consciousness shuddering with terror as it faces pain, danger, death, cosmic indifference, and nothingness. "The volcano trembled in another ether, / As the body trembles at the end of life" (*CP* 314), he writes. Extrapolating from themes introduced by Burke, Kant pointed out in his *Critique* that volcanoes were sublime as long as the observer could ponder their fury from a position of security and conclude that their power, although considerable, was no match for the mind's conceptual power.

This is precisely the situation at the beginning of Stevens's "Esthétique du Mal." Stevens depicts the soldier reading paragraphs from treatises on the sublime (no doubt by Burke and Kant), and responding to those, like Ransom at *The Kenyon Review*, who seem to value only charming beauties:

> He was at Naples writing letters home
> And, between his letters, reading paragraphs
> On the sublime. Vesuvius had groaned
> For a month. It was pleasant to be sitting there,
> While the sultriest fulgurations, flickering,
> Cast corners in the glass. (313–14)

Ransom's correspondent had complained that *Kenyon Review* poets refused to countenance pain, so to spike the guns of his combative critics, Stevens addresses pain five times in the first ten lines and makes the soldier-critic his aesthetic hero:

He would describe
The terror of the sound because the sound
Was ancient. He tried to remember the phrases: pain
Audible at noon, pain torturing itself,
Pain killing pain on the very point of pain. (314)

While Stevens provides the soldier with a platform to air his views, he also subtly questions them. Is his painful "baptism by fire" real or imagined? The soldier implied in his letter to Ransom that his experiences were real. Stevens, an inveterate skeptic, is not so sure. In his epistemological inquiry he contends that the soldier's pain is mediated by the phrases he reads and writes. Artifice can heighten pain, order it dramatically, and infuse it with awe and terror, Stevens implies, but it can also anesthetize; it can act as a painkiller. Although Stevens goes much further than Ransom in satisfying the soldier's request for a "baptism by fire," he nevertheless affirms that the baptismal fire is, at least in part, artificial, the product of an imagination under duress, and that the sublime "phrases" transfigure and thereby diminish the pain.

If Ransom finds sublimity in dense textures of words that seem to transcend their formal constraints, and if Tate finds sublimity in rhetorically dazzling compositions regardless of subject or author, Stevens finds sublimity in the void created by the death of traditional ideas, rhetoric, and form. He admires the iconoclastic courage to destroy the sort of mythical and ritualistic orders Ransom and Tate extolled. He plays the Blakean Romantic deconstructing classical, hierarchical concepts when he says: "now both heaven and hell / Are one, and here, O terra infidel" (315). His sublime arises from an awareness of the "total past" (314) blowing up, as in a volcanic eruption or bomb blast. After this negative apocalypse, the mind that faces the abyss in all its terrible beauty attains sublimity merely by imagining it. "If pain, no longer satanic mimicry, / Could be borne" (316), then human consciousness can prove its strength as a "capable imagination" (249). He accuses sentimentalists of mystifying and distorting the painfulness of reality, and thereby eradicating the possibility of sublimity. The "true sympathizers" (317), on the other hand, commune with the void, with the death of traditional ideas and their traditional rhetorical dress, and they try to communicate this death with "the words of all / The soldiers that have fallen, red in blood" (318–19).

As with Lowell, Stevens's sublime is entangled in tragic ambition and satanic ordeals. But when he posits, "The death of Satan was a tragedy / For the imagination. A capital / Negation destroyed him in his tenement" (319), he is conferring sublimity not on Satan but on the nihilist who denies and thereby destroys him. Somewhat like Wordsworth, Stevens's nihilist attains a degree of egotistical sublimity by returning to a maternal nature ("the most grossly maternal, the creature / Who most fecundly assuaged him") to be "born /Again in the savagest severity, / Desiring fiercely" (321). He is a born-again realist rather than a born-again Christian. As Vereen Bell demonstrates, for Lowell, too, the nihilist is a hero; he destroys old ways of perceiving the world in order to approach it with searing candor. Romantic etiquette and love of nature, as espoused by Ransom in "Artists, Soldiers, Positivists," are not for him. Heroic nihilism, however, provides a paltry substitute for the ideologies it deposes. It, too, is subject to attack by Lowell's questioning intellect, which leads Bell to conclude that a "demoralized ambivalence . . . is the salient characteristic of Lowell's work" (*Nihilist* 2).

Lowell, who was far more susceptible to violent, satanic fixations than Stevens, early in his career published a review of *Transport to Summer* that dwelled on "Esthétique du Mal" and, surprisingly, chastised the older poet for his intellectual vagaries. Lowell's attack was aimed at Stevens's tendency to withdraw into an imaginary world of ideas. Although he was not a "logical lunatic," according to Lowell he was excessively rational, idealistic, and aloof. "As with Santayana," Lowell writes, "one feels that the tolerance and serenity are a little too blandly appropriated, that a man is able to be an imagination and the imagination able to be disinterested and urbane only because it is supported by industrial slaves. Perhaps if there are to be Platonists, there must always be slaves. In any case, Stevens has little of the hard ugliness and virtue of Socrates. His places are places visited on vacation, his people are essences, and his passions are impressions" (*CP* 13). Having thrown his darts, Lowell then pulls back and applauds the "grand manner" of "Esthétique" that manages to get off its stilts and examine the common ugly world of pain: "*Esthétique du Mal* is . . . almost as good and important as T.S. Eliot's *Four Quartets* or 'Ash Wednesday.' Its subject is: How shall the imagination act when confronted with pain and evil?" (15).

Stevens's answer—that the imagination should aim for sublimity by testing its strength against adversity, and do so in an existential way without an armory of archaic symbols and rituals to bolster it—was a sentiment Lowell no doubt sympathized with because he was writing the review a year after his painful decision to divorce Jean Stafford and abandon the Catholic Church. He twice quotes the line "The death of Satan was a tragedy / For the imagination," and when he remarks that Stevens's "speculative world [is] . . . closer to the philosophy and temperament of George Santayana than to Plato" (*CP* 13), he may be recalling Santayana's discussion of the sublime and beautiful in Carritt's *Philosophies of Beauty*. Tragedy and evil are occasions for the sublime, Santayana argues, when the mind reduces them to ideas of serene contemplation: "There can be no difficulty in understanding how the expressions of evil in the object may be the occasion of this heroic reaction in the soul. . . . The more [one] . . . is able to look back upon [the tragedy] with calmness, the more sublime that calmness is and the more divine the ecstasy in which he achieves it" (Carritt 203). Tragic literature, provided it is articulated in "the grand manner," can mediate and sublimate any amount of horror. Santayana asserts: "Any violent passion, any overreaching pain, if it is not to make us think of a demonstration in pathology . . . must be rendered in the most exalted style" (Carritt 202).

During his New Critical phase, which in some ways he never abandoned, Lowell subscribed to this view. He dramatized the tragic nature of his "pathological enthusiasms," fueled as they were by the hubris of "sublime ambitions," with stylistic brio. Exaltation of any sort, however, would soon prove too hard to manage. As his enthusiasms struck with increasing frequency, he struggled to express them in less frenetic form. Whereas *Land of Unlikeness, Lord Weary's Castle,* and *The Mills of the Kavanaughs* grow out of Ransom's and Tate's New Critical allegiance to a "substantival sublime" and show signs of Stevens's existential confrontations with pain, terror, and the void (so important to Burke's conception of the sublime), *Life Studies, For the Union Dead,* and *Near the Ocean* illustrate his attempt to "sing softer." Although Lowell shifts his style from the rhetorical densities of Tate and Ransom to the less stentorian, less opaque felicities of Williams and Bishop, he sees this change in terms of the sublime as well. As his interest in the New Critical sublime wanes, his interest in the egotistical sublime, which he finds as entrenched in Bishop's personality and poetry as in his own, waxes. While working on *Life Studies,* Lowell composed many drafts of "The Two Weeks Vacation," a poem for Bishop in which he expressed an affinity as well as an antipathy for her solitary, muted sublimities. An early version begins with the intimacy of a letter:

> Dear Elizabeth,
> Half New Englander, half fugitive
> Nova Scotian, wholly Atlantic sea-board—
> Unable to settle anywhere, or live
> Our usual roaring sublime. . . . (H 2199)

In this instance, Bishop abides by the well-mannered etiquette and aesthetics of those other Fugitives, the Southern New Critics, but in later versions she mingles with the devil's company—with Lowell's mad/bad company— and is branded with Keats's anti-Wordsworthian stigma. Here Lowell speaks confessionally for himself and for Bishop, too:

> Wholly Atlantic, though half a fugitive
> From Nova Scotia, I have tried to live
> Our country's egotistical sublime.
> I raised the great sail, and there came a time
> Unanchored and unmoored to any hope—
> My total memory lashed me fast with rope;
> The four bad Georges ruled my horoscope. (H 2238)

The regressive impulse behind political and psychological egotism is renounced for an outgoing sea journey. But if the goal is political—to sail from the doldrums of the solitary ego toward society, like Odysseus lashed to the mast, passing the Sirens on his way home to Ithaca—the consequences of all sublime quests seem the same, whether the quester is Odysseus, Lucifer, Ahab, Bishop, or Lowell himself. Bad tyrants and mad gods determine the hero's destiny and destination, and both are tragic.

Lowell's journey toward sublimity, early and late, zigzagged between two principal poles: the solitary and the politicized self. Narcissistic withdrawals into the "dark downward and vegetating kingdom" (*FUD* 70), as he writes in "For the Union Dead," were matched by equal and opposite tendencies to push toward responsible political action. Lowell was irreparably divided. He could be mad, tyrannical King George as well as his opponent, "bad," rebellious George Washington, and many other patriarchal figures, too. He could be a woman drawn to the egotistical sublime as well as a man opposing it. His sympathies with the aesthetic and ideological principles of the New Critics were countered by equally strong sympathies with the principles of Emersonian Romantics like Stevens. Southerner and Northerner, traditionalist and iconoclast, aristocrat and democrat, classicist and romanticist dueled in his psyche for his allegiance. Symbolic unities like Dante's mystical rose or Eliot's "crowned knot of fire" (*FQ* 59) were beyond his purview. His reconciliations between warring factions were always fragile. The classical, Longinian sublime of stylistic panache that Ransom and Tate advocated, for example, proved to be little different from the Romantic, Burkean, and Kantian sublime of Stevens, which arose from the deification of the self-reliant mind. Lowell pursued godly rhetoric, godly ideals, and godly personae with equal passion.

The New Critics' reverence for organic form and Stevens's reverence for the abyss that form was supposed to displace, in Lowell's work attain a startling expression. "Ahab's void" (*LWC* 14) and Satan's hell were just as compelling as the formal cosmos of symbols and rituals designed to civilize them. Although Lowell may have yearned for the traditional allegorical journey from chaos to cosmos, he found himself vacillating constantly between the two extremes. Like Sisyphus, he pushed his boulder to the summit of sublimity and then followed it back to the valleys of depression and contrition. Sublimity was his muse, his divine enchantress, inspiring psychological frenzies as well as his poetic masterpieces. It ruled his horoscope.

4

The Politics of the Sublime

Contradictory Stances

During the early 1960s, when Kennedy and Khrushchev squared off over Russian missiles in Cuba and Americans prepared for imminent Armageddon, Robert Lowell recorded a dream that typified the way he wrestled with phantasmal strongmen for the boons of sublimity. On the back of a draft of "Returning," a poem later collected in *For the Union Dead*, he jotted:

> World has ended, or wasted suffered a disaster. Two groups, one American (?) which I head, the other Russian, headed by Krushev, much bigger and physically stronger than in life. . . . Struggle to survive, in second part of dream, the corner has been turned, stench receding, also barrenness, very fond and intimate with K. . . . I rely on K. as a weight to test myself against, as some one to talk to, somehow in the end as my guide. (H 2284)

Like many dreams, this one smacks of juvenile megalomania. Lowell is Jack Kennedy taking on a muscular Russian foe, a little like Rocky Balboa in the boxing ring several decades later. What is odd and yet characteristic is the way Lowell achieves self-aggrandizement by identifying with both antagonists, as if moral considerations vanished before those of power.

Throughout his life Lowell cozied up to stereotypical enemies, glamorizing and supplicating their power. Surveying history, as his dream intimates, he obsessively measured himself against political "supermen"—Alexander, Caligula, Nero, Napoleon, Hitler, Mussolini—registering his ambivalence toward "friend"—Roosevelt, Eisenhower, Kennedy, Johnson, Nixon—and "foe" alike. The imperious military and political figures that march through his poems all seem exaggerated versions of his father, whom he describes facetiously in "91 Revere Street" as a "sublime man" (*LS* 18). As in the dream of combating and then befriending Khrushchev, his poetry offers a motley group of patriarchs (and matriarchs who possess patriarchal traits) that, in typical oedipal fashion, he attempts to dethrone. What most critics have ignored is that Lowell's attitudes toward these politicos fluctuate with the terror, awe, envy, and glorious assimilation that characterize the dialectic of the sublime.

Determining Lowell's "sublime politics" is a difficult business, mainly because his political stances shifted as frequently as his manic-depressive moods. In his well-known portrait of Lowell inspired by their 1967 march on the Pentagon to protest the Vietnam War, Norman Mailer found in the quixotic Lowell a political kinsman. He speaks for himself as well as for Lowell when he declares: "Each had a delight in exactly the other kind of party, a posh evil social affair, they even supported a similar vein of vanity (Lowell with considerably more justice) that if they were doomed to be revolutionaries, rebels, dissenters, anarchists, protestors, and general champions of one Left cause or another, they were also, in private, *grands conservateurs,* and if the truth be told, poor damn emigre princes" (29). As Mailer probably knew, at times Lowell's sympathies were with dictators and generals, at others with democratic presidents and pacifists. A draft of "Mania in Buenos Aires" tells of his propensity for "aimless aristocratic anarchy" (H 2532); a poem like "Rebellion" reveals a propensity for revolutionary idealism.

For a period in his twenties Lowell toed the ideological line of Catholic conservatives; later, in moments of mania, he sided with Hitler and Mussolini. Although it is tempting to blame Lowell's love affair with tyrants on his mental illness, thereby exonerating him, the situation is not so simple. Sensitive to his sexual and political excesses, and to his Plath-like insistence that unconsciously every man and woman "adores a Fascist" (Plath, *Ariel* 50), Marjorie Perloff astutely comments: "The strong-man scenario would not . . . have shown up as consistently as it did, had Lowell not had, even in his sanest moments, an elitist, isolationist, New England Puritan-turned-Southern agrarian sense of America's destiny" (113). Mania, it would seem, simply lifted the lid on a Pandora's box of fascist ghouls. Nevertheless, in sane moments the ghouls haunted him as well, even though they took more politically acceptable forms.

Lowell zigzagged between political Symplegades. One side of him revered America's radical ideals while the other realized their dangers and pined for authoritarian ways of controlling them. Williamson rightly observes that "Lowell harbors within himself an Eliot-like conservative's insistence on forms of integrity lost in historical 'progress'; a revolutionary's vision of apocalyptic community and hunger for poetic justice; and a liberal's sharp, impersonal scruples" (*Pity* 2). If "A foolish consistency is the hobgoblin of little minds" (*CW* 33), as Emerson professed, Lowell would give his contradictory selves equal time to air their multiple views. To Stanley Kunitz he echoed Walt Whitman's famous apology for contradiction, and explained:

> One side of me, for example, is a conventional liberal, concerned with causes, agitated about peace and justice and equality, as so many people are. My other side is deeply conservative, wanting to get at the root of things, wanting to slow down the whole process of mechanization and dehumanization, knowing that liberalism can be a form of death too. In the writing of a poem all our compulsions and biases should get in, so that finally we don't know what we mean. ("Talk" 54)

Getting at the root of things, as Lowell surely knew, is the etymological meaning of "radical." Lowell's wordplay shows how oxymoronic his conservative/radical politics could be.

Sooner or later meditations on politics come around to questions of power: how one gains, maintains, and loses it. Power, of course, is also the provenance of the sublime, as Lowell would have learned by reading Burke. (Burke wrote: "I know of nothing sublime which is not some modification of power" [Carritt 90].) Recent commentators on the sublime have been particularly sensitive to the political ramifications of Burke's aesthetics. Terry Eagleton, for one, argues that for Burke, sublimity corresponded to the political values of "enterprise, rivalry and individuation," and that "As a kind of terror, the sublime crushes us into admiring submission; it thus resembles a coercive rather than a consensual power, engaging our respect but not, as with beauty, our love" (*Ideology* 54). A terroristic repressiveness, in turn, spawns revolutionary ferment.

Eagleton could be explaining the dialectic of Lowell's sublime politics when he points out: "If freedom transgresses the submission which is its very condition, the repressiveness of the sublime can be invoked; but this ultimate efficacy of power is also its potential downfall, breeding as well as subduing rebellion. Power is thus a kind of riddle, of which the mystery of the aesthetic, with its impossibly lawless lawfulness, is an apt sign" (56). For Lowell, King George was one such figure who instigated a bid for the sublime by paradoxically attempting to crush it. America's "sublime ambitions" grew from English shackles. If the origins of America's culture lay in its revolutionary struggle to overthrow "sepulchral" traditions, then according to Lowell's jaundiced view, America had come full circle. It had become a "sepulchral" tradition itself. A modern superpower, America was now as imperial and imperious as King George's England. It had grown so used to flaunting its Luciferian powers that its sublimity was now a tedious intoxicant.

Eagleton, as sensitive to the vices of capitalism as Lowell's Agrarian friends, sees a disguised attempt to promote capitalist enterprise and its attendant alienations and violations in the aesthetic of sublimity. Investigating Kant's description of the dialectic of the sublime, Eagleton also allegorizes the sublime, interpreting its aesthetic effects by translating them into a political register: "The [Kantian] subject of the sublime is accordingly decentered, plunged into loss and pain, undergoes a crisis and fading of identity; yet without this unwelcome violence we would never be stirred out of ourselves, never prodded into [capitalist] enterprise and achievement" (90). For Eagleton capitalism satiates consumers with "beautiful" commodities; to avoid "complacency, the [Kantian] sublime is always on hand with its intimidating power; but the dangerously demoralizing effects of such power are in turn tempered by the subject's joyful consciousness that the power in question is that of its own majestic Reason" (93). The final effect legitimizes, naturalizes, and rationalizes a mad scramble for power that, according to Eagleton, is neither legitimate, natural, nor rational. Lowell's jeremiads against American capitalism and its Protestant roots in New England have all the sting of this Marxist critique.

Although Lowell told Alvarez that "The two thinkers, nonfictional thinkers, who influence and are never out of one's mind are Marx and Freud" ("Talk" 40–41), his Marxist qualms about the sublime's oppressions were frequently derailed by his countervailing love of its terrifying stimulus. His aesthetic compulsions and ideological principles often collided and fused. Throughout his life he strained for beautiful orders as well as the sublime forces that demolished or transcended them. Having read Carritt, who characterized the history of aesthetics as divided between Aristotle and Longinus, classical advocates of mimetic order (the beautiful) and Romantic advocates of expressive disorder (the sublime), Lowell realized that his personality subsumed both sides of the debate. For Longinus the "Really sublime and transcendent natures" depended on democratic politics—"the kindly nurse of genius" that fostered "noble minds . . . with high hopes . . . [through] mutual rivalry and eager competition for the foremost place" (247–49). For Lowell an enthusiasm for democratic freedom and the sort of competition that inspired the sublimities of genius was little different from an enthusiasm for totalitarian supremacy. The former led dialectically to the latter. Like Burke, Lowell tended to conjoin rather than differentiate enthusiasm, fanaticism, and sublimity, and to link all three to the patriarchal and capitalist strength he condemned and craved. For Burke sublimity issued from "The authority of the father" (111) and all other imposing figures that produced terror through "an unnatural tension and certain violent emotions of the nerves" (134). Burke's analysis of the sublime, however jejune it may seem in hindsight, would have struck a sympathetic chord in Lowell, who constantly dramatized his agon in authoritarian terms.

A hankering for the sublimity of authoritarian figures, needless to say, compromised Lowell's liberal agenda. How could he campaign for the peace candidate, Senator Eugene McCarthy, as he did in 1968, while following the example of Pound and other modernists by flirting with Hitler and Mussolini? Although his fascist sympathies were inspired by mania, he states that his sober, principled testimonials for democracy and liberal humanism were inspired by mania as well. Did his enthusiasm for all ideals and ideologies, whether conservative, liberal, or radical, arise from the same lust for power and publicity? His 1943 letter to President Roosevelt typifies his contradictory stances. Here he bristles against the "diabolical adversaries" of freedom, wars that lead to "totalitarian slavery," and the "exploitation by Money, Politics and Imperialism" of other nations. He praises the "fundamental principle of our American Democracy, one that distinguishes it from the demagoguery and herd hypnosis of the totalitarian tyrannies, that with us each individual citizen is called upon to make voluntary and responsible decisions on issues which concern the national welfare" (*CP* 368–69). His invocation of "higher laws" seems eminently rational, moral, and liberal-minded. Yet in the more confessional mood of *Life Studies* he admits, "I was a fire-breathing Catholic C.O., / and made my manic statement, / telling off the state and president." He ends his poem with an eerie identification with the formerly violent and now "sheepish[ly] calm" Czar Lepke of "Murder Incorporated" (*LS* 85–86), as if the once homicidal but now thoroughly tranquilized Czar embodied Lowell's political vacillations between peace and violence, "the tranquilized *Fifties*" and his fire-breathing forties.

Anthony Hecht has suggested insightfully:

> When he calls himself a fire-breathing C.O. he is talking about the ridiculousness of being a conscientious objector and a militant one at the same time [he had tried to enlist for military duty over half-a-dozen times during World War II before his sudden conversion to pacifism]. . . . He sees himself as slightly ridiculous, and at the time of course he was. . . . There are less self-aggrandizing ways of refusing to fight, but Lowell wanted to provoke attention and give offense, and there was this quality in him, this

insubordination, that expresses itself in all kinds of poetry. And some of it is about his own father, but some of it is about any kind of authority that he wants to rebel against, including organized society itself. ("On Lowell" 3, 7)

Twenty years after "telling off" Roosevelt, Lowell would protest another president's war policy by refusing to attend Johnson's White House Festival of the Arts. Again ambivalence and self-aggrandizement lay behind his rebuke. First he accepted the invitation; several days later he rejected it. He claimed in an open letter: "I am very enthusiastic about most of your domestic legislation and intentions" (*CP* 371), knowing full well that enthusiasm was what normally pushed him *toward* rather than *away from* authoritarian figures like Johnson.

Lowell's political personae (Johnson among them) oscillated on a kind of Yeatsean gyre from hawkishness to doveishness, which, as the Chinamen on their mountain in "Lapis Lazuli" know, is the tragic cycle of imperial history. His moral abhorrence of the destructiveness he was capable of when feeling sublime, and his embarrassed perception of how ridiculous he looked when he donned the emperor's robes or the revolutionary's beret, forced him to adopt the more ordinary wardrobe of a liberal citizen. Although Lowell's poetic career progressed through several dramatic stylistic shifts, his political attitudes, orchestrated as they were by his ambivalence toward the sublime, remained consistently inconsistent. Despite his poetic gifts, Lowell lacked the temperament to take one principled stand and abide by it. As John Thompson, a friend from Lowell's Kenyon days, put it: "He was the great poet of our time. . . . He covered everything: politics, which he didn't know beans about. . . . He wrote about it anyway" (24). Aware from an early age that his sublime pursuits were perhaps little more than vaunting and posing, Lowell joined his critics and satirized himself accordingly. He had the grace and humor to see himself both as he was and as he wished.

An Imperial Anti-Imperialist

Although critics have made much of Lowell's early Catholic politics, especially because they gained impetus from Weber's thesis that the individualistic spirit of Protestantism led ineluctably to the excesses of capitalism, his politics are usually informed by Marxist and Freudian principles. As Lowell made apparent in his letter to Roosevelt when he qualified his praise for his family's long tradition of military service, because it was partially tarnished by "Money, Politics and Imperialism" (*CP* 368), politics was something that began in his patrician home. Oedipal and class struggles, insurrections against biological fathers and capitalist patriarchs, arduous attempts to empower the self by seizing the means of (re)production, for Lowell were all intimately tied to conflicts with his parents and relatives. Society was fundamentally an extension of his Boston family. A Marxist Lucifer or Freudian Ahab, Lowell pitted his political energies against authoritarian figures in order to usurp their power. Lowell could express animosity toward capitalist and imperialist plunder as well as "envy [for] the conspicuous / waste of our grandparents on their grand tours / . . . breezing on their trust funds through the world" (*LS* 3). Rather than progress dialectically beyond class struggle to a socialist utopia, Lowell, more in Freudian than in Marxist fashion, sought to outdo his aristocratic forebears by becoming even more imperial and patriarchal than they. If his father was merely a naval officer and bourgeois businessman, Lowell would join forces with his mother, whose identifications with Alexander and Napoleon were carried to ludicrous extremes. He would unseat his father and set himself up as the new Caesar or Oedipus in the House of Lowell.

Eagleton's and Jameson's Marxist descriptions of the "bad sublime" as capitalism's terrifying yet astonishing ability to proliferate commodities, wealth, and bafflingly intricate systems to keep moneymakers in power, apply to Lowell's notions of a sublime that both offends and entices. Even early in his career, America's "military-industrial complex" aroused this sort of paradoxical response. His poem "Sublime Feriam Sidera Vertice," written at Kenyon three years before he announced his conscientious objection to the Second World War, casts doubt on the warrior ethic he had extolled five years earlier in the youthful essay "War: A Justification." His allegorical account of Ahab's whale hunt in the poem interrogates the sublime power of America symbolized by the whale. Should he submit to it or incorporate it? He makes use of Hobbes and Hegel as he contemplates the pros and cons of military sacrifice:

> Great Commonwealth, sail on and on and roll
> On blood, on my free blood; my heart misgave,
> Confessed itself a slave,
> And Hegel proved State an invested soul,
> Oh mortmain, patron and gaoler of the grave. (17)

The poem is cramped by New Critical obsessions with paradox and compression, but the heart's misgivings over whether to freely sacrifice its blood to keep America's leviathanic "ship of state" afloat are relevant to Lowell's subsequent political postures. A later revision, "Leviathan" in *Land of Unlikeness*, alludes to the final scene in *Moby Dick*—the *Pequod* going down with its flag flying—to stress Lowell's conviction that the violent pursuit of sublime ideals, either by an Ahabian America or by its enemies, whether initiated out of necessity or out of free choice, usually ends in madness and death.

"The Quaker Graveyard in Nantucket" is Lowell's most accomplished attempt to dramatize his schismatic view of the American sublime and its political manifestation in the country's "military-industrial complex." It is an early instance in which he projects his political compulsions onto Ahab and charts the tragic consequences of his "leap for the sublime." Another is "The Boston Nativity," in which he rouses a sardonic "clap for Freedom and Democracy" in a beast-filled, Ark-like ship of state that once again "lists / Into the sea." "Soon the leviathan / Will spout American" (*LU* 9–10), Lowell jests, as if Moby Dick is the Ark and America, too. The suggestion, so often repeated in Lowell's political allegory, is that America's pursuit of the sublime will turn nation and world into a brutish leviathan. In its mad, idealistic campaign to convert all nations to democracy (so they can all "spout American" language and culture), America will destroy itself in the process of destroying others. "The Boston Nativity" imagines America swallowed and regurgitated by an apocalyptic beast of its own making.

Lucifer and leviathan jockey for command in these early poems. As in "The Quaker Graveyard," Lowell typically expresses empathy for both predator and prey, just as Melville does in *Moby Dick*. Ahab—that monomaniacally bellicose Quaker pacifist, indifferent to but participating in Captain Peleg's and Captain Bildad's capitalist enterprise—becomes a persona for Lowell's political antinomies. The leviathan becomes Lowell's symbol for the sublime wonder and terror of political power he alternately despises, reveres, and envies. His early reading of *Moby Dick* no doubt encouraged this symbolic connection between the whale and the American sublime. Melville frequently discourses on the "unimaginable sublimity" (30) of the whale. Its whiteness, he insists, is "sublime . . . [and exists] to heighten that terror to the furthest bounds" (158). For Lowell the sublime whale would metamorphose into Hobbes's Leviathan, a fit emblem for the awesome and awful powers in the American state.

Because modern civilization is so painfully aware of the ravages of authoritarian and imperialist regimes, Thomas Weiskel argues in *The Romantic Sublime* that it is now hard for informed poets to approach the sublime's magisterial presumptions without irony. In revisions of "The Cloister" written at Kenyon, Lowell's emphatically ironic evaluation of the politicized sublime dovetails uncannily with Weiskel's. For Lowell, the collusion of poetic and political rhetoric in leading millions toward catastrophe is reminiscent of Hitler's, Mussolini's, and, by guilty association, his own oratorical performances, which also could mesmerize. As Lowell journeyed through history, contemplating the "sublime ambitions" of political notorieties, he always seemed to encounter himself. In his early poetry, Hitler and Napoleon appear most frequently as mirrors of his own egotistical drives for power. A passage from a chapter in his unpublished autobiography titled "Rock" (the name of the place where his grandfather had a farm) admits, "I wanted to live at Rock twelve months of the year. I wanted to be the Napoleon of my day-dreams" (H 2220). As a boy, he filled a whole notebook with information about Napoleon's troops. A poem that went through many drafts at Harvard explicitly connects a youthful romanticism, in which, as Wordsworth wrote in "Resolution and Independence," "By our own spirits are we deified" (167), with political megalomania. One version, entitled "Dada-Age Derived from Romance," ends:

> Hitler, Napoleon, Wordsworth and Freud
> You fruited us with alloyed fruit; our age
> Droops nude beneath your savage light, negroid
> In sex and sense, her soiled her sacred gauge. (H 2046)

What this nearly impenetrable quatrain suggests is that the four figures were Luciferian light-bringers or new Adams tempting the modern age with the bitter fruit of carnal knowledge. They revealed the savage, sexual animal beneath the civilized fig leaf. The fall into knowledge they engendered was a fall into a perception of evil and chaos. Rather than inspiring a Christian redemption, this latter-day fall inspired further political and artistic plunges into anarchy. Racist as the poem is, it shows Lowell grappling with the politics of the egotistical sublime, marshaling Freud in his effort to understand the Romantic underpinnings of his authoritarian and imperialist enchantments.

Another notebook from Lowell's undergraduate period at Harvard juxtaposes discussions of Romanticism's "reawakening of boundless imagination," Rousseau's organic, back-to-the-soil creed, and the French Revolution in an even more shocking rendition of "Dada-Age." Entitled "Our 20th Century Is a Derivation from Romantic Decadence," it argues:

> Herr Hitler was
> Just a reproduction of romance
> A trustworthy rustic
> Wordsworthian sheep-herder

In a verduous vegetarian Germany
Chewing a rural cheese. . . . (H 2045)

Another draft proposes: "Herr Hitler was / But an exponent and just a victim / Of the bigger better / Napoleonic" (H 2045). Lowell's sardonic tone distances poet from imperious patriarch, but only because the Napoleonic superman beguiles him so intensely. Although one might assume that Lowell was simply following the anti-Romantic dictates laid down by modernists and New Critics, on another level he was exposing the way the Romantic sublime gets smuggled into the authoritarian views of modernists and New Critics, and expressing solidarity with both Romantics *and* modernists. At Harvard, Lowell transcribed parts of Pound's *Cantos* into his notebooks and imitated Pound's style of political invective in his poems; simultaneously he applauded those Romantics, like Wordsworth, whom Pound thought most discardable. One uncollected poem begins:

> If I were great as Wordsworth
> And had done what he had done
> Multitudes would stand before my portrait
> In public where it hung
> And they would speak my name in awe. (H 2044)

Although the voice belongs to his poetry teacher at St. Mark's, Richard Eberhart, the obsession with Wordsworth's egotistical sublime and oratorical grandeur is Lowell's. In his pantheon of awesome and potentially awful personae, democratic Wordsworth takes his place alongside imperialists like Napoleon and Hitler. From the ideology of the sublime to the politics of tyranny is but a short step.

The fact that Wordsworth envisioned the French Revolution as an apocalypse that would issue in a new world order of republicanism and that Hitler envisioned the Second World War as an apocalypse that would solidify the power of the Third Reich for a millennium mattered little to the young Lowell. In his typological way of drawing analogies in history, "daemonic agents" who battle and quest for apocalyptic political ideals are not distinguished by their moral values; they are all lumped together as if they constituted different parts of a whole, or different masks worn by the same person—Lowell. The poems in *Lord Weary's Castle*, as Jarrell pointed out, keep telling "one story and one story only," and this story of oppressive and liberating forces clashing in history is the story of Lowell's sublime politics. What Jarrell refrains from discussing in his review is his friend's sympathies with both sides. When Lowell told Alvarez that "The world seemed apocalyptic at that time [during and shortly after the Second World War], and heroically so. I thought that civilisation was going to break down, and instead I did" ("Conversation" 35), he implied that although the forces of civilization had defeated the forces of barbarism, the war continued unabated within his psyche. His failure to decide which side to support arose in part from his inconsistent appraisal of the sublime.

One of the best examples of Lowell's political antinomies, their apocalyptic proportions, and the way Lowell struggles to reconcile them is "To Peter Taylor on the Feast of the Epiphany." Like Yeats contemplating the horrors of political events in the early twentieth century (Yeats may be one of "the Irishmen" alluded to in the poem), Lowell expresses both love and loathing for his "rough beast . . . [that] / Slouches toward Bethlehem" (Yeats 187) to reveal itself in a new "Epiphany." Political periods and identities merge in Lowell's allegorical version of recent history. America, Italy, Germany, and Japan are all rough beasts; their apocalyptic war might end time as we know it and might initiate a new beginning as well. As in Yeats's cyclical view of history, nativity and apocalypse are two ends of the same gyre. The fundamental theme of the poem, however, is fear (a word that appears at the beginning, middle, and end). Lowell could be responding to his nemesis, Roosevelt, who believed that the only thing Americans had "to fear is fear itself." Just as he had rebuffed the president's war policy, now he rebuffs his policy on fear. His point is that the fear of war is also, paradoxically, its attraction. Although he mocks all daredevils who lust for fear, he confesses that he also reveres what should be feared. Lowell begins his epistolary meditation on the cataclysm of the Second World War as if he were considering the fearful and wonderful aspects of the sublime:

> Peter, the war has taught me to revere
> The rulers of this darkness, for I fear
> That only Armageddon will suffice
> To turn the hero skating on thin ice
> When Whore and Beast and Dragon rise for air
> From allegoric waters. Fear is where
> We hunger: where the Irishmen recall
> How wisdom trailed a star into a stall
> And knelt in sacred terror to confer
> Its fabulous gold and frankincense and myrrh. . . . (LWC 52)

Lowell ironically cherishes the Luciferian rulers of darkness—presumably Roosevelt as well as Hitler, Mussolini, and Hirohito—because their mutual evils might provoke apocalyptic redemption. If Lowell imagines America and himself as Christ-like heroes skating rather than walking on icy water, he implies the opposite as well—that such heroes are emissaries of the devil, and only a conflagration like Armageddon will "turn" or "convert" them from their current dangerous track.

The "sacred terror" of Lowell's magi before the Christ Child parallels his own sacred terror before the satanic politicians who wage the Second World War. Daemons, whether godly or ghoulish, exert a didactic force; they teach Lowell to fear and revere and, like Christian in *Pilgrim's Progress*, to travel the difficult path toward God. Lowell, however, refuses to stay on the one, right path. He skates on thin ice. The poem's allegoric quest for the sublime leads to an entrepreneur who, like the warmongers Lowell detests, makes money off people drawn to the fear that war instills. The rides he offers on "pre-war planes" seem to be for amusement. Lowell's message is that the old men who nostalgically hark back to the romance of war are ridiculous. Like Warren in his poem on Emerson and airplanes, he mocks their pursuit of sublime altitudes. Satanic, Christian, and secular forms of the sublime collide as Lowell attempts to explain the religious foundation of his politics. His "barker" at the end might as well be the devil. Although he transports his customers (whom Lowell mocks as rich daredevils) into heaven, Lowell implies they are headed toward hell:

> And the sharp barker rigs his pre-war planes
> To lift old Adam's dollars for his pains;
> There on the thawing ice, in red and white
> And blue, the bugs are buzzing for the flight.
> December's daylight hours have gone their round
> Of sorrow with the sun into the sound,
> And still the grandsires battle through the slush
> To storm the landing biplanes with a rush—
> Until their cash and somersaulting snare
> Fear with its fingered stop-watch in mid-air. (*LWC* 52)

The grandsires "snare" their moment of ecstatic fear mechanically and monetarily. Presumably the paid flight is timed with a stopwatch. Lowell wants to praise the frisson of sacred as opposed to profane fear because, contrary to what Roosevelt said, he believes that it can lead to something positive. It can precipitate a communion with the terrible God of apocalyptic judgment. And apocalypse may scare or punish the corrupt back to the path of righteousness.

The complex layering in Lowell's allegory makes it difficult to determine his political stance. Is he a Fascist sympathizer (several years before writing the poem he had backed Franco in the Spanish Civil War)? Does he solicit "The rulers of this darkness," as Yeats occasionally did, because things must be brought to a terrible climax before they can improve? Is he a zealous fundamentalist quaking in sacred terror before an epiphany of God? Is he a liberal democrat bemoaning the financiers who capitalize on the machinery and romance of war? Is he a Poundian reactionary or Southern Agrarian attacking all entrepreneurial warmongers? Or is he simply a political satirist weighing and mocking all these stances for their faults? It is difficult to tell. In the end the only conclusion may be that there is no conclusion. After investigating his contradictory political ideas, rather than resolving them, Lowell leaves them in suspension.

Lowell's quester in *Lord Weary's Castle* usually staggers through an apocalyptic present that strikes him as good only insofar as its fearful demolitions promise renovation. The murderous anarchy of revolutions, however, inspires a nostalgia for the sort of rigid, aristocratic orders they intend to overthrow. In "The Exile's Return" Lowell adopts the regal persona of Louis Philippe, who left France for a life in exile in England in 1848 as revolutionary leaders set up a republican government at the Hôtel de Ville. When Lowell surveys the war-ravaged building, he longs nostalgically for an imperial past, much as Yeats did in poems about great houses in Ireland. He pines for ceremony and hierarchical order rather than the "sublime ambitions" of revolutionaries. The bellicose winter storm menacing the Hôtel is deadening rather than apocalyptically renovative:

> There mounts in squalls a sort of rusty mire,
> Not ice, not snow, to leaguer the Hotel
> De Ville, where braced pig-iron dragons grip
> The blizzard to their rigor mortis. (*LWC* 9)

The "gray, sorry, and ancestral house / Where the dynamited walnut tree / Shadows a squat, old, wind-torn gate" (*LWC* 9) is a reminder of aristocratic splendors in decline rather than democratic virtues in ascendance. The allusion at the poem's end to the inscription on the gate of hell in Dante's *Divine Comedy*—"Abandon all hope, ye who enter"—aligns Lowell with other pilgrims who took the trip to the underworld. Confronting the satanic energies released by wars, the poet's persona remains politically ambiguous. He could be a monarchist or a republican, an aristocrat or a revolutionary, a Louis Philippe or an "unseasoned liberator" (*LWC* 9), a Nazi invader or a resistance fighter. In any case, the hell of postwar Europe has little Blakean élan. Its horrors are banal rather than thrilling.

The Second World War and Lowell's conflicting judgments of it instill the poems in *Lord Weary's Castle* with an air of furious tension. In poems like "The Quaker Graveyard in Nantucket," for instance, Lowell depicts himself stretched to the breaking point by issues of power. He wants to embrace Ahab's all-out onslaught on monstrous evil, but in his allegorical interpretation of the war the monster is everywhere ("its corruption over-runs this world," *LWC* 18). With its policy of carpet bombing German cities and incinerating thousands of Japanese civilians with atomic bombs, Ameri-can idealism has metamorphosed, according to Lowell, into the sort of imperialistic destructiveness it allegedly fought against. The overpowering menace of stormy, nocturnal seas is Lowell's traditional site for a sublime agon. The elements, like the Germans or the Japanese, are enemies: "The sea was still breaking violently and night / Had steered into our North Atlantic Fleet" (*LWC* 14). America is an enemy as well. To emphasize this point, Lowell elegizes his American cousin who was killed by American rather than enemy weapons.

Ahab and his Quakers fascinate Lowell because they possess America's self-destructive will to pursue political ideals that are virtuous as well as vicious. His funeral at sea mourns innocent as well as knowing victims of sublime conflicts, and in turn elegizes his own potential victimization because he, too, is a self-destructive Ahab. He admonishes nation and self in a mood of existential despair, or what Bell calls "Christian nihilism" (*Nihilist* 31):

> Sailors, who pitch this portent at the sea
> Where dreadnaughts shall confess
> Its hell-bent deity,
> When you are powerless
> To sand-bag this Atlantic bulwark, faced
> By the earth-shaker, green, unwearied, chaste
> In his steel scales: ask for no Orphean lute
> To pluck life back. (*LWC* 14)

What is so startling in the poem is Lowell's almost prurient fascination with the violent power struggles on earth as well as in heaven, his Catholic empathy for all victims—he mourns for Ahab as well as "the hurt beast" (*LWC* 15)—and his anti-Catholic and antielegiac attitudes concerning the efficacy of redemptive rituals. When he asks "Who will dance / The mast-lashed master of Leviathans / Up from this field of Quakers in their unstoned graves" (*LWC* 17), his answer at various points in the poem is "no-one." "Only bones abide / There, in the nowhere, where their boats were tossed / Sky-high, where mariners had fabled news / of IS, the whited monster" (*LWC* 16). Jehovah is Moby Dick, a whited sepulcher as well as a mon-strous, bellicose world-power that may toss bones and boats toward heaven but in the end sinks them in the void.

Throughout the poem Lowell teases us with intimations of redemption, of relief from the world's agonistic blood feuds, and then undercuts them with existential doubt. "In the great ash-pit of Jehoshaphat / the bones cry for the blood of the white whale" (*LWC* 18), but these Quaker bones yearning for the Last Judgment could be crying out for revenge on Moby Dick and Jehovah as much as for an absolving baptism in the beast's Christ-like blood. In this world of elemental strife the statue of "Our Lady at Walsingham" is as impotent as the Quakers' bones. Lowell states: "There's no comeliness / At all or charm" or power to redeem "in that expressionless / Face with its heavy eyelids" (*LWC* 19). In the battle to wrest sublimity from an adversarial power—traditionally an affair for men only—Lowell introduces a woman who promises the sort of transcendence expressed by his earlier hero, St. Simeon. The episode "is wracked by a sense of failure." Axelrod is prescient when he apprises us of "the extreme improbability and even, perhaps, the undesirability of faith" communicated by the statue. Although the Virgin "presents the only existent alternative to human chaos, it is not an alternative Lowell can endorse with whole heart" (61). Lowell's failure to endorse the woman has agnostic as well as misogynist roots. Although his description of women in world affairs (such as the political and military affairs of the Second World War) may be historically accurate, his description of their failure to rise above a passive, moribund role is also demeaning. Just as he had chided Bishop for failing to "live / Our usual roaring sublime" (H 2199), now he satirizes a similar woman for withdrawing from the "roaring" violence of the Atlantic. The ocean's violent turbulence, he suggests, is too much for her. As a result, she regresses to her customary role of somnolent spectator.

Feminists interested in the sublime have pointed out that the genre typically excludes women just as Lowell's poem does. In her essay, "In the Twilight of the Gods: Woman Poets and the American Sublime," for instance, Joanne Feit Diehl shows how Emersonian and Freudian theories of the sublime agon confine themselves to the way new Adams and new Oedipuses grapple with patriarchal tradition to achieve patriarchal power, but pay little attention to women. If Emerson and Freud believe that sublimity arises from an identification with an Other (the "not-me" of nature and tradition) or an adversary (the Father), which leads to transcendence (they seem to say "if you can't beat them, join them and then beat them"), Diehl argues that traditionally women either have been unable to identify with male precursors or have been crushed by them:

> Consider the possibilities—if authority is associated with the patri-
> arch, then the woman poet cannot so easily experience the identity between

self and all-powerful other; instead, his presence may seem so "ravishing" (a term long associated with the workings of the sublime), that she is vanquished. As avatar of the patriarch, his power remains external to hers, for she is not the son who joins that male company of descendental poets known as poetic tradition. If, on the other hand, the woman poet experiences this external power as feminine, as the mother, her "inspiration" does not impart the gift of tradition. (177)

On the other side of the gender fence:

The male poet resolves his difficulties—the terrifying discontinuity in his selfhood—by aligning himself with the culturally assumed identity of the patriarchal voices of authority, thus at once reclaiming his own superiority without denying his access to the reciprocal relationship between the imagination and the natural world. Not so, the woman poet. Faced with an overdeterminacy born of a relationship where her position as passive, receptive self mirrors her culturally assumed identity, a relationship where the authoritative power *is* the masculine other, she becomes either silenced by the incursions of the sublime or radicalized by the process. (177–78)

Lowell's "Quaker Graveyard" reveals in abundant detail how men fight for their trophies of tragic sublimity in a sea crowded with challenging patriarchal powers. Women, on the other hand, are consigned to the sidelines, where—if their "heavy eyelids" offset the forces of sleep long enough to allow for a moment of consciousness—they merely witness the contest in stony silence.

The virgin at Walsingham in many respects resembles the wrung-out, ineffectual Christ figures in Lowell's *Land of Unlikeness*. She has sacrificed her life in this world for a life in the next. For a critic like Barbara Freeman, this feminine sacrifice is built into the sexist dynamics of the sublime. In her provocative essay "The Rise of the Sublime: Sacrifice and Misogyny in Eighteenth-Century Aesthetics," one of her focuses is Kant's *Critique:*

From the outset, Kant's formulation of the sublime presupposes an interplay between two highly personified faculties of mind, the imagination and reason. This dyad is in fact a barely disguised hierarchy that provides the grounds for debasing one half of the couple at the expense of the other. For the attainment of the sublime is dependent upon a sacrifice; its cause is the collapse of the imagination's capacity to connect empirical reality with the realm of abstract ideality, and reason's subsequent amplification occurs only because the imagination has been unable to comprehend reality. Indeed, Kant links the defeat of the imagination to the very possibility of representing what had belonged previously to the domain of the unrepresentable. (84)

As with Lowell and other commentators, Freeman's interpretation of the sublime amounts to an *allegoresis*. She admits: "The interaction between the reason and the imagination in the sublime is itself an allegory of gender relations" (85). Mining novels written at the time the sublime was being disseminated and discussed in England, Freeman concludes: "The role of the imagination in the Kantian sublime reflects the very notion of feminine inferiority that women writers of the period were beginning to resist, and that their concurrent development results from a reaffirmation of traditional constructs of gender at the very moment when these were being powerfully, and institutionally, threatened" (92). The sexual politics of "The Quaker Graveyard" are deeply traditional; the Lady's sacrificial impotence allows the various masculine characters to pursue the sublime unchecked. If "Kant's sublime tells the story of internalized oppression, one of the principal strategies through which patriarchy reproduces itself" (90), then "Our Lady at Walsingham" represents a Kantian imagination overwhelmed by the onslaught of worldly experience, repressing itself out of a sense of customary subservience inculcated by the patriarchal culture that storms around it, and making it possible for masculine forces to step in and assert their dominance.

Does Lowell's poem submit unreservedly to the sort of misogynist values Freeman finds encoded in the sublime? Again, it is difficult to tell where Lowell stands. At times he appears to be as critical of the patriarchal power struggles intrinsic to the sublime as is Freeman. What is disturbing about Lowell's poem, at least from a feminist perspective, is its indulgence in a rhetoric—the "harsh, grating, powerfully disruptive kinaesthetic diction" (46), as Staples calls it, that betrays an enchantment with the sort of patriarchal conflicts the poet supposedly opposes. Numerous critics have noticed that Lowell takes a certain gothic pleasure in describing the horrors of the whale hunt, even though he castigates the men who conduct it. What is also disturbing is the poem's denial of any practical political means of ameliorating the horrors of such enterprises. Men will be men, Lowell implies, and will continue to hunt and fight for the sublime as their fathers did; women will be women and stay behind. They will maintain roles of voiceless stoicism as they have done for centuries. Although Lowell casts a cold, realistic eye on the cyclical violence of history, he adopts both masculine and feminine roles to express his divided temperament (as a conscientious objector he was a bystander, like the Virgin at Walsingham, while his peers wreaked havoc around the world). He expresses his and his culture's embattled factions but gives little hope for their resolution in a more viable future.

History's Masquerade

History in *Lord Weary's Castle* is a cycle of encounters in which idealistic and usually Christian factions battle satanic forces, but do so with such enthusiasm that they become satanic themselves. Lowell is still an allegorical Everyman, history a masquerade in which he dons a multitude of different costumes, his message usually being that the masks of hero and villain are made from the same mold. According to Kant's dialectical notion of the sublime, everything "that blinds or binds: the Old Law, imperialism, militarism, capitalism, Calvinism, Authority, the Father" would confer sublimity if the antithetical mind, like "the perfect liberator whom the poet calls Christ" (Jarrell 20–22), could release its power to conceive and thereby transcend all those things that blind or bind. Sublimity for Kant arises from acts of pure reason. Lowell tirelessly emphasizes that the ideas and ideals of pure reason, when enforced politically, bathe the world in blood. He goes to the Second World War, the First World War, the American Civil War, the Revolutionary War, King Philip's War, and back to the earliest encounters between Pilgrims and Native Americans in order to document the conflagrations caused by sublime ideals. In poems like "Christmas Eve Under Hooker's Statue," Lowell's liberal endorsement of Northern idealism quickly turns into a pessimistic critique of all causes, which is hardly alleviated by the final glimmer of hope: "our fields are running wild: / Till Christ again turn wanderer and child" (*LWC* 23). The Christ-like Hooker (the Union general who was defeated at Chancellorsville) overlooks an Eden transformed into a wasteland, and knows that supposedly innocent, Christian children are the cause rather than the cure of such disasters. Lowell reflects on his own Christian childhood with sarcasm in "The First Sunday in Lent," where, surrounded by instruments of destruction in his attic, he seems more satanic than Christ-like (he relishes "A Luger of a Hun, / Once blue as Satan" that "breaks Napoleon / My china pitcher" (*LWC* 21). If the child is father to the man, Lowell berates both for the bloodshed caused by their Romantic ideals.

In "Salem," "Rebellion," and other poems interrogating the dynamics of the Revolutionary War, Lowell continues his assault on the fatal cost of history's allegedly sublime ideals. In one of his most concise examinations of the origins of American culture, "Children of Light," Calvinist Pilgrims, who for Lowell are as much agents of Lucifer as of God, confront a sublime continent of wonders and horrors and, according to the biblical paradigm of the Fall, turn Eden into a godless "land of unlikeness." The "inner light" Protestants destroy everything natural and fruitful—everything they mistakenly believe belongs to Indian and devil—in their quest for transcendence: "Embarking from the Nether Land of Holland, / Pilgrims unhoused by Geneva's night, / They planted here the Serpent's seeds of light" (LWC 34). Unhoused and unhoused (denied the Eucharist) because of their benighted Calvinist beliefs, these bellicose voyagers copy Cadmus, who planted dragon's teeth only to see warriors spring from the ground and murder each other. The survivors who go on to build the doomed city of Thebes are progenitors of those founding fathers of a doomed America. "The pivoting searchlights" (LWC 34) or lighthouses, which Lowell no doubt saw from the Connecticut coast when he resided there during the war, remind him of illuminated skies over embattled European cities. Contemporary wars, he argues, are legacies of "Our fathers [who] wrung their bread from stocks and stones / And fenced their gardens with the Redman's bones" (LWC 34) and of those earlier fathers descended from the "landless blood of Cain" (LWC 34). Unhoused exiles, they find spiritual sustenance in instruments of violence rather than in the traditional bread of the Eucharist. Like his Pilgrim ancestor Josiah Winslow (governor of Plymouth and enthusiastic supporter of King Philip's war), they deploy theology to justify their colonial atrocities.

The "Serpent's seeds of light" transform the American and global Eden into a poisonous garden. To Lowell, "inner light" Protestant enthusiasts, some of them Quakers like Ahab, tend to translate inward apocalypses into outward holocausts. Their sublime ambitions pit them against what they consider to be daemonic terrors (like the Native Americans) in the original American wilderness. By conquering those terrors, they attain the sublime but relegate themselves, as power passes from antagonist to protagonist, to the satanic status of their enemies. As usual, Lowell traces his own genealogy here. Some of his ancestors, after all, were among the original Pilgrims on the *Mayflower*. He grew from their "seeds of light," which for him are biological as well as Gnostic (the phrase is often used by Gnostics to describe that divine "spark" or "pneuma" in the self that makes possible a return beyond the fallen Creation to God). Mazzaro identifies these seeds as "the seeds in Matthew (13:5–6) which fell upon rocky ground . . . [and which] signify those who have heard and accepted God's Word, yet who could not withstand tribulations and persecutions" (30). Lowell's satanic "seeds of light," however, spark tribulations and persecutions with rabid abandon. They kindle his desire to be God or at least to be with God, and his antithetical attempts to restrain his violent Protestant hubris with Catholic rituals. As Cosgrave argues, the poem shows that "Catholic beliefs and [Protestant] Predestinarian impulses were at war with him" (82).

Expositors of this Gnostic, Protestant, and thoroughly American religion have shown that the enthusiast's obsession with an inner God who reveals Himself to the self in solitude translates into a political obsession with freedom, democratic individualism, and what Bloom has called in *The American Religion* "The flag and the fetus, our Cross and our Divine Child" (47). Brooding on America's founding Protestant enthusiasts and their quests for Gnostic sublimity, Bloom expresses a Lowellish despair: "The religion of the spark or pneumatic self [or "seed of light"] consistently leads to a denial of communal concern, and so perhaps to an exploitation of the helpless by the elite. . . . What I have called the American Orphism [a creed stressing the potential divinity of the elite or elect self] has led on to what is most distinctive in our cultural and aesthetic achievement, but it may have had a miserable fallout upon our political morality" (58). For Lowell, too, the American religion informs and contaminates American political ideology. Allegorizing the sublime into political, religious, psychological, and literary contexts, like Bloom he maps and critiques that obsessive quest for the inner light of God that burns most intensely in the solitary self. With a plethora of historical examples he shows how an enthusiasm for noble ideals fostered by a freedom from society and tradition is politically explosive. Carried to narcissistic and schizophrenic extremes, American self-righteousness promotes an egotistic sublimity that in turn leads to domestic and international debacles. Like Bloom, Lowell knows how close his own religion of agonistic sublimity is to fundamentalist politics. Both develop their allegorical interpretation of the sublime to scrutinize the ramifications of their ideals, and try to temper the reactionary as well as revolutionary elements of their temperaments with a liberal social conscience.

If the American way sanctions the freedom to regress from social responsibilities so that the Gnostic spark within every individual can return to its divine origin before the Creation, and if this regression promotes holier-than-thou jihads fought in the name of democracy, is a benevolent dictatorship preferable? What is better—an organic, homogeneous community bound by strict laws or a loosely knit conglomeration of individuals pursuing their heterogeneous agendas? For Lowell the decision came down to embracing the fascist politics of mentors like Pound, the aristocratic, reactionary politics of mentors like Eliot and Tate, and the more democratic politics of mentors like Williams. If Lowell had never recognized the tragic repercussions of American idealism, he could have sanctioned the democratic "pneuma" or "spark" with a clear conscience. For Lowell, however, the allegorical quest for such sublime ideals was part of a cycle that spun inevitably toward revolution, anarchy, and reactionary calls for order.

Although *Lord Weary's Castle* registers vehemently opposed responses to the political quest for sublimity, its flamboyant rhetoric betrays an enchantment with the sublime that Lowell found impossible to repress. His later volumes deploy a more subdued, conversational style that atones for his and America's penchant for the grandiose without repudiating it completely. In his allegorical interpretation of the sublime he continues to identify with America's bifurcated role as revolutionary republic and reactionary empire, and continues to deploy Lucifer as his persona. Starting with *The Mills of the Kavanaughs*, Lowell strives to offer a more confessional self-portrait; he begins to focus more directly on the private turmoil beneath the political mask. Myth is still important—especially the myth of Hades's rape of Persephone—but domestic rather than international politics dominates the scene. In Lowell's complicated drama he and his dead father coalesce into a ghost that haunts Anne Kavanaugh (a composite of Stafford and Lowell's mother) as she plays solitaire and reminisces on her married life in hell. Events that biographers speculate are true—Lowell's attempted rape of Stafford during their period together in Damariscotta Mills, Maine, and his attempt to strangle her in bed when she dreamed of another lover— give the poem its gothic flair. Despite or perhaps because of their conflicts, both Lowell and Stafford were extremely productive during this period, which is no doubt why the vegetation myth involving Hades, Persephone, and Demeter appealed so strongly. For Stafford, Lowell represented a satanic power, both horrifying and seductive, which aroused her Persephone-like fertility. At first a "violated bride / Uncertain even of her hold on hell" (*MK* 86), later in the poem she becomes adept at stealing fire from her enemy and putting it to productive use. As in the fertility myth, the infernal marriage allows for spring's recrudescence. Lowell documents her productivity as follows:

> Weary and glorious, once, when time was young,
> She ran from Hades. All Avernus burned.
> Black horse and chariot thundered at her heel.
> She, fleeting earthward, nothing seemed to steal,
> But the fruition that her hell had earned. (*MK* 86)

In the previous stanza Lowell's persona admits "I am married to myself" (*MK* 86), and in the drama he oppresses his wife with a fury that is unconscionable. In his sublime egotism, however, he merges with his opponents;

he, his wife, and his mother form a daemonic constellation that glows with his own Luciferian light. Although the domestic politics are ignominious, he shows that the divided parties are unified in their hellish enthusiasms.

Jarrell criticized this amalgamation as a major flaw in the poem: "There is a sort of monotonous violence and extremity about the poem, as if it were a piece of music that consisted of nothing but climaxes. The people too often seem to be acting *in the manner of* Robert Lowell. . . . You feel, 'Yes, Robert Lowell would act like this if he were a girl; but whoever saw a girl like Robert Lowell?'" (*"The Mills"* 42). Although Jarrell's sarcastic volleys hit their mark, they do so willy-nilly. *The Mills* is certainly flawed dramatically. Lowell's allegorical way of rendering domestic strife lacks the compression and persuasiveness that he had achieved in earlier dramatic lyrics. What Jarrell objects to is true about all Lowell's poetry, and certainly true about *Lord Weary's Castle*, which Jarrell adored. From the beginning, Lowell's poetry suffered from a "monotonous violence" (or a "monotonous sublime," as he would call it later), and his characters almost always mirror his own manners, or lack thereof.

If "The death of Satan was a tragedy / for the imagination" (*CP* 319), as Stevens maintained, Lowell repeatedly resurrects a politicized Satan as an example of the way individual power can triumph over external pressure. Lowell's middle confessional period is not so much an aberration as a continuation of this theme in a different key. The political convictions that lend the poems their sardonic pathos come from a Lucifer in liberal guise. His deepening awareness of sexual politics in America provokes guilty avowals of collusion in patriarchal vices. A poem like "Going to and fro," for instance, sketches his vacillations between devilish desires and liberal principles. It also illustrates his more muted style. Like Stevens's satanic, soldierly poet in "Esthétique du Mal," who experiences "Pain /Audible at noon, pain torturing itself, / Pain killing pain on the very point of pain," Lowell feels a hellish Vesuvius erupting in his own bowels:

> the intestines shiver,
> the ferry saloon thugs with your pain
> across the river—pain,
> suffering without purgation,
> the back-track of the screw.
> But you had instants,
>
> to give the devil his due—
> he and you
> once dug it all out of the dark

> unconscious bowels of the nerves:
> pure gold, the root of evil,
> sunshine that gave the day a scheme.
>
> And now? Ah Lucifer!
> how often you wanted your fling
> with those French girls, Mediterranean
> luminaries, Mary, Myrtho, Isis—
> as far out as the sphynx!
> The love that moves the stars
>
> moved you!
> It set you going to and fro
> and up and down— (*FUD* 29–30)

God's cosmic love moves this Luciferian poet in a dialectic way; it incites him to rebel against God and love until the only god within is "pathological enthusiasm."

When Lowell writes in "New Year's Eve" about his second wife, Elizabeth Hardwick, "when we joined in the sublime blindness of courtship, / loving lost all its vice with half its virtue" (*FL&H* 25), he is elegizing as well as deriding satanic sublimities, as he had done in "Waking Early Sunday Morning." "Myopia: A Night" in *For the Union Dead* delivers another elegy and eulogy to Lucifer, whose sexual politics fill Lowell with a mix of nostalgia, guilt, and sardonic humor. To the backward-looking Lowell, paradise lost is not so much Eden lost as Lucifer lost. His sublime light, which for Lowell is the light of sex sublimated into political enthusiasm, has dwindled before the light of conscience. Lowell yearns for a lost Gnostic splendor, as if Lucifer were his paradoxical hero of enlightenment:

> I see the morning star . . .
>
> Think of him in the Garden,
> that seed of wisdom, Eve's
> seducer, stuffed with man's
> corruption, stuffed with triumph:
> Satan triumphant in
> the Garden! In a moment,
> all that blinding brightness
> changed into a serpent,
> lay grovelling on its gut. (*LWC* 32)

The sonnets at the end of Lowell's career continue this elegiac examination of a prelapsarian paradise, emphasizing that political hubris creates a history punctuated by triumphs and disasters.

Lowell's mode in *History* is apocalyptic once again; he conjures up daemonic figures from history's hellish pandemonium and judges them like a cynical Jehovah. As Vendler said: "These poems live neither on ideology nor on logic . . . ; instead, they yield to the lawless free associations of the rocked and dangerous mind. . . . Lowell's data are not primarily historical . . . ; they are symbolic. Cain, Nero, Caligula, Jesus, and Napoleon all serve equally as projections of Lowell himself" (132, 135). Compared with *Lord Weary's Castle*, the style of the sonnets appears slapdash, the aperçus tossed off at random, the narrative structure jerrybuilt. Nevertheless, the theme of the sublime persists. Saturated with terror and grandeur, history is a daunting graveyard of monuments to events and heroes against which Lowell measures his own aspirations. Emblematic of his fantasies and fears, history's great men and women receive equal doses of charity and mockery. It is as if Lowell recognized his own features either magnified or dwarfed in history's statues. Again and again he trains his acerbic, dialectical wit on political figures who attained sublimity through magnificent displays of power, whether for republican or despotic ends.

Several examples from *History* can serve to illustrate Lowell's new way of expressing his myriad-minded stance toward the autobiographical and political facets of the sublime. An early sonnet, "Death of Alexander," commemorates a hero with whom Lowell had identified from the time he was a boy. "The young man's numinous eye is like the sun" (*H* 40), Lowell remarks, as if to praise Alexander's visionary power. By the end of the poem, however, the quest for the sort of power symbolized by the sun arouses a flurry of ambiguous reactions. About this tragic political hero, Lowell says:

> He soon dies,
> this after all, perhaps, the "better thing." . . .
> No one was like him. Terrible were his crimes—
> but if you wish to blackguard the Great King,
> think how mean, obscure and dull you are,
> your labors lowly and your merits less—
> we know this, of all the kings of old,
> he alone had the greatness of heart to repent. (*H* 40)

It is better that Alexander die young, because death will put an end to his terrible crimes before they proliferate further. Nevertheless, early death ensures his martyrdom (to which Lowell quickly subscribes) and the perpetuation of his heroic example. Alexander's sublime accomplishments, as honorable as they are horrific, make Lowell's seem puny. Commending Alexander because he repudiated the "crimes" that made him famous, Lowell by extension exonerates his own lowly labors because they seem penitential. Lowell draws back from the terrible heights of the sublime to the lower ground of moral probity, all the while asserting that he is on common ground with his hero.

He establishes this common ground in poem after poem so that *History* becomes a kind of elysian fields where Lowell mingles casually with all the imperious dead. Later in *History*, for instance, he scrutinizes the "sublime ambitions" of Stalin as if they were his own:

> Stalin? What shot him clawing up the tree of power—
> millions plowed under with the crops they grew,
> his intimates dying like the spider-bridegroom?
> The large stomach could only chew success. What raised him
> was an unusual lust to break the icon,
> joke cruelly, seriously, and be himself. (*H* 143)

The Russian state here is a jungle and Stalin a predatory animal whose appetite for power drives him murderously to the top. His iconoclasm (against the church and the old ways of the tsarist aristocracy), his satirical humor, and his contradictory personality link him to Lowell. He is one more example of a Luciferian revolutionary who strives for sublime ideals by fighting the old oppressive order, only to institute his own reign of terror in its place. This is "Revolution returning to grand tragedy," as Lowell states in his meditation on the French Revolution "Robespierre and Mozart as Stage." He comments sardonically: "Robespierre could live with himself: 'The republic / of Virtue without *la terreur* is a disaster. / Loot the chateaux, dole bread to Saint Antoine'" (*H* 76). Here again Lowell stresses the dialectical energies at work in his "one story." The pursuit of sublime ideals is a revolutionary struggle against overbearing powers, but in wresting sublimity from one oppressive system the "daemonic agents" simply transfer it to their own.

Late poems that dramatize the trials of poet friends like Bishop and Jarrell also take the political sublime to court and reach equally ambiguous verdicts. In "Soliloquy" (H 2238), Lowell sets Bishop's feelings about the sublime in the context of both personal and political power struggles, and speculates that she represses her erotic love for him because he represents an awesome, overpowering tyrant—the sort of patriarchal power that she bemoans in poems like "Roosters" and "Brazil, January 1, 1502." Since Lowell aligns himself with an egotistically sublime Wordsworth as well as a mad, despotic King George, he casts Bishop as his (and their) opponent and allows her to articulate her reservations about his joyous but ferociously mad sublimity: "I will serve/ England's true genius, I desire to bend / With humorous awe to love's contingency, // Yet cringe disloyally from his fierce joy" (H 2238).

According to "Soliloquy," Wordsworth finds sublimities in "the shooting lights" of his sister's "wild eyes," *and* Bishop finds her "wild lights" in Lowell's manic eyes, but they remind her not so much of Wordsworth's "elevated thoughts" and "intimations of immortality" as of her mother's madness, triggered by the death of her father. Immediately after comparing her transcendent love for Lowell to a star, she recollects similar homicidal and imperial tendencies in her mother, as if her mother were another American Caligula or Lucifer, another "mad Mussolini" unfurling "the eagle of Caesar," or another Ahabian Lowell primed with idealistic violence:

> Starlike the eagle on my locket watch,
> Mother's sole heirloom. I hear her, "All I want
> To do is kill you!"—I, a child of four;
> She early American and militant. (H 2238)

By the end of the poem Bishop realizes that her mother is within her, a muse comparable to the sublimely mad King George. Possessed by the same sort of political daemon or inner god as Lowell's other Pilgrim enthusiasts, Bishop supplicates as well as represses her "genius begging for its cap and bells" (H 2238). By the end of the poem Lowell has erased sexual and cultural differences to the point that he and Bishop are one.

A poem to Jarrell drafted in the mid-1960s, shortly after his discussion of American culture with Alvarez, extends a sympathetic hand to another friend similarly embroiled in the politics of the sublime. As with Bishop, Lowell projects his idiosyncrasies onto Jarrell. Similarly well versed in Freud and Marx, and similarly enlightened about the moral and political dialectic that can transmute earnest child into odious father, principled worker into dictatorial boss, sublime saint into tragic rebel, Jarrell is another Ahab or Lucifer whose enthusiasms plunge him toward death. One draft declares in self-reflexive fashion: "Easy to picture you as old, / still enthusiastic, spare, / snow-shocked" (H 2764). Addressing Jarrell's Marxist enthusiasms for workers, which like Lowell's were compromised by aristocratic biases, he asks:

"The work stands, but the workers?"
Those hewers of wood and stone
once so sublimely far from the sublime,
were contented with their lowly task
of building the Parthenon
in Nashville Tennessee . . .
and choosing you, Randall, as their model
for Ganymede. (H 2764)

Two sublimes vie for dominance as the transient workers, who are satisfied with the "lowly" sublimity of patiently doing their job (Lowell mockingly suggests they are sublimely or blissfully ignorant of sublime art), make way for the more glorious and permanent artifice of the poet. Like the workers on the American Parthenon, Lowell sculpts Jarrell as he was once sculpted—as a cupbearer to the gods transported to Olympus by Zeus's eagle—and thereby bestows upon him a measure of sublimity (a replica of the Parthenon was actually erected in Nashville and Jarrell as a child did indeed serve as the model for Ganymede). In later drafts Jarrell appears as a worker sublimely free from all sublime obsessions until his end, when he falls prey to them and joins the other mad, suicidal poets of his generation. Jarrell's devotion to great art like the Parthenon, which recalls Hugh Selwyn Mauberley's irascible determination "to resuscitate the dead art/ . . . to maintain 'the sublime'/ . . . In a half savage country" (Pound 61) leads to a tragic plunge in front of a car on a North Carolina highway. Lowell emphasizes Jarrell's contradictions to the end:

Then to escape, and never to escape
the eyes, lights piercing through the overpass,
while, black-gloved, black-coated,
you peer with harsh luminosity
into the blank vacuity of the tunnel
and plod stubbornly out on the thruway. . . . (H 2764)

The extremes of visionary "luminosity" and "blank vacuity" are obviously Lowell's as much as Jarrell's.

Lowell's classical commitment to the political world and his conservative appraisal of human follies dovetailed with the Kantian sublime—the apotheosis of individual reason and patriarchal morality—and the aesthetic ideology of the New Critics. Repeatedly undermining this outward drive toward political conservatism, however, was the Romantic's egotistical sublime, its pull toward narcissistic delusions in which Lowell cavorted as radical or reactionary strongman. The classicist in Lowell enlisted the intellect in a noble battle against such back-sliding. From Weiskel's Freudian and Lacanian perspectives, this battle for a Kantian sublime engages the Law of the Father and through an oedipal struggle allows an even stronger patriarch to reign in the superego. On the other hand, the egotistical sublime depends on a regression toward the Lawlessness of the Mother, toward the apolitical solitudes of the passionately uninformed. In Kant's stridently masculine and nationalist sublime, the feminine Other is politically offensive—a beautiful femme fatale who spawns peacefulness and "debasing self-interest, cowardice, and effeminacy, and tends to degrade the character of the nation" (113). For Lowell it created an abyss for the imagination to fill with patriarchal fantasies of political power. In the end, Lowell's regressive quests for a maternal sublime and progressive quests for a paternal sublime circled toward the same point.

Because Lowell liked to confuse the genders of his parents, conferring upon his mother a Napoleonic splendor and upon his father a bungling effeminacy, to a certain extent he deconstructs the sublime's gendered stereotypes and oppositional models. To Weiskel's contention that the sublime quester proceeds through castration anxiety at the hands of a fantasized father, entertaining oedipal patriphobia and matriphilia along the way to "an identification with the superior power" (93), Lowell might say that the Electra complex serves as an apt model as well. In his poems castration leads to fantasies of feminine power as often as of masculine power, to his mother as often as to his father. The original drafts of "Caligula," for example, depict a mad Lowell in Buenos Aires boasting of how he "lopped the civic power" representd by "Cleopatra's needle in the main square, / [which] rose like a phallus without flesh or hair" (H 2290). The phallic power is masculine, feminine, and neuter at the same time, and in this case castration precipitates a daemonic upsurge of sublimated energy.

Scrambling gender stereotypes and overturning hierarchies of power that traditionally maintain them, Lowell also deconstructs the antinomies of reason and enthusiasm, morality and mania, divine order and daemonic fanaticism. As for Blake, his heavens and hells are symbiotic, interchangeable. His sublime Ahab is also a satanic fool, his Edwards an objective scientist and maniacal enthusiast, his Caligula a divine emperor and brutal killer. His typical response to this Elysium of patriarchs and matriarchs is always a paradoxical one of withdrawal, confrontation, and moral evaluation. He will sigh "for the dark downward and vegetating kingdom / of the fish and reptile" (*FUD* 70) as if it represented the amoral, womblike, egotistical sublime, but then ascend to face historical conundrums and their political correlatives in the present. Sublime power crushes and invigorates him; it drives him back toward daemonic possession as well as forward toward poetic and political mastery. "The true sublime," he would agree with Longinus, "elevates us: uplifted with a sense of proud possession, we are filled with joyful pride, as if we had ourselves produced the very thing we heard" (Longinus 139). Lowell's all-too-joyous identifications with authorial masters and authoritarian tyrants also bear out Longinus's warning that sublimity "in the light of day . . . gradually declines from the terrible to the ridiculous" (29). The sort of political dialogue Lowell conducts with himself and others is poignantly sketched at the end of a draft of "Caligula":

> Oh why are you so lofty and unkind?
> I had high-spirits, courage of a kind;
> though circumstances doomed me to abuse
> my power and run amok, I could amuse. (H 2290)

Implicit in these lines is a diagnosis of sublimity, of the biological and cultural "circumstances" that conferred upon Lowell and his dubious heroes both tragic grandeur and ridiculousness. As he told Kunitz, political poems should "contain all our compulsions and biases" ("Talk" 54). Throughout his career he weighed different political leaders and ideologies in the balance of his often unbalanced mind. Putting on and stripping off political masks, whether feminine or masculine, with a boyish gusto that baffled his friends and critics, Lowell nevertheless struggled toward principled judgments, subjecting the sublime urges within his culture and himself to a trenchant moral critique.

5

The Psychopathology of the Sublime

A "Freudian Papa"

For Lowell, the sense of *hypsos* bestowed on those who actually believed they became the masterful authors or political orators who dazzled them was cause for psychological inquiry. Freud was the most helpful guide in his analysis of this sublime uplift, and Lowell imitated the psychoanalyst by mapping the oedipal neuroses and psychoses behind it. Bell has claimed that "Lowell was the celebrant of the psychopathology of everyday life" ("Robert Lowell" 240), but Lowell also conducted a psychopathology of the sublime in which he appeared as both Dionysian celebrant and Apollonian analyst. To Lowell's Freudian perspective, the desire to appropriate the rhetorical power of a "master" corresponds to impulses at work in the family romance and the origin of culture. Lowell no doubt recalled Freud's speculations in *Totem and Taboo* and *Civilization and Its Discontents* when he discussed the origins of American culture and the dynamics of the American sublime with Alvarez. Near the end of *Totem and Taboo*, Freud affirms: "The beginnings of religion, ethics, society and art meet in the Oedipus complex" (202). The various totem figures in early cultures are avatars of an original father; the various taboos against killing the totem animal and against sexual intercourse with totem cohorts of the opposite sex are vestiges of prohibitions against parricide and incest. A desire to transgress these prohibitions, however, persists. Although "the totem religion had issued from the sense of guilt of the sons as an attempt to palliate this feeling [of reverence and murderous hate for the father-god] and to conciliate the injured father through subsequent obedience" (187), the sons continue to harbor animosity toward religious commandments and rituals. Like oedipal heroes in tragic art, they still entertain plans to kill the father and abscond with the mother.

99

On the psychological level of Lowell's "one story," the sublime moment comes in the son's actual or fantasized displacement of the father, the identification with the internalized image of the father, and his abduction of the mother. To Longinus's description of beneficent influence and Kant's confidence in triumphant reason Lowell adds his Freudian stamp. Usurping a patriarchal "master" or dictatorial reason is predicated on oedipal mutiny rather than harmonious communion. Lowell's autobiographical essay "91 Revere Street" exemplifies his way of translating the sublime into a Freudian context. The reminiscence of his family home in Boston tells how Lowell's mother "suitably sublimed" (*LS* 18) his father to Napoleonic and Wagnerian proportions, and how, having forged an oedipal alliance, mother and son collaborate in overthrowing him. The collaboration is incestuous; Lowell's mother wants to play Jocasta to his Oedipus. When Commander Lowell returns to his post at the Naval Yard one Christmas Eve, Mrs. Lowell rushes into her son's bedroom: "She hugged me. She said, 'Oh Bobby, it's such a comfort to have a man in the house'" (*LS* 24). Lowell, only a child, resists his mother's advances. "I am not a man. . . . I am a boy" (*LS* 24), he said. As if to make up for lost possibilities, the late sonnet "1930's 9" records a fantasy of their sublime, orgasmic liaison: "It makes one larger to sleep with the sublime; / the Great Mother shivers under the dead oak" (*H* 112). This fantasy precedes the sonnets in *History* about Lowell's fight with his father over his early girlfriend, Anne Dick, near the end of 1936: "I knocked my father down. He sat on the carpet— / my mother calling from the top of the carpeted stairs, / their glass door locking behind me, no cover" (*H* 112). An oedipal assault on the father and a subsequent pursuit of a motherly woman who promised sublime dispensations was a strategy that recurred in Lowell's life and art.

After attacking his father (in an early uncollected poem he uses the naval metaphor of torpedoing), Lowell met with the psychiatrist and sonneteer Merrill Moore, who not only eased family tensions but helped the young Lowell launch his literary career. All origins, Lowell implies, involve sins of violation and self-aggrandizement, of upstart powers overthrowing reigning ones. Ahab's and Lucifer's bellicose attempts to subdue superior powers illustrate both the madness and the nobility of these originating endeavors. Even as a teenager Lowell was aware of the madness and destruction that pursuits of sublimity could unleash. In the sonnet "For Frank Parker 2," which appears shortly before "1930's 9" in *History*, Lowell derides his first attempts to capture Melvillean sublimities: "as we drifted I tried to put our rapture in verse: / *When sunset rouged the sun-embittered surf.* / This was the nearest we got to Melville's Nantucket" (*H* 111). Later he referred to this period as steeped in "pathological enthusiasm" (Hamilton

226–27). Several sonnets later, rehashing the anger over his father's romantic meddlings, he confesses his early alliance with Milton: "That morning nursing my dark, quiet fire / on the empty steps of the Harvard Fieldhouse in / vacation . . . saying the start of *Lycidas* to myself / fevering my mind and cooling my hot nerves" (*H* 112). These private agons have more public ramifications when Lowell compares them (as in his early "Rebellion," rewritten as "Father" in *History*) to the American Revolution and the birth of American culture. Just as Milton fought against kings, defending regicide in his inflammatory *Defence of the English People* and romanticizing Satan in *Paradise Lost* (and nearly suffering the consequences of his insubordination when Charles II took the throne after Cromwell), Lowell fought against his "suitably sublimed" father figures and suffered the consequences, whether in jail or mental hospital.

The second section of Weiskel's *The Romantic Sublime*, titled "The Psychology of the Sublime," offers a penetrating analysis of the sort of struggle that lay behind Lowell's ambitions to become the "masterful" power he opposed and revered. Alluding to Burke and Kant, Weiskel argues that the sublime moment depends on "a positive 'identification' with the Father, an identification which both presupposes the renunciation of parricidal aggression and facilitates an escape from the imagined consequences of a murder" (91). This identification makes way for an introjection of the superior power and the formation of the superego, which through a complex process of sublimation ends up being more daunting than its actual model. For Kant, this superego is the seat of reason, morality, and divinity; it can transcend life's terrors by reducing them to concepts and repressing them. For Freud the formula for the sublime might be: Let ego be where id is and let superego be where ego is. The superego's sublime civilizing powers, however, are wedded to the forces of oppression. Once the judgmental father is inside and once the son *is* the father, the superego will turn on itself, punishing the psyche for its aggressive usurpation. "Pathologically," Weiskel comments, "this results either in obsessional neurosis—when the ego refuses to acknowledge guilt—or in melancholia—when the ego accepts the guilt" (96).

Lowell's leaps for the sublime are partly motivated by his wish to transcend melancholy; his descents, partly by his guilty recognitions of the antics and crimes he committed while doing so. In an essay on Yeats, Jahan Ramazani points out that "mania corresponds to the sublime" because, as Freud showed, mania has access to "the whole quota of anticathexis which the painful suffering of melancholia had drawn to itself from the ego" (165). Once released from despair, the liberated, cathected ego flies toward a phantasmal empyrean. For Lowell this heaven beyond melancholy was populated with tyrannical patriarchs, Nietzschean supermen, and great writers (usually white and male); it was more a Blakean hell than a Christian heaven. While manic, as he was at Yaddo in 1949, he hobnobbed with tradition's august masters, a ghost among familiar ghosts. Alfred Kazin recalls: "He was at the top of a psychic crest down which he would slide the next season; but at this peak he talked in tongues; he was of the great company, with Milton and Hardy and Eliot; he was wonderful and frightening. He was not just damned good. Suddenly famous and deserving his fame, he was in a state of grandeur not negotiable with lesser beings" (251). Once again he had grasped an illusory sublimity.

Because Lowell struggled throughout his life to outdo his real father and the paternal image he internalized, forgoing the ordinary oedipal resolution, he soared and plummeted repeatedly. His manic-depressive cycle, although fundamentally chemical, was magnified by his unwillingness to repudiate his sublime models—his Caligulas, Napoleons, Mussolinis, and Hitlers. If his father was a benign naval officer, Lowell would be a menacing martinet or imperial commander in order to triumph over him. As Hamilton's biography attests, Lowell was always deeply embarrassed by his manic charades when he was clearheaded enough to reflect on them. Nevertheless, when lithium was prescribed near the end of his life, as Esther Brooks reveals, "He became more and more careless about its use and the consequent effects were subtly noticeable to those who knew him well. The well person and the unwell person seemed to rub together in a strange kind of muted euphoria" (285). This carelessness is not unusual, as Kay Jamison points out in her study of manic-depression, *Touched with Fire*. In a chapter that refers several times to Lowell, she asserts that some "writers and artists stop taking their medications [like lithium] because they miss the highs or the emotional intensity associated with their illness, or because they feel that drug side effects interfere with the clarity and rapidity of their thought or diminish their levels of enthusiasm, emotion, and energy" (7–8). Like others similarly afflicted, Lowell was reluctant to sacrifice the intoxicating energies he associated with the sublime. Along with many of his contemporaries (Roethke, Berryman, Plath, Sexton), he equated creative inspiration with manic power, and in order to achieve *hypsos*, he allowed hubris to catapult his imagination beyond the ego's limits, toward delusion and breakdown.

Although various eighteenth-century writers had "tried to establish sublime poetry upon enthusiastic emotion" (235–36), as Samuel Monk remarks in *The Sublime*, some of the principal commentators of the age detected, as Lowell did two centuries later, the pathological pitfalls of such endeavors. Although Burke celebrates obscurity as sublime because "In reality a great clearness helps but little towards affecting the passions, as it is in some sort an enemy to all enthusiasms whatsoever" (60), and celebrates the "fanatic preacher" who incites sublime passion among the ignorant because "It is our ignorance of things that causes all our admiration" (61), he also recognizes the dangers of such enthusiasms. He predicts Freud, Weiskel, and Lowell when he argues that the sublime rouses us out of "melancholy, dejection, despair" and other moribund moods of the "relaxed state of body" (135), only to plunge us into incapacitating frenzies and further depressions. Like psychopathologists after him, Burke knows that the euphoria of sublimity can become an addiction, an obsession that instigates neurotic repetitions: "This is the reason of an appearance very frequent in madmen; that they remain whole days and nights, sometimes whole years, in the constant repetition of some remark, some complaint, or sin; which having stuck powerfully on their disordered imagination, in the beginning of their phrensy, every repetition reinforces it with new strength; and the hurry of their spirits, unrestrained by the curb of reason, continues to the end of their lives" (74). Weiskel and Lowell make similar connections between the mind's need to reenact powerful stimuli, its longing for sublimity, and obsessional neurosis.

As Lowell grew older, his models for the sublime changed from those representing intellectual and moral power to those representing sexual and political power. The gods, as he explains in the late sonnet "Words," are not the reasoning saints and philosophers of former eras but "daemonic agents" like Hitler and Mussolini, whose "compulsive syndromes" are truly virulent. The logic of Lowell's oedipal psychodramas was such, however, that he felt compelled to outmaneuver his father by allying himself with those who could be construed as sublime only by a mind deranged by mania. He resisted an oedipal resolution partly because identifying with his father was too mortifying to countenance. The concluding lines of a poem like "Home After Three Months Away" express his fear that after recovering from a manic transcendence of all his father stands for, he will now have to submit to the kind of impotence and absurdity his father represents. Like his father in retirement, Lowell confesses: "I keep no rank nor station. / Cured, I am frizzled, stale and small" (*LS* 82). "Commander Lowell" again traces a complex family romance in which, as a seven-year-old boy, "bristling and manic," Lowell becomes the sublime Napoleon, a surrogate husband for his mother, who, in her "hysterical, unmarried panic" (*LS* 70), renounces her real husband. Commander Lowell is a parody of the great military leaders who populate his wife's and son's fantasies of masculine power. His naval exploits are confined to the bathos of the bathtub:

> "Anchors aweigh," Daddy boomed in his bathtub,
> "Anchors aweigh,"
> when Lever Brothers offered to pay
> him double what the Navy paid.
> . . . .
> He was soon fired. Year after year,
> he still hummed "Anchors aweigh" in the tub— (*LS* 71)

Ironically, the Commander's son also "used to enjoy dawdling and humming 'Anchors Aweigh' up Revere Street after a day at school" (*LS* 20), as Lowell reveals in his autobiographical essay in *Life Studies*.

Lowell's transports purport to avoid the ridiculous deflations his father succumbed to by steering toward more magnificent surrogates. Such quests, however, go astray because of the intensity with which he conducts them. Much to his sardonic chagrin he ends up in the same tub as his father. When Lowell becomes a father, when he internalizes that image of his actual father as a ridiculous loser, superego and ego war in his psyche, necessitating new surges toward transcendence. The late sonnet "Symptoms" in *The Dolphin* reveals Lowell in the same bathetic position as his father. He is in the bath, similarly deflated, similarly pathetic. His whining, in fact, expresses a sense of defeat even more overwhelming than his father's robust singing. He complains like a spoiled child:

> I have no mother to lift me in her arms.
> I feel my old infection, it comes once yearly:
> lowered good humor, then an ominous
> rise of irritable enthusiasm . . .
> . . . .
> I soak,
> examining and then examining
> what I really have against myself. (*D* 18)

What he has against himself is a guilty sense of failure. He cannot win, at least morally, because to embrace his mother's expectations of manhood would turn him into a patriarchal monster, and to acquiesce to his father's example of mindless, even-tempered resignation would turn him into an effeminate clown. He tries to do neither and ends up doing both.

A Patriarchal Mother

If Lowell's "pathological enthusiasms" drove him to imagine sublime triumphs over his father, over other patriarchal figures in his poetic and political culture, and over a superego fabricated from all of these, they also engaged him in phantasmal battles and rapprochements with a "suitably sublimed" mother. "Where did his torrent of energy come from?" his old St. Mark's friend Blair Clark asked. "That astonishing drive's main source was certainly his mother, but the hysterical dynamo in her had no outlet and was therefore destructive of herself and of those around her—especially, of course, her husband and her son" (254). The agon between Lowell and his mother led to something similar to the egotistical sublime, which, as Weiskel explains, is a version of Freudian narcissism. Because of a traumatic loss, libido once attached to its object returns to a primary, painless state or it returns to a heightened, sublimated conception of the ego. Freud speculates that the lost object, whether mother or lover, is retrieved through introjection. In his essay "The Theory of the Libido: Narcissism," he avers that mania and melancholia issue from the oscillations of love and hate for the lost, introjected object: "The melancholic has indeed withdrawn his libido from the object, but . . . by a process which we must call 'narcissistic identification' he has set up the object within the ego itself, projected it on to the ego. . . . The ego itself is then treated as though it were the abandoned object; it suffers all the revengeful and aggressive treatment which is designed for the object" (*General Introduction* 434). In Weiskel's adaptation of Freud and Lacan, the egotistical sublime culminates in a love of self that is womblike in its obliviousness to painful, external stimuli (the pain of loss is removed by the gainful internalization of the Other or Mother that originally abandoned the ego). It can also be divisive and deathly, since the ego turns its animosity on the internal image of the betrayer.

Many of Lowell's poems dramatize this ambivalence toward the mother and those who act as her surrogates. In "Symptoms," Lowell's bath is both a womblike "bag of waters" and tomblike "grave of waters" as he laments the death of his mother ("I have no mother to lift me in her arms"). His enthusiasm is partly for the remembered mother within. Nevertheless, despair ensues because Lowell also disapproves of her, just as he disapproves of his obsessive, narcissistic self-examinations. Hardwick in *Sleepless Nights* recalls how Lowell would experience "seizures of optimism" when he fell in love with younger women and then, "Alerted to rejection on the very heels of enthusiasm and hope, he would then have to retreat" (45). She once told Frank Parker that her husband "had a way of making his girlfriends his mother" and that his first wife had understood this "and fought it all the way." Parker concluded it was "a losing fight. He was making [Stafford] into a mother and could therefore repudiate her. . . . And he had to have someone else—whom at once he tried to make into his mother" (Roberts 239).

Although Lowell loved his mother through other women, and in his manic phases repeatedly allowed younger women to fan the fires of his maternal enthusiasms, he also despised himself and his motherly lovers because of it. The "compulsive quality" of his affairs, according to Jay Martin, can be traced to two possible determinants: "first, his childhood fear that he would lose his mother's love and need to win it over and over; and second, the wish that he could indicate to his mother—and then to his wives, substitutes for his mother—that he did not, after all, need her love, that he could easily replace her with another woman. He would force Mother—and then other women who loved him subsequently—to experience the pain of loss of love that had once so tortured him" (42). Whatever the reasons, along with his invidious supermen, his surrogate mothers were dangerous sirens drawing Lowell toward the sublime's pathological delusions. His response included both frenzied submission and principled resistance.

The roots of the problem may be traced in Lowell's autobiographical essay "Antebellum Boston." Lowell says: "When I was three or four years old I first began to think about the time before I was born. Until then, Mother had been everything: at three or four, she began abruptly and gratingly to change into a human being. I wanted to recapture the Mother I remembered and so I began to fabricate" (CP 293). Partly abetted by his mother's own fantasies, Lowell transfigured her into the strong patriarchal figures that his father was incapable of assuming. She was Alexander: "Mother, her strong chin unprotected and chilled in the helpless autumn, seemed to me the young Alexander, all gleam and panache. . . . Mother, also, was a sort of commander in chief of her virgin battlefield" (CP 295). She was also Napoleon: "She began to bolt her food, and for a time slept on an Army cot and took cold dips in the morning. In all this she could be Napoleon made over in my grandfather's Prussian image" (CP 297). In this complicated oedipal drama, Lowell's mother yearned for her charismatic father—"her Freudian papa," as Lowell calls him in "Beyond Fever" (LS 80)—whom she nicknamed "Napoleon." Lowell also longed for his Napoleonic aura, so much so that his grandfather became a surrogate father. "He was my Father. I was his son" (LS 65), he says frankly in "Dunbarton." To make family and gender matters even more complex, his mother, as battlefield commander, also played surrogate father.

Among these changing variables, the women who became the objects of Lowell's enthusiasms resemble his "suitably sublimed" mother, whose gender remained ambiguous because of her propensity for patriarchal roles. Lowell rehashed his bizarre family drama in an early uncollected short story, "The Raspberry Sherbet Heart." The narrator, Charles, who acts as Lowell's persona, contemplates marrying Rose Sharon, then hesitates: "He thought, 'Maybe I'd rather marry Mummy. Daddy could stay around, if he wanted to.'" Having replaced lover with mother, he now treats mother and father with equal indifference. "He thought about what fun it would be to call his father 'Mummy,' and his mother 'Daddy.' 'You can do anything with them, if you scramble them and mix them up'" (H 2229). Collectively, Lowell's fatherly mothers and motherly lovers compose a mythical, androgynous Great Mother for whom he incestuously and guiltily yearned.

In his analysis of Burke's aesthetic of violence, terror, and pain, Weiskel argues that the sublime apotheosis repeats that moment in the child's oedipal development when, having desired the mother and rejected the father, he overcomes the fear of punishment by the father—his castration anxiety—by realizing it was simply a guilty fantasy: "The fantasy of injury ends in the simultaneous perception of defeat and the realization that the threat is not, after all, a real one. This makes possible a positive resolution of the anxiety in the delight . . . which is psychologically an identification with the superior power" (93). Obsessed with castration and power struggles with his parents and their surrogates, Lowell also expressed a desire to be free of them, and free of sublime (phallic or "phallogocentric") power in general. His purification mania aimed at purging the priapic roots of mania; his sublime battles, at defeating the forces instigating sublimity. Yet the sublime's enchantment never died. An uncollected fragment of an autobiographical essay written for *Life Studies* mentions "an attack of pathological enthusiasm" suffered in 1949 in Bloomington, Indiana, during which Lowell "shouted again and again: 'Cut off my testicles'" (Hamilton 156) to police trying to subdue him. In this manic seizure, he became a Jehovah figure "crying out against devils and homosexuals" and "evil, unexorcised, aboriginal Indians" (Hamilton 156), as if trying to publicly orchestrate the sort of Last Judgment he described privately in his poems. Although rejecting his real father in this moment of lunacy, Lowell identified with the aristocratic, Puritan, sexist, and racist "forefathers" of his New England heritage—whom he usually excoriated—and set out to surpass them by taking on the apocalyptic force that they had tried to appropriate as well. "I suspected I was a reincarnation of the Holy Ghost, and had become homicidally hallucinated," he admitted after the experience, adding contritely: "To have known the glory, violence and banality of such an experience is corrupting" (Hamilton 157).

Drafts of "Caligula" recount a similar experience of purification mania in Buenos Aires. Castration, Lowell believes, will initiate a purity that will make possible an influx of divine, imperial power. The poet proceeds to the tub, his favorite place for negotiating with sublime enthusiasms, and confesses:

I . . .
took a cold bath, and rolled my genitals
until they shrank to peas, or little balls
of icey glass. Marble and purified
I marched into the bedroom of my bride:
"Let's live like eunuchs, I abolish sex."
I moved that crushing millstone from our necks.
I knew the old Olympians were a fraud.
I was Caligula, the living god. (H 2290)

Promiscuity, according to Lowell's delusional logic here, precludes power. He concludes that the licentious Olympian gods must have been fakes, because sexuality and godly power do not coexist. Sex is like a millstone crushing the possibility of cerebral potency, which paradoxically depends on the equally millstone-like punishments of castration and repression. Earlier Lowell metamorphoses into "The God, Adonis," who is gored in the thigh and resurrected, at least in Lowell's myth, as an emperor blazing with violent enthusiasm. Again Lowell subscribes to a paradoxical law of compensation whereby the sublime energies he once associated with sex are internalized so that they may invigorate his egocentric fantasies of imperial grandeur.

Because for Lowell the sublime was always enmeshed in the banality of violence, or what his friend Hannah Arendt called "the banality of evil" (Lowell, when manic, *could be* the Nazi war criminal of Arendt's investigations), and because it often issued from an inflated, narcissistic view of his sexual capacities, an ascetic detumescence in ideology and style was a moral alternative that proved increasingly tempting to Lowell in his middle and later periods. His most overt poetic debate with the sublime came in "Waking Early Sunday Morning." In his intriguing discussion of the "consciously intended Freudian imagery of phallic power and castration in the poem," Williamson argues that Lowell "fears being castrated if he reveals his full powers and ambitions, literary or ideological; when he prefers subjects without apparent 'purpose' or 'meaning,' he is essentially protecting himself by pretending to be castrated already" ("Reshaping" 49–50). Lowell may fear castration (the powerful father figure in this case is the infuriated President Johnson, whose policies Lowell had denounced); contradictorily, he may also welcome castration. As Williamson rightly points out, "Lowell is, again, deliberately conflating his own faults with those of his adversaries" ("Reshaping" 53). The repudiation of sublime potency that has become "monotonous" amounts to a desire for self-castration. Rather than castrate others, Lowell implies it would be better if they castrated themselves. Johnson's violent wars and Lowell's manic attacks assure "the blind / swipe of the pruner and his knife / [will be] busy about the tree of life" (*NO* 23). Self-castration might remove the seed of bellicose animosity. Implicit in this grotesque moral fantasy is a possible resolution of Lowell's oedipal drama with his parents: a growing desire to identify with his father's postmilitary serenities and to reject his mother's "hysterical, unmarried" obsessions with "suitably sublimed" heroes, including her incestuous flirtations with her father and her son.

A factor in Lowell's argument with sublimity must have been Jarrell's early criticism of his friend's proclivity for gothic excess. From the start Jarrell pronounced it tedious. Lowell could have been acknowledging his friend's and his own impatience with tiresome psychological extremes when he confessed in "Eye and Tooth": "I am tired. Everyone's tired of my turmoil" (*FUD* 19). Unfortunately, his disillusionment with sublimity often led to enervated poems, and other critics soon pounced on the monotony of his mellower style. Some conjectured that lithium was the culprit, blunting Lowell's psychological and prosodic energies with the same blow.

In his early review "The Kingdom of Necessity," Jarrell predicted the way Lowell would dramatize his psychopathology of the sublime for the remainder of his career. He contended that Lowell's mind was "so traditional, so theocentric, and anthropomorphic that no images from the sciences, next to none from philosophy, occur in his poems." Rather playfully, he observed: "*Bodily Changes in Fear, Pain and Anger* may let the poet know more about the anger of Achilles, but it is hard for him to have to talk about adrenalin and the thalamus" (25–26). Lowell knew that his mania was caused by a combination of environmental and chemical factors that were largely irremediable. Wallingford informs us: "But just as Lowell was inevitably disillusioned by psychotherapy's failure to effect a permanent cure, so was he forced to learn that lithium would prove no panacea either; although it acted initially to moderate the course of Lowell's illness, he was never to be 'cured,' never to be free from the threat of mania and its aftermath, crippling depression" (11). Lowell knew, however, that unlike the phenothiazine drugs he had previously taken, lithium dampened his manic-depression without too many deleterious side effects (except perhaps stylistic ones). He probably knew that his "pathological enthusiasms" resulted from norepinephrine or other chemical transmitters generating barrages of nerve impulses along his synapses.

Knowledge about the chemical causes of manic-depression, however, was sketchy in the mid-1960s, as the psychiatrist Mogens Schou reveals in a "Special Review of Lithium in Psychiatric Therapy and Prophylaxis" (1968), first published a year after Lowell began taking lithium. Although conceding that little was actually "known about the biological disturbance

underlying manic-depressive disorder," he pointed out that "Much specu-
lation has centered around the role of monoamines in affective disorders,
and recent studies disclose an interference of lithium and monoamine me-
tabolism and the activity of monoamine neurons in the brain. . . . These
data suggest that lithium may decrease noradrenaline levels at the receptor
sites" (387). Rather than choose biogenic amines and lithium salts for his
personae and construct a *psychomachia* out of chemical antagonists, Lowell
drew on the more traditional Freudian model—obsolescent as it may be for
many current psychiatrists—because it focused on the sort of wrenching
family relations that he knew all too well. Obsessed with history, myth,
religion, and literature, as Jarrell commented, Lowell interpreted and alle-
gorized the sublime from a humanistic rather than a scientific point of view.
His psychopathology, like Freud's, deployed a "mythical method" to illumi-
nate personal and familial conflict. Standing behind the drama of sublimity
like a sphinx that he, a latter-day Oedipus, wanted both to decipher and to
ruin was the compound ghost of his parents. In the end, as in the begin-
ning, all the tumult in his psyche was "only (only) a mix of mother and
father" (*H* 115).

6

The Religious Sublime

Catholics and Protestants

Along with politics and psychology, religion composed a facet of Lowell's allegory of the sublime. Full of sanctimonious ambitions, Lowell had his eye on Catholic saints and Protestant enthusiasts from the start. Even in poems written as early as his teens and early twenties, however, he found it prudent to deflate the religious sublimity he craved. A poem written in 1936 at Harvard, "The Flame-Colored Stain of Lust," for example, mocks the "Antipodean solitude sublime" that "Blankets the ladder to beatitude" like so much sticky candy. He calls it "mellow taffy" (H 2020), as if the religious sublime were a cloying seduction for the narcissist's palate. He also ridicules its transcendentalism. Those who aspire to such heights are as illusory as flying saucers and as dizzy as spiraling buzzards. "Sublimely saucering the stratosphere / Divinest, dizzy, southern buzzards spire" (H 2020), he says of these unlikely pilgrims who ascend divine spires toward religious sublimity. His self-conscious mockery recalls Pope's in *Peri Bathos, or The Art of Sinking*, a satirical takeoff on Longinus's *Peri Hypsos*. Around this time, in fact, Lowell studied the way the eighteenth century poet punctured all grand schemes with his rapier wit. An exam book from either St. Mark's or Harvard (it is undated) praises Pope for bringing the "sublime and absurd" (H 2787) into collision. As an undergraduate, when Lowell extols religious sublimity, he invariably attacks it, deems it illusory or, if real, unattainable. In "Great Britain's Trial," he hails "the sublimest Thirteenth Century" because of poets and theologians such as Dante and Aquinas who, like his early hero St. Simeon, are monuments to divine reason. Nevertheless, in the same breath he scoffs at "Scholastic pedant-parrots" (H 2133) cloistered in the Sorbonne who only adulterate religious sublimity in facsimiles and commentaries. He would like to be Dante, although he implies

111

he can only parrot his magnificent allegorical style. When he tries to fly with Dante to the heights of religious verse, he admits, he squawks like a ridiculous bird.

Not long after his disquisition on St. Simeon, Lowell began conferring sublimity on Ahabian and Luciferian heroes. The transformation of Lowell's concept of the sublime from the pillar saint's "true light," which radiated from an ascetic intellect high above the boorish "men of authority who misuse their power" for "the advancement of evil or petty ends" ("The True Light" 129), to those tragic heroes who try to dethrone the "true lights" and become the "men of authority" themselves, is remarkable. Since Lowell's first published reference to the sublime is in a predominantly religious context, it is worthwhile to trace his evolving conception of the religious sublime and its part in his "one story." A clue to his preoccupation with religious sublimity surfaces in his unfinished autobiography written in the mid-1950s. Hamilton recalls that the book "would cover his early life up to 1934, the year of his first summer in Nantucket with Frank Parker," a summer Lowell believed was marked by boundless enthusiasm or "extreme religious zealotry" (226). Lowell obviously considered this outbreak of religious passion to be a milestone in his career. It no doubt compelled him to rethink the devilish and angelic attributes of religious enthusiasm.

In Lowell's early writing "enthusiasm" was a virtue rather than a vice. His "War: A Justification," composed in 1935 with an ingenuous ignorance of European events like Hitler's ascent to power, found evidence for its argument (as Longinus did in *Peri Hypsos*) among the sublime phrases, events, and heroic characters of Homeric poetry. Of Ulysses, Lowell wrote: "He is by no means perfect, but he radiates life, energy, and enthusiasm" (158). His speech that won the oratorical contest at Kenyon College in 1940, "Moulding the Golden Spoon," chastised aristocratic students at St. Mark's for not being aristocratic enough, and for approaching courses like English literature "without enthusiasm or perception" (35). Soon Lowell's attitude toward enthusiasm and, by extension, religious sublimity would alter drastically. Enthusiasm became a threat to sanity, as the early uncollected poem, "Veterans," claimed. Here it has all the incendiary force of a bomb:

> Each spring the earth bursts into flame.
> The mortal's seasons are the same:
> Its effete fabric must outlast
> Sexual enthusiasm's blast. (H 2161)

As these fiery manic explosions became more brutal and more frequent, Lowell began to brood on the lives of Protestant enthusiasts, but primarily to confess and condemn what he considered, as a Catholic, to be at best a tragic flaw and at worst a heinous sin.

He began to allegorize his agonizing quest for God in terms of other similarly motivated "daemonic agents" whose compulsions for the sublime matched his own. If on the political level he interpreted his and America's quest for the sublime as a battle with daunting foes that culminated in a transfer of power to the rebellious underdog, and on the psychological level as an oedipal struggle in which the son appropriated power from his father by deposing him, on the religious level the bellicose quest involved displacement and transference as well. Throughout his career Lowell was fascinated by those godly pilgrims, evangelical ministers, and holy communicants whose attempts to unify with the divine led to magnificent and horrific displays of religious passion. According to Kant, the sublime depended on the overpowering splendors of an external God and His creation that awakened the perception of godhood within the mind. For Kant that awakening of the god within (the *en-theos*) could erupt in delirium and mania; for Lowell it was the beginning of self-aggrandizement and the sort of self-righteousness that sparked private and public jihads. Lowell's inner God had a habit of stealing power from the outer One and, with newly acquired convictions of omnipotence and omniscience, assaulting the world with judgmental violence. Lowell's apocalyptic outbursts had religious parallels in American and world history, and one of his poetic purposes was to relate them typologically.

According to Ronald Knox's influential study, *Enthusiasm*, which Lowell probably read, "Enthusiasm did not really begin to take shape until the moment when Luther shook up the whole pattern of European theology; did not (in that age of repression) come out into the open till more than a century later. Not until the days of the Commonwealth can it be studied in its full context. Then, for a hundred and fifty years, it becomes the major preoccupation of religious minds" (4). The Quakers lit the enthusiastic torch and passed it on to Methodists like George Whitefield and the Wesleys. Lowell's Ahab in "The Quaker Graveyard in Nantucket" was in his own way a Quaker enthusiast. Another enthusiast was Lowell's early model, Jonathan Edwards, whose Great Awakening in the middle of the eighteenth century derived inspiration from the impassioned sermons of Whitefield. Within the eighteenth century an incipient dialectic already stirred between classical and Romantic, conservative Anglo-Catholic and radical evangelical Protestant, the tribe of Pope and the tribe of John Dennis. These contrary factions drew much of their animus from differing attitudes toward sublimity and enthusiasm. Several centuries later the debate would play itself out with similar vehemence in Lowell.

Although "sublime" and "enthusiasm" were critical terms that emerged in tandem and then meandered into different fields, the two terms were originally aligned by Longinus when he compared the religious experience of the Pythian priestess conjuring divine power from her oracle to the literary experience of conjuring power from oracular authors. Gods and great poets, for Longinus, imparted authorial if not authoritarian sublimity. Burke, whose famous *Enquiry* was begun during the heyday of religious enthusiasm (in the late 1740s), praised the sort of dark, terrifying religious passions that scattered the classical tenets of the Enlightenment to the winds. Several decades earlier Anthony Shaftesbury, comparing religious sublimity with religious enthusiasm in his "Letter Concerning Enthusiasm," warned that these experiences of divinity could easily spawn delusion and madness in melancholy temperaments. He wrote of the divinely inspired mind:

> Something there will be of extravagance and fury, when the ideas or images received are too big for the narrow human vessel to contain. So that inspiration may be justly called divine enthusiasm; for the word itself signifies divine presence, and was made use of by the philosopher whom the earliest Christian Fathers called divine, to express whatever was sublime in human passions. . . . But to know it as we should do, and discern it in its several kinds, both in ourselves and others; this is the great work, and by this means alone we can hope to avoid delusion. For to judge the spirits whether they are of God, we must antecedently judge our own spirit, whether it be of reason and sound sense; whether it be fit to judge at all, by being sedate, cool, and impartial, free of every biassing passion, every giddy vapour, or melancholy fume. By this means we may prepare ourselves with some antidote against enthusiasm. And this is what I have dared affirm is best performed by keeping to good-humour. For other wise the remedy itself may turn to the disease. (38–39)

Lowell may have learned of Shaftesbury's ideas concerning the sublime when he studied under Ransom because he was represented in Carritt's *Philosophies of Beauty.*

Lowell's early religious poetry patched together a marriage between New England Puritanism and Roman Catholicism (which the poet adopted in 1940 and spurned in 1947, shortly after publication of *Land of Unlikeness*). Catholicism appealed to Lowell not only because it represented a tradition antithetical to his Puritan heritage and close to the Eliotic principles that his mentors, the Southern Agrarians, espoused, but also because it offered an antidote to the *en-theos* or "inner light" that possessed him with such daemonic force. To the manic anarchy that he increasingly associated with Protestant sublimity he brought the intellectual authority of the Catholic Church, hoping that its long tradition of rational theology and strict rituals could govern the inner God always threatening to overpower him. As a Catholic in the early 1940s, Lowell fortified himself with the theological writings of Gerard Manley Hopkins, John Henry Newman, Christopher Dawson, E. I. Watkin, Jacques Maritain, and Etienne Gilson, whose *Spirit of Mediaeval Philosophy*, *Philosophy of Thomas Aquinas*, and *The Mystical Theology of St. Bernard* proved particularly riveting.

In one way or another all these writers argued for what deconstructionists have labeled the logocentric tradition in Western metaphysics—the view that truth, reason, divinity, and the Word form a unified and privileged order. Gilson is particularly at pains to show that "theology . . . will long continue to inspire metaphysics" (*Mediaeval Philosophy* 18) and that "the imagination of the classical metaphysicians was absolutely possessed by the idea of the Biblical Creator-God" (16). He traces the metaphysical suppositions of Gottfried Leibniz, George Berkeley, Kant, as well as St. Augustine, St. Aquinas, and other Church Fathers, back to Plato's conception of divine reason and Aristotle's notion of the prime mover—the *anima* or soul—insisting that Christians fulfilled or perfected the principles laid down by Greek philosophers. For these thinkers the central, original *logos* inheres in God the Father, the Word, and the rational mind. Reason, as opposed to enthusiasm, is paramount. Like Kant, Gilson attempts to yoke rational theologian with rational philosopher when he declares: "The content of Christian philosophy is that body of rational truths discovered, explored or simply safeguarded thanks to the help that reason receives from revelation" (35). "Christian revelation," he repeatedly stresses, is "an indispensable auxiliary to reason" (37).

A rational faith whose revealed truths could be ascertained and ritualized under the authoritarian aegis of the Catholic Church satisfied Lowell's need, albeit briefly, for psychological stability. Without the pillar of the church his intellectual St. Simeon would come crashing down. His Kantian sublimity would be demolished. Lowell's problem was that he devoted himself to austere Catholic disciplines with the zeal of an enthusiastic Protestant. He became a reasoning fanatic, an Ahab or Lucifer clamoring for the inner and outer light of divine truth with such ferocity that he finally broke down. If he repressed Protestant passions to serve Catholic principles, his repressions returned in psychotic form. As Lowell matured, Catholic rationality receded as the Freudian *logos* advanced. Although Lowell repudiated both Protestantism and Catholicism in the middle of his life, and recruited Freud as his new religious guide, he would never entirely repudiate the church's enchanting rituals and symbols. He often invoked them nostalgically, elegizing their former capacity to console broken hearts and broken minds.

"Religion," Freud declared in "The Future of an Illusion," is "the universal obsesssional neurosis of humanity; like the obsessional neurosis of children, it arose out of the Oedipus complex, out of the relation to the father" (43). Lowell's religious obsessions, however, were more complicated; they had patriarchal as well as matriarchal sources. As Lowell in his teens and twenties tried to triumph over that introjected image of his Protestant mother and father—his superego—hoping somehow to attain an intellectual transcendence he associated with Catholic saintliness, he became ever more suspicious of religious enthusiasm. Nevertheless, his battles with parents only incited his enthusiasms, and these episodes sent him packing to the madhouse. As if to prove Freud right—that "devout believers are safeguarded in a high degree against the risk of certain neurotic illness; their acceptance of the universal neurosis spares them the task of constructing a personal one" ("Future of an Illusion" 44)—Lowell vacillated between Protestant, Catholic, and existential neuroses. After Lowell renounced Protestantism and left the Catholic Church, his neurosis became more personal, more idiosyncratic. Oddly enough, it continued to involve bewildering identifications with Catholic saints and Protestant satans, holy ghosts and unholy ghouls, democratic presidents and fascist tyrants.

Lowell may have rejected Catholicism and theologians like Gilson because their cheerful abstractions reminded him too much of his smiling, platitudinous father. The benign Gilson was devoted to a metaphysically reasoned "Christian optimism"; he believed in the "Christian affirmation of the intrinsic goodness of all there is" (*Mediaeval Philosophy* 112). To counter the cerebral innocence of Church Fathers, Lowell supplicated more experienced gods—the Hegelian and Nietzschean supermen of history whose terrifying acts filled him with awe. Having rejected actual father, Judeo-Christian Father, and sundry Church Fathers, like Lucifer he populated his vacuum with nefarious daemons. Lowell possessed the sort of restless, dialectical imagination that, in Stevens's words, "to find what will suffice, / Destroys romantic tenements / Of rose and ice // In the land of war" (*CP* 238–39). Following Lucifer, he refused to inhabit one place for long. Tenure in a "romantic tenement," whether it be the Catholic's rose-windowed cathedral or the Puritan's icy clapboard church, was short-lived because the religious sublime, like all other sublimes, grew monotonous. The mind craved fresh stimuli, fresh challenges, fresh horrors in its furious drive to experience and create.

Apocalyptic Leviathans

The early poem "Sublime Feriam Sidera Vertice" ("with my head raised so high then shall I strike the stars," from Horace's dedicatory *Ode*) predicted the Janus-like stance Lowell would take throughout his life toward the religious sublime. Although the title suggests that he might extol the intellectual transcendence of his former hero St. Simeon, because he now knows that Hitler and Mussolini are ravaging Europe, the transcendence found in the "free" act of contemplation espoused by Kant, Schopenhauer, and Hegel rings hollow. In Lowell's poem, God, nature, and humanity are embroiled in a power struggle for survival that is as much a parody as an imitation of the sublime paradigm. "Nature charged brute devotions to the soul," Lowell writes, but due to the "satanic partnership" that this godly Nature finds in the first humans, He "put out a fall, an Ark, a flood" and then "put them out" by extinguishing them with "Christ Jesus and his golden rule" (17). Christ in "Sublime Feriam" is an early example of Lowell's dualistic concept of the religious sublime. Typologically related to both wounded Ahab and wounded whale, He is both "patron and gaoler of the grave" (17). Wielding apocalyptic force at the Second Coming, He patronizes graves by filling them up; He also patronizes the dead by liberating them, like a jailer, into heaven or hell according to their deeds. Christ, Ahab, and Moby Dick are in turn terrifying and awesome, and for Lowell embody the tragic relation between enthusiasm and destruction.

Lowell's revision of "Sublime Feriam," titled "Leviathan," amounts to a prophecy of doom. Here the murderousness of the world during the war and Lowell's murderous attitudes toward his father are aligned allegorically in terms of religious figures—Cain, Abel, and God. Once again the blood of destruction mixes with the blood of redemption. The murdered Christ on the cross is the murderous Christ of the Apocalypse; Ahab the monstrous predator joins Moby Dick the monstrous prey. America and Ahab may enact Christ-like paradigms as they combat evil foes and purge the world of leviathanic sins; they also threaten to bring "the world down in ruins." The final lines of "Leviathan" echo the manic imperatives and moral injunctions of the earlier poem, although in the later version Hegel has been oddly metamorphosed into an octopus:

> The Ship
> Of State is asking Christ to walk on blood:
>
> Great Commonwealth, roll onward, roll
> On blood, and when the ocean monsters fling
> Out the satanic sting,

Or like an octopus constrict my soul,
Go down with colors flying for the king. (*LU* 36)

In this bitter appraisal of the sinning world, dire prophecies have turned to sarcastic commandments of annihilation. About a year before this poem appeared, the American "ship of state" threatened to ship Lowell overseas to fight in the Second World War. Although he had praised the "enthusiasm" of war heroes in "War: A Justification," his newly acquired Catholicism rebelled against the terrible bloodshed of civilian bombing. A manic "fire-breathing Catholic C.O." (*LS* 85), as he called himself a decade later, he took on an American president rather than combat more destructive "monsters" abroad.

If there was self-aggrandizement in Lowell's "telling off the state and president" (*LS* 85), there was also self-aggrandizement in his identifications with Christ, Satan, Ahab, Moby Dick, America, and God. The antidote of Catholic theology and ritual could not counteract and expel Lowell's megalomania. Catholicism, in fact, simply led to another self-righteous entrenchment, an empowering of a newly fortified conscience that would judge the self with the same violent, apocalyptic fervor with which it judged nation and world. Robert Fitzgerald could be diagnosing his friend's early addiction to the religious sublime when he comments: "After his first grave manic attack in 1949, after his first hospitalization, all concerned grew wary on his behalf, as indeed he did himself, of excitements religious, political, or poetic. He could no longer be a Catholic because, as he told me, it set him on fire" (Williamson, "Reshaping" 47–48).

Lowell's Catholic and Calvinist penchant for impersonating the great sinners of the world led to a mischievous sublimity. In his Blakean "marriage of heaven and hell," Satan became his antithetical God, a messiah who promised deliverance from the more benevolent, weaker gods simulated by his father. "Milton's Messiah is call'd Satan," Blake proclaimed in his "Marriage" (150), and Lowell agreed; both poets found in Satan an embodiment of exuberant, amoral energies. Perhaps the main reason for his obsession with the Calvinist Edwards was due to his fellow New Englander's enthusiasm for a God whose commingling of horror and majesty made Him, as for Blake, a hybrid of Jehovah and Satan. The odd marriage of Catholicism and Protestantism in Lowell's poetry derived from this oedipal dialectic in which the benign, rational God of the Church Fathers spawned its opponent—a satanic Protestant son whose rebellion was tragically heroic. Catholicism and Protestantism produced a sublime and countersublime that Lowell struggled unsuccessfully to purge.

Although "The Quaker Graveyard in Nantucket" allegorizes the sublime from a political perspective, it also dramatizes the religious sublime and its tragic consequences. Indebted to Milton's "Lycidas" and Melville's *Moby Dick*, Lowell's persona—the megalomaniacal Ahab—is also close cousin to Milton's Satan, that "sublime ambition" doomed to fall in violent combat with "IS, the whited monster" (*LWC* 16)—a composite of Jehovah and white whale. Ahab's tragic flaw is the hubris that comes from his fanatical enthusiasm, a sin attributed to Quakers who could quake deliriously when possessed by the inner *theos*. In his historical account of enthusiasm, Knox reveals: "The Quakers were the first in the field, with their rude challenge to all the institutional churches" (4). The Shakers were implicated, too. The Quaker Ahab resembles the Edwards-like Father Mapple of the early "Sermon" chapter in *Moby Dick* who "cried out with a heavenly enthusiasm" (57) at Ishmael and the rest of the congregation. Ahab's divine madness also aligns him with the Shaker in "The Jeroboam's Story" who fanatically believes he is the archangel Gabriel. In "the preternatural fervors of real delirium" and "gibbering insanity, [he is also heard] pronouncing the White Whale to be no less a being than the Shaker God incarnated" (249, 251).

For Ahab, too, Moby Dick is a god who inspires furious enthusiasms. Like those writers of the eighteenth century who, as David Morris records in *The Religious Sublime*, took Dennis's lead in praising the Bible as "the ultimate source of sublime poetry" (63) and championing Milton "for having carried away the Prize of Sublimity from both Ancients and Moderns" (67), and like the Augustans who "increasingly resigned such terms as *inspiration, enthusiasm*, and *je-ne-sais-quoi* in favor of Longinian sublimity" (30–31), Melville blends manic enthusiasm with august sublimity in the character of Ahab. Melville also disparages sublimity and enthusiasm, underscoring the hypocrisy of Quakers like Peleg, Bildad, and Ahab. "The Ship" chapter points out that the duplicitous Quaker, "Though refusing, from conscientious scruples, to bear arms against land invaders, yet himself had illimitably invaded the Atlantic and Pacific; and though a sworn foe to human bloodshed, yet had he in his straight-bodied coat, spilled tuns upon tuns of leviathan gore" (76). In Ahab, Lowell could see his own contradictory temperament reflected, and in "The Quaker Graveyard" he brilliantly mastered a Longinian rhetoric to embody the dialectic of terrifying power, awed subjugation, and godly triumph that defines the religious sublime.

The ambiguities and paradoxes in "The Quaker Graveyard" that unify combative oppositions into a network of identities (so that, as Bell puts it, they "seem finally to function as the agents of a single inexorably ruthless force" [*Nihilist* 28]) are a direct consequence of the religious sublime.

Lowell's Catholic sympathy for all victims and his Catholic notions of just and unjust wars, which he stated were behind his conscientious objection to the Second World War, draw him toward the war's losers. The rhetorical force of the poem and the hostility it expresses toward brutal patriarchal figures, on the other hand, draw him toward the winners. An organic unity of paradoxes, of course, was a goal to which New Critical poems aspired. A series of unlikely identifications was also normal in the sort of pastoral elegy Lowell chose to imitate. Poet, nature, deceased, and Christ (or some other agent of resurrection) customarily joined in a symbolic descent and ascent, a rhythm of despair over mortality and hope for immortality.

What distinguishes Lowell's poem is the way it deconstructs the Catholic and pagan hierarchies that support the elegy's traditional promise of redemption. "Ask for no Orphean lute / To pluck life back" (*LWC* 14), Lowell says at the beginning, and then, when he is about to offer a traditional apotheosis of the dead in "Our Lady of Walsingham," he depicts the holy statue as a lifeless imitation of a lifeless God. The whole poem is a complicated, symbolist ritual of communion that, in the absence of the Word of a traditionally benevolent God, places all the burden of redemption on the poet's sublime rhetoric. Although Mazzaro faulted the poem for its "ideological . . . insistence that contemplation [guided by Our Lady of Walsingham] is the only method of achieving . . . the new covenant with God" (43), Lowell in fact indicates the contrary: that peaceful contemplation with a peaceful God is no longer possible. And although Cosgrave attacked the poem for failing to organize the "ambiguously evaluated symbolic nuances" into "a final and comprehensive statement of meaning" (104), it is the clash of contraries that, like steel against flint, ignites the poem's rhetoric—a rhetoric that in fact *does* encompass ambiguities in a single blaze.

The story of *Moby Dick* provided Lowell with a compelling narrative of daemonic communion in which wounded Ahab and wounded whale are more alike than unlike in their terrifying grandeur. With Milton's elegiac and epic models in mind as well, Lowell juxtaposed awesome and awful powers. Lowell's "sea is . . . divine and demonic" (*Pity* 38), as Williamson remarks. In the very first lines, natural strife is equated with military strife, and shortly afterward Poseidon ("the earth-shaker"), Jehovah (the "hell-bent deity"), Ahab (as "hell-bent" as God), and Lowell's cousin Winslow ("the drowned sailor" violently clutching "the drag-net" [*LWC* 14]) coalesce to form a bizarre alliance. Later in the poem the biblical Leviathan, worldly corruption, Moby Dick, and the Quaker whalers all come together in the figure of Jonas Messias, a cross between Jonah and Christ. Williamson correctly notes that the figure of the slaughtered, messianic whale "culminates that confusion of the divine and the Satanic, the aggressor and the victim, which has haunted the poem" (*Pity* 43). This typological unity inspired Albert Gelpi to claim: "The hunting of the whale becomes the supreme symbolic enactment, at once grotesque and sublime, of the Incarnation in history" (61). Although there are intimations of transcendence at Walsingham, Lowell's early sublime moments normally occur in the presence of patriarchal rather than matriarchal figures. Unity with a Catholic Mother like "Our Lady of Walsingham" may provide a mystic "peace that passeth understanding," as in Eliot's timeless moments. Lowell, however, searches the temporal world for a male solution to his male problems. If there is any resolution, it comes ambiguously at the end, through an uneasy "at-one-ment" between Lowell and his numerous father figures, and a difficult recognition that creation is wedded to destruction just as redemption is wedded to crucifixion, mania to despair, poetic survival to ardent struggle.

The poem recollects some of the "pathological enthusiasm" experienced during Lowell's 1935 summer on Nantucket when he struggled to absorb Homer, the Bible, Shakespeare, Blake, Keats, Coleridge, and Wordsworth, and to write a long poem called "Jonah." Nantucket is his Blakean Eden of ferociously contending contraries as well as a Darwinian arena of origins, struggles for survival, and deaths. "Here in Nantucket," he writes at the end of the poem, you can

> cast up the time
> When the Lord God formed man from the sea's slime
> And breathed into his face the breath of life,
> And blue-lung'd combers lumbered to the kill.
> The Lord survives the rainbow of his will. (*LWC* 20)

This satanic Jehovah is capable of Darwinian survival precisely because he does not relax after he has established his covenant with Noah. Although he promises never to destroy the world again after the flood, he retains the right to renege in order to endure. God is not dead, as some presume. If he prepares a "will," it assures his beneficiaries he will live on like a fierce animal. He competes and violates because, like Lowell who imitates Him, he knows that aggressiveness is necessary for supremacy. "God has rescinded the benign promise of the 'rainbow' of the covenant and survives, instead, as the omnipresent, destructive element of Lowell's sea" (*Nihilist* 30), Bell speculates. Although rainbows are beautiful, God's lightning bolts and thunderstorms are sublime. They indicate real as opposed to sentimental signs of endurance.

The Second World War, according to Lowell, provides ample evidence that an apocalyptic struggle between humans and God persists. In this case "blue-lunged" humans led by Satan lumber from the ocean to kill God, His edenic natural world, and all Christian values. Their goal is to become gods themselves. God, however, prevails, sacrificing beautiful concords like the covenant of Genesis in order to visit destruction upon the earth and to maintain His sublime dominance. What perplexes and disgruntles is the poem's refusal to find unambiguous fault or unambiguous felicity on one side or the other. "Lowell's Jeremiad against God's sinning children modulates into an exposure of the cruel Father (63)," Axelrod says; yet Lowell is both child and father, and both child and father have virtues as well as vices. Perhaps all we can conclude is that the poem offers a searingly honest account of human complexity and that the many conflicts in Lowell's psyche and world are "not logically resolved in the poem but imaginatively undergone." According to Axelrod, "The poem has no 'answer'" (64) other than its own strident eloquence.

Another of the paradoxical correspondences forged in "The Quaker Graveyard" is between "IS, the whited monster" (*LWC* 16) and Edwards's tyrannical Calvinist deity popularized in his sermon "Sinners in the Hands of an Angry God" (1741). When Lowell in the third section depicts the naval guns that "rock / Our warships in the hand / Of the great God" (*LWC* 16), he recalls the sort of violent judgment of worldly evil that Edwards so graphically portrayed. Lowell's fascination with Edwards no doubt arose from his recognition of a fellow New England enthusiast whose oedipal obsessions with patriarchal powers led to madness (Edwards was pronounced insane at the end of his life). His sense of kinship, in fact, led to his spurious claim of kinship. In a letter to Santayana written in 1948, he said: "long long ago Jonathan Edwards was one of my ancestors" (Wallingford 4). Wallingford believes the claim may have been a preliminary sign of mania (he would suffer an acute manic-depressive breakdown a year later). Nevertheless, "His desire to claim Jonathan Edwards as an ancestor, when it is not clear that any such relationship existed in fact, indicates the affinity that Lowell believed existed between them" (4). If Edwards delivered his apocalyptic judgments on New England through the persona of Jehovah, Lowell followed suit two centuries later.

Although Perry Miller and other scholars have shown that Edwards was more skeptical of the enthusiastic evangelists of the Great Awakening than his critics allowed, his enemies branded him an enthusiastic and satanic madman. Chauncey, who once called Edwards "a visionary enthusiast" (Miller 177), led the attack when he aimed his Harvard commencement address in 1742, titled "Enthusiasm Described and Caution'd Against," at everything Edwards stood for. Like Shaftesbury three decades before, Chauncey distinguished between the genuine sublimity of those enthusiasms that provoked biblical prophets to testify and the false enthusiasms that inspired pathological fools to blather. The prophets, he claimed, "were under a divine Influence, [and] spake as moved by the HOLY GHOST" (Chauncey 105). On the other hand, "inner light" fanatics were mad, bad-tempered impostors. He railed against the religious charlatan who "mistakes the workings of his own passions for divine communications, and fancies himself immediately inspired by the SPIRIT OF GOD, when all the while, he is under no other influence than that of an over-heated imagination" (105). According to Miller, Chauncey deployed the scholastic philosophy of medieval Catholicism, elevating reason over imagination and will in order to dethrone Edwards. Lowell had tried the same strategy to cure his own enthusiasms, but it had backfired.

Gods in the Land of Unlikeness

If in his first collection, *Land of Unlikeness*, Lowell was "consciously a Catholic poet" following the cultural precepts of Christopher Dawson and opposing the "democratic poets who enthusiastically greet the advent of the slave-society" (*LU* i–ii), as Tate claimed in his introduction, in his second, *Lord Weary's Castle*, he was more conscious of his own enthusiasms seething irrepressibly under his Catholic mask. Lowell borrows his first title from St. Bernard's concept of *regio dissimilitudinis*, which Gilson had explained as a "land of unlikeness," a wasteland in which modern folk wandered aimlessly away from God. "The central point in St. Bernard's doctrine," Gilson claimed, "is that the Image of God in us can never be lost . . . but the Likeness to God in us can be lost" (*Saint Bernard* 51). Although we are "*made* to the image [of God]—one alone *is* this Image Itself, namely the Word, because the Word alone is an adequate and subsistent expression of the Father" (52). Gilson warned that the root of all evil is hubris because it can prompt human reason to transgress proper (Catholic) limits, "setting itself above God" (57). Rather than wander hopelessly and pathetically through the "land of unlikeness" with those hollow men who "suffer not only the loss of God but also the loss of themselves" (58), Lowell periodically declared his likeness to God and soared toward Him in a blaze of manic energy.

The force with which he supplicated God, as his early poems attest, made Lowell both godly and ungodly. Cognizant of this paradox, his Catholic confessionalism aimed to draw a genealogical connection between himself, his satanic Protestant ancestors, and his country's origins. For example, in the third part of his elegy "In Memory of Arthur Winslow," which appears in both *Land of Unlikeness* and *Lord Weary's Castle,* Lowell projects family history onto American history so that he can better judge the lineage of his sins. "In his judgement of New England history, Lowell is essentially using the same technique of judgement that he condemns in his ancestors" and, Cosgrave adds, this "is the [poem's] real weakness" (62–63). His confession of mutual faults, however, is carried out with stylistic virtuosity, which is the poem's strength. Lowell records how his maternal grandfather, who made a fortune in mining, sanctioned his assault on the environment by drawing on the antinatural ideology of Puritan fathers like Mather and Edwards. Lowell insinuates his own unnatural acts into this religious context. Because the Winslows married into the Stark family, one of whom was a prominent Revolutionary War general, Lowell punningly declares: "Then from the train, at dawn, / Leaving Columbus in Ohio, shell / On shell of our stark culture struck the sun / to fill my head with all our fathers won / When Cotton Mather wrestled with the fiends from Hell" (*LU* 4). The allegorical shells are principally the shells of metal train cars that remind Lowell of precious metals Winslow "shelled" from ore (they might also remind him of bullet shells), but what is important is that they fill Lowell's head with dreams of power, of triumphs over nature and family, of Mather-like sublimations even though Mather and Winslow are satanic. In the end Lowell's attempts to subvert the divinely ordained "natural" order of things resemble Satan's just as much as Winslow's mining for gold resembles Mammon's grubbing for gold in the underworld.

In his early poems, the battle for religious sublimity is essentially a *psychomachia* in which Lowell remains tensely uncommitted to either God or Satan. When Lowell adopts the voice of Edwards in "After the Surprising Conversions" to give a psychological portrait of the enthusiastic Josiah Hawley (Edwards's suicidal uncle), he portrays personal conflicts he is unable to reconcile. In a sermon titled "The Unreasonableness of Indetermination in Religion," which, according to Mazzaro, Lowell incorporated into his poem, Edwards declared: "There are but two masters, to one of which we must be reputed the servants, Beal and Jehovah, God and Mammon: There are but two competitors for the possession of us, Christ and the devil" (Mazzaro 71). Although Edwards actually names more than two, Lowell implies that they are all, in fact, one. Intimating that Jehovah and Satan join forces to punish humanity, Lowell's persona claims: "At Jehovah's nod / Satan seemed more let loose amongst us. God / Abandoned us to Satan." Hawley's delirious enthusiasm allows Satan to oust Jehovah from his psyche and then act as if he were Jehovah at the Last Judgment: "through that night / He meditated terror, and he seemed / Beyond advice or reason, for he dreamed / That he was called to trumpet Judgment Day / to Concord" (*LWC* 66–67). The sublime delusion arises from melancholy ("He came from melancholy parents," Lowell says) and returns to it; Hawley finally cuts his throat. Lowell's "Mr. Edwards and the Spider" and, indeed, most of the religious poems in both *Land of Unlikeness* and *Lord Weary's Castle* demonstrate how Jehovah's apocalyptic violence makes God more satanic than Satan. They diagnose the sublime quests of Puritan enthusiasts who, as Miller asserts, "mistake some mechanical or psychological disturbance for the voice of God" and believe they are "a moral absolute, freed of restraint, incapable of sin" (143).

Lowell's later poems on Edwards combine the empathy of dramatic monologues with the hindsight characteristic of elegies. "Jonathan Edwards in Western Massachusetts," for example, intimates judgment as it elegizes that enthusiast's vehement ambition to establish a Promised Land in America. It simultaneously elegizes Lowell's early enthusiasms for transcendental ideals, whether Protestant or Catholic, and establishes similarities as well as differences between the two New Englanders. Lowell's backward look is winsome, ironic: "Ah paradise! Edwards, / I would be afraid / to meet you there as a shade. / We move in different circles." Although they quest for similar paradises, their enthusiasms have pitched them into different circles of hell. For Lowell as for Blake, heavenly and hellish manias are married. In Edwards's case, too, the way up and the way down are the same. "You stood on stilts in the air, / but fell from your parish. / 'All rising is by a winding stair.'" The Yeatsian echo is matched by a Yeatsian desire for tragic joy and a redemption through artifice: "I love you faded, / old, exiled and afraid / to leave your last flock, a dozen / Houssatonic Indian children // afraid to leave/ all your writing, writing, writing" (*FUD* 40–44). The late sonnet "The Worst Sinner, Jonathan Edwards' God" in *History* once again conflates sin and virtue so that the Puritan's aspirations for godhood merge with those of Satan. "The blood of the shepherd matched the blood of the wolf" (*H* 73), Lowell remarks, reflecting on his own saintly and wolflike enthusiasms as well.

In the "one story" delineated in *Lord Weary's Castle*, the oedipal drama skews the traditional biblical narrative of God the Father and Jesus the Son so that the former represents "everything that . . . blinds or binds" and the latter "everything that is free or open, that grows or is willing to change" (Jarrell, "Kingdom" 19). If God is a bloodthirsty shepherd, his son is a free-spirited wolf in sheep's clothing. Lowell sometimes adapts Yeats's dialectical scenario from "The Second Coming" to imagine Christ as a wolfish "rough beast . . . [that] / Slouches toward Bethlehem to be born" (187) in order to liberate the earth from the shepherd's nightmarish history. In "The Holy Innocents," for instance, he allegorizes a simple scene of oxen drawing a hay cart up a hill in a Maine town so that it parallels Christ bearing the burden of human sins up purgatory. The father figure in the poem is "King Herod shrieking vengeance at the curled / Up knees of Jesus choking in the air" (*LWC* 10). Although the war-ravaged "world out-Herods Herod" (it is 1945), its animus is little different from the vengeance of Edwards's "great God" who, at least in "The Quaker Graveyard," orchestrates the cataclysm from behind the scenes. Against this patriarchal force the innocent Christian beasts (like Yeats's magi searching for another incarnation of "The uncontrollable mystery on the bestial floor" [126]) and born-again Christ have little chance to flourish:

> the oxen near
> The worn foundations of their resting-place,
> The holy manger where their bed is corn
> And holly torn for Christmas. If they die,
> As Jesus, in the harness, who will mourn?
> Lamb of the shepherds, Child, how still you lie. (*LWC* 10)

As in Eliot's "Journey of the Magi," the Christian birth is overshadowed by death. The implication in Lowell's poem is that neither beast nor Christ has the capacity to stop the Herod-like slaughter of innocents that in the Second World War has gone beyond even Herod's most bloodthirsty dreams. The oxen and Christ Child in the crèche, according to Lowell, will probably be slaughtered as well. Their stillness at the end, like the rhyme on "die" and "lie," suggests sacrificial impotence rather than capable resistance. Many of his religious poems reveal a Lowell confronting Christ with the hope of discovering His sublime power and going away disenchanted. In the allegorical battle between an apocalyptic liberating Christ and a world mired in satanic murder and corruption, the Christ Child can redeem only by overpowering and neutralizing the forces of darkness. One of Lowell's dilemmas during the war arose from his own religious violence that he saw reflected in both Allied and Axis powers. He chose pacifism, but his poems acknowledge belligerence. They concede that pacifism is a lie, a weakness, a strategic mistake. Nothing sublime can be gained from it.

Lowell's temperament was divided between the innocent Christ Child and the daemonic Christ of the Apocalypse, who often appeared as a strange hybrid of Jehovah and Satan. A poem like "Colloquy in Black Rock" tries to articulate this bizarre, needless to say blasphemous, conjunction. The colloquy, which in traditional Catholic meditation is the dialogue following union with God, is hardly peaceful even though it occurs while Lowell is on parole for refusing to go to war. His opening parody of 1 Corinthians (13:1) depicts the inner God of his devotions at one rather than at odds with the violence around him:

Here the jack-hammer jabs into the ocean;
My heart, you race and stagger and demand
More blood-gangs for your nigger-brass percussions,
Till I, the stunned machine of your devotion,
Clanging upon this cymbal of a hand,
Am rattled screw and footloose. All discussions

End in the mud-flat detritus of death.
My heart, beat faster, faster. (LWC ll)

The cacophany of his beating heart indicates that Lowell, according to the cliché, has "a few loose screws." Like a mad conductor of a brass band that clangs inside his head, he tries to increase the tempo, to turn the internal melee into all-out mayhem.

By poem's end Christ's innocence and violence reveal themselves in the Eliotic figure of the Fisher King: "Christ walks on black water. In Black Mud / Darts the kingfisher" (LWC ll). To reinforce this bifurcated notion of bellicose pacifism and transcendental destructiveness, Lowell also borrows Eliot's figure from the Four Quartets of the Holy Spirit's Pentecostal fire descending in the form of a German bomber. Lowell writes: "The mud / Flies from his hunching wings and beak—my heart, / The blue kingfisher dives on you in fire" (LWC ll). Transformed from an innocent "king of speechless clods and infants," Christ is now a pilot dive-bombing and fire-bombing Lowell's heart just as his satanic double bombs civilians in Europe. Moving from colloquy to confession, Lowell acknowledges guilty collusion with the enemy, as if in the quest for sublime ideals the forces of good—America, Christ, Lowell—have metamorphosed into the forces of evil—Germany, Japan, Satan. Mazzaro takes issue with Lowell's religious strategies because by making "union with God the end rather than the means of Truth," the poem forfeits "peace and understanding and truth" (46). What Mazzaro fails to realize is that Lowell's union is morally dubious and that it *does* lead to truth, albeit a bizarre and unpleasant one. The startling truth is that when religious ecstasy is achieved through contemplation, at least in Lowell's feverish mind, Christ turns out to be another Luciferian light-bringer. An enlightened pacifist, Lowell has become another belligerent enthusiast. In the religious sublime, as in its other manifestations, opposites unite.

The companion poem "Christmas in Black Rock" expresses these conjunctions and conundrums more clearly, at least at the end, when Lowell declaims:

> O Christ, the spiralling years
> Slither with child and manger to a ball
> Of ice; and what is man? We tear our rags
> To hang the Furies by their itching ears,
> And the green needles nail us to the wall. (*LWC* 12)

The dialectical situation again is Yeatsian. The gyring or "spiralling years" have been "vexed to nightmare by a rocking cradle" (187), as Yeats claimed in "The Second Coming," and now the impotence of an otherworldly Christ calls out for a new reincarnation, a rough beast to combat the world's evils on its own ground. But with the world's military beast everywhere in evidence, Lowell implies that the years of "stony sleep" may be preferable. Was his impotent pacifism morally superior to potent resistance? Lowell cannot decide. As it turns out, he wants and does not want a new Christ to be born. He wants to "hang the Furies" the way "Christ God's red shadow hangs upon the wall" (*LWC* 12) at the beginning of the poem, yet he finds *himself* hanged or crucified at the end. Christian pacifist and Christian soldier, Christ as innocent child and Christ as apocalyptic redeemer, compete as before for Lowell's allegiance.

With his Catholic conscience trained on war crimes committed by all sides in World War II, Lowell in his early poems finds his paradoxical Christs, Lucifers, and Leviathans raging everywhere around him. "And the Leviathan breaks water in the rice / Fields, at the poles, at the hot gates to Greece," he says in "The Crucifix" (*LWC* 54). Although Roman legions "Under the eagles of Lord Lucifer" have retreated from the world's battlefields, new imperial powers have advanced to take their place. Lowell declares that "Satan is pacing up and down the world" despite the fact that Christ the "fisherman / Walks on waters of a draining Rome / To bank his catch in the Celestial City" (*LWC* 55). When Lowell wrote his confessional poems about a decade after *Lord Weary's Castle*, shifting his rhetoric away from religious iconography toward the facticity of prose, much of his allegorical concern for the sublime quest and battle remained. Although his symbolism now derived more from personal, everyday experience than from Judeo-Christian tradition, he did not abandon religious sublimity; he simply expressed it in more secular terms.

A poem like "Skunk Hour" (*LS* 89–90), for example, narrates the same agon between a satanic mind and sterile, nominally Christian culture that appeared in the earlier poems. Animals and ordinary people, rather than traditional religious figures, now serve as emblems of sublimity. The "daemonic agents" who transcend the overpowering horrors of Lowell's "dark night" are the skunks. Although they may be "ironic emblem[s] of unmediated nature" (*Nihilist* 69), as Bell believes, they are also totems of Luciferian potency, both fiendish and noble. They "will not scare," although they surely scare others with their powerful stink. Their "search / in the moonlight for a bite to eat" parallels and parodies the poet's quest for spiritual sustenance in the small, lifeless Maine town. Searching for signs of sacred and profane love, he follows St. John of the Cross's meditative journey toward divine love in *The Dark Night*, but in an ordinary way (by driving his Ford up a local hill) rather than in a Catholic, mystical way. On "the hill's skull," which recalls Golgotha, love is not so much crucified as resurrected in the form of necking teenagers in "love-cars." Lowell fails to reach Christ or any other meaningful god of love, yet his discovery of the animal power to resist the human wasteland in the skunks that live and thrive off human refuse is a triumph. "A mother skunk with her column of kittens swills the garbage pail," he says. While the town declines into poverty, she offers "rich air" to a poet used to finding sublimity in what offends conventional taste.

In her essay "Mephistophilis in Maine," Sandra Gilbert echoes John Berryman's claim that in "Skunk Hour" "Lowell works rather in parable form than in forms of allegory. There is no point-to-point correspondence, the details are free" (Berryman 320). She proposes: "there is . . . 'more to' Lowell's skunks than . . . a neatly definable, almost allegorical meaning," but then offers a brilliant bit of *allegoresis:* "Lowell's skunks . . . are Hell's totemic animals, fiery familiars who emerge from the shadows of the graveyard . . . flaunting their demonic triumph" (77). The Lowellish speaker who identifies with the skunks is "not *just* Hamlet or Hamlet's cousin but also, what is more important, the descendent or reincarnation of a more crucial and burning figure: Mephistophilis, or Lucifer, or Satan, the very model of a Romantic major poet" (76).

As in his other *psychomachias,* Lowell approximates allegory without enslaving himself to its archaic machinery. His chains of correspondences are "free," as Berryman stipulates, but also characteristic in that traditional opponents join hands by the end. In one camp he lumps Lucifer, skunk, and himself. "I hear / my ill-spirit sob in each blood cell, / as if my hand were at its throat. . . . / I myself am hell," he confesses with Milton's Lucifer, who said something similar when he was about to destroy God's handiwork in Eden. The "moonstruck eyes' red fire" of the skunk emits a daemonic intensity similar to that of Lucifer and the mad, "moonstruck" Lowell. "I'm a skunk in the poem," Lowell candidly admitted in a letter to Bishop (quoted in Kalstone, 185). Against this impassioned trinity stands a trinity of waste-land figures that may, as Lawrence Kramer suggests, represent Lowell's mother, father, and self (90). "Nautilus Island's hermit / heiress," the deceased "summer millionaire, / who seemed to leap from an L.L. Bean / catalogue," and the "fairy / decorator" who earned "no money" and would "rather marry" than persist in his unrewarding business approximate aristocratic mother, moribund father, and confused son.

Looming over the derelict town is "the hill's skull," whose graveyard, like "the chalk-dry and spar spire / of the Trinitarian Church," symbolizes the absence of a traditional Christian spirit rather than its resurrection and perpetual presence. In this existential dark night, God is dead mainly because Lowell has stolen His fire and internalized it in inverted form. Kramer argues that Lowell's oedipal drama is manifest in oblique form in the figures that populate his hellish landscape: "His self-images—Jesus, Saint John of the Cross, Marlowe's Mephistophilis and Milton's Satan—are outsize figures" (and obviously contradictory ones) meant to serve as substitutes for his unimpressive father. According to Kramer, Lowell renounces these "phantoms of a trumped-up narcissism" but then encounters "only a void." Fortunately he finds in the skunks "the perfect compromise between . . . untenably grandiose identifications . . . and . . . intolerably depressive ones" (91). In a sense he finds a happy image for himself and for his ambivalence toward the sublime.

Once again Lowell tells the story of his Luciferian ascent toward religious sublimity—how his "Tudor Ford climbed the hill's skull"—and how he ends with "moonstruck eyes." His attitude toward "sublime ambition" is typically double-edged. Although it depends on the sort of "pathological enthusiasm" that gripped Josiah Hawley in a suicidal frenzy, Lowell nevertheless finds its power hard to shake off. The "mother skunk with her column of kittens" is creative and triumphant despite, and perhaps because of, her offensiveness. She is another mother for Lowell to love, and in some ways more lovable than his actual mother. Like Satan storming heaven and like Lowell attacking peers, parents, wives, and presidents, this matriarchal skunk resists all opponents with her potent aroma. Although this is "something less than affirmation" (20), as Cosgrave posits, it is definitely much more than despairing capitulation. It resembles Satan's defiant triumph in hell.

Like Milton, Blake, and Yeats, Lowell confers tragic joy—a kind of countersublime—on a Luciferian hero. Orthodox Christianity along with its orthodox heaven are unattractive wastelands to Lowell's disillusioned eye, places where wealthy hermits thirst "for / the hierarchic privacy / of Queen

Victoria's century" and buy "up all / the eyesores . . . / and let them fall."
Although Lowell usually blames the ruined hierarchical order on the sa-
tanic id, in "Skunk Hour" he extols the id's rebellious power as productive,
however repugnant it may be. The skunk does not instigate the town's
collapse but accepts its ruins and flourishes despite them. The often slighted
animal teaches Lowell to "recognize the beautiful and the exotic in the
disgusting and ordinary" (Yenser 164). And as Gilbert points out, the skunk
teaches the reader "To find the magic of hell, albeit a sordid, morbid, even
misogynistic magic . . . in the tranquilized fifties" (78). In the end, Lowell
and his skunks confront their infernal environment with buoyant equanimity.

Following his departure from Catholic and Protestant churches, Lowell's
critique of former religious models was often harsh. The ascetic Catholic
intellectual who transcended libidinal temptations through a reasoned faith
later suffered a Marxist and Freudian deflation. To his later view, traditional
religious sublimity was a massive delusion, a neurosis protecting civilization
from more painful neuroses. Lowell's sardonic analysis of the religious sub-
lime achieves another complex expression in "Beyond the Alps," versions of
which appeared in both *Life Studies* and *For the Union Dead*. The second,
longer version begins with a quotation from Napoleon, "Au dela les Alpes
est l'Italie" (*FUD* 55), and could just as well begin with Napoleon's earlier
"Du sublime au ridicule il n'y a qu'un pas," which Lowell translated and
appended to the end of "The True Light" (129). As Lowell crosses the
Alps—those traditional sites of sublimity for Romantic questers—he ridi-
cules the sublime in both its religious and its political guises.

Evaluating the paradoxical forces behind the poem, Williamson con-
tends: "The hubris, or hypertrophy of the cerebral . . . can create not only
a greater power to kill but a greater desire; for its narrow drive to perfect
its own splendor requires an indifferent, or even a Neronic, experimental
attitude toward most human individuals" (*Pity* 94). Aware of this, Lowell
struggles to free himself from the traps of hubris, but finds them set wher-
ever he goes. Divine City and Earthly City, pope and emperor are equally
threatening. Because Rome elicits memories of domineering powers, Lowell
declares: "Much against my will / I left the city of god where it belongs. /
There the skirt-mad Mussolini unfurled / the eagle of Caesar. He was one
of us / only, pure prose."

Pound, who had tried to maintain his "old sense" of the sublime by
advocating the satanic policies and purifications of Mussolini and Hitler,
and the policy that poetry should be as well written as prose, is no doubt
part of the reason Lowell rejects Rome. The city may remind him of Pound's
megalomania and his treasonous broadcasts on behalf of Mussolini on Rome
radio. Infused with the heady moralism of Winters, a critic like Cosgrave

finds "nothing but nihilism" in Lowell's shocking confessions, and therefore judges "Beyond the Alps" "a 'bad' poem" (128). He obviously misses the point. The journey away from Rome is itself a moral one, instigated primarily by a recognition of the sublime's potential destructiveness. Lowell is attempting to leave behind religious mania and institutions like the Roman Catholic Church that, in his case, encourage it. He is following the example of the Swiss mountaineers who, after trying to climb Mt. Everest—a mountain even more daunting in its sublimity than the highest Alps—"throw the sponge in" rather than risk sure destruction.

A year before 1950, when "Pius XII defined the dogma of Mary's bodily assumption" (*FUD* 55), as the poem's note explains, Lowell underwent an "assumption" or "ascent" of his own. Having abandoned the church, an event the poem represents geographically, and after suddenly rejoining it, Lowell suffered what Tate called a homicidal bout of "purification mania" (Hamilton 156). Robert Fitzgerald revealed that his brief return to Catholicism provoked the "strain and exaltation of religious experience . . . when he felt that God spoke through him and his impulses were inspired" (Hamilton 149). This was the period when he thought he "was a reincarnation of the Holy Ghost" and that he could paralyze cars by raising his arms in the middle of an Indiana highway (Hamilton 157). Crossing the Alps, Lowell attempted to put the Catholic impulses that impelled these sublimities and sublimations behind him.

No wonder Lowell mocks Mary as a gorgeous, angel-winged jungle bird in "Beyond the Alps" (*FUD* 55–57) and later links her to Pallas Athena and her Roman double, Minerva, the goddess of purity as well as of warfare. She resembles Lowell and also his mother, whose identifications with legendary warriors and hysterical pursuits of purity enter into other poems. The sublime alpine altitude, symbolic of his mother's "pure mind and murder" and his own homicidal purification mania, is something he obviously wants to abandon. Mary's assumption into heaven (which corresponds to his mother's death in 1954) leaves Lowell to wrestle with various father figures: the Holy Father (Pope Pius), Saint Peter, the Jehovah-like Duce (Mussolini) who "herded his people to the *coup de grace*," and Apollo, god of light, science, and reason. In the second version of the poem, Apollo is introduced after an exiled Ovid appears to denounce the poets and politicians of Rome, "the *black republicans* who tore the tits / and bowels of the Mother Wolf to bits— / Then psychopath and soldier waved the red / of empire over Caesar's salvaged bog" (56). The psychopathic poet condemns himself here, and condemns his oedipal conflicts with his various symbolic mothers and fathers that led to obsessions with "caesars" like Caligula and Mussolini. "Tired of the . . . blear-eyed ego kicking" in oedipal nightmares, he wants to wake with the morning light of Apollo and "plant his heels / on terra firma" (57). Although Apollo and Minerva are gods of enlightened civilities like those represented by Paris, the city of Lowell's destination, they never appear in unadulterated redolence. As the black soot is scrubbed from Parisian buildings and the nightmare of history dissolves from Lowell's waking consciousness ("Paris, our black classic, [is] breaking up / like killer kings on an Etruscan cup" [57]), vestiges of murderous power struggles remain in lines that imagine their effacement. The eponymous Paris, after all, provoked rather than terminated a war. Apollo's light only makes history's darkness more visible. As Nietzsche speculated, Apollo governs the Dionysian "breakings" of tragedies ("black classics") by illuminating them.

In Lowell's agonistic quest for religious sublimity, civilized orders break up and individual psyches break down. The manic desire for transcendent purity that some have called the sin of "angelism"—"the refusal of the creature to submit to or be ruled by any of the exigencies of the created natural order" (Hill 4)—was a danger for Lowell and everyone around him. This is the main point of Bishop's "The Armadillo," a poem dedicated to Lowell, whose "frail, illegal fire balloons" are "Climbing the mountain height, // rising toward a saint / still honored in these parts" (103). Containing the same sort of "moonstruck eyes' red fire" that Lowell depicted in "Skunk Hour" (a poem written in response to "The Armadillo"), the fire balloons symbolically trace the ascent of a manic psyche (like Lowell's) in its destructive quest for religious sublimity. The balloons "solemnly / and steadily forsaking us, / or, in the downdraft from a peak, / suddenly turning dangerous" (103), destroy themselves as well as others in the "created natural order." "The Armadillo" amounts to a disguised portrait of Bishop's manic friend. "Skunk Hour," while dedicated to Bishop, offers a defensive riposte of sorts because it concludes with an act of heroic defiance that is aimed to protect rather than destroy the animals and their habitat.

Although Lowell abandoned Catholicism and Protestantism in midcareer, they continued to exert an irresistible tug on his imagination. Rather than allegorize his conflicts solely in Marxist terms of class struggles or Freudian terms of oedipal struggles, Lowell often found his most compelling rhetoric in the religious traditions he spurned. In his "one story" a "compulsive syndrome" drove his "daemonic agents," as Fletcher would say, to commune as well as clash with God. According to Lowell, the desire to play God or king after traditional gods and kings had been ousted was at the heart of American culture, American enthusiasm, and the American sublime. Milton's Satan and Melville's Ahab captured in archetypal form "the American Religion," an ideology of apocalypse whose ends are inspiring and whose means are cataclysmic. Its principal expositor, Bloom, traces his book on the subject "back to my purchasing and reading Monsignor Ronald Knox's *Enthusiasm* in 1960" (*American Religion* 47). He explains:

> The American Religion is, in many respects, a continuation into the nineteenth and twentieth centuries of what was termed Enthusiasm in Europe, particularly during the seventeenth and eighteenth centuries, when the term tended to be used in disapproval. In its literal sense, Enthusiasm suggests divine inspiration or even possession, but genteel Christians of the Enlightenment gave the term its figurative force of emotionalism and even fanaticism. (47)

Later Bloom contends: "The American version of religious 'Enthusiasm' has been so prevalent for two centuries now that it is identical with the American Religion itself, whether that manifests itself as the Mormons or the Methodists, Assemblies of God or the Baptists, conservative Protestants or liberal Protestants" (218). For Bloom the American Christian is engaged in a Gnostic quest for the abyss before creation where the God within can be unified with the God without. What holds the various sectarian strands of Protestantism together is "the American persuasion, however muted or obscured, that we are mortal gods, destined to find ourselves again in worlds as yet undiscovered" (103). Bloom treats the different Protestant swerves from orthodoxy as manifestations of Romantic iconoclasm; Lowell treats them similarly but emphasizes their vices. The oedipal agon driving the American Religion, in Lowell's view, is shameful, as is his own attempt to be a "mortal god." Although during his mad moments he was convinced he could out-Jehovah Jehovah, the rest of the time he realized that measuring his powers against the omnipotence of Jehovah was a doomed and ludicrous enterprise.

Lowell's conversion to Catholicism and persistent fascination with the church after his departure from it arose from his personal knowledge of the dangers of Protestant individualism. Cut off from the authoritarian decrees of the Catholic Church, compulsively solipsistic or egocentric individuals like Lowell were prone to chaotic behavior. Because his enthusiasm for a position of moral superiority from which he could judge the world and punish its sinners was so rabid, the ascetic rationality of the Catholic Church's long, prestigious tradition of scholastic philosophy had an obvious appeal. This sort of sublimation, however, with its necessary regimen of repression, proved to be both cure and disease. Lowell seemed destined by his biological and cultural endowments to keep questing for the authoritarian grandeur of godhood, even though it plunged him, as it had his Luciferian precursors, into hell. This paradox, as Williamson explains, underlies "the conflict between Lowell's religious impulse—which centers around a desire to live in apocalyptic moments when all energy is liberated and the self and the world are no longer distinct—and his rationalistic fear that this desire is obscurely married to the worst elements in himself, to a primitive destructiveness" (*Pity* 6–7). Although he satirized and condemned the enthusiasm behind his tragic quest for apocalyptic moments, saturating his poetry with personal and historical examples of enthusiasm's dire consequences, like others similarly afflicted Lowell could not totally renounce the ecstasy promised by such moments. The inspiration afforded by lofty, liberating ideals, however delusory, made him into one of the most compelling, insightful, and prolific poets of his generation. Why renounce the power that produced one's greatest efforts? With others in his tragic generation Lowell sacrificed mental health at the altar of enthusiasm and sublimity.

7

The Postmodern Sublime

Lowell, Wilson, and Jameson

Although for many critics Lowell is the central poet of the postwar era, consolidating advances made by modernists and pushing beyond them, whether he is postmodernist is open to debate. Arguing against the very terms of this debate, a critic like James Breslin unwittingly places Lowell at its center by fastening on a topic repeatedly scrutinized by theorists of postmodernism—the sublime. Quoting the 1965 interview with Alvarez in which Lowell differentiates American culture from English culture, Breslin concludes: "Lowell's theory [of the American sublime] is most valuable when understood as a projection onto the American past of his own struggles as a beginning poet" (113). If Lowell's early poetry courted the apocalyptic violence the sublime entails, making him one "of Ahab's party without knowing it" (113), his later poetry (from *Life Studies* on), according to Breslin, renounces the sublime and embraces the prosaic: "It discards rhetorical sublimity and religious myth in a quest to enter a demystified present. Lowell touches what had hurt him most, the prosaic and everyday, and he finds that his fiery creative self can survive within the quotidian" (124).

Does this tell the whole story? Can Lowell's career be divided so neatly between sublime ascent and prosaic descent, religious myth and demystified fact, or did his ambivalence toward the sublime simply decrease in intensity without ever really disappearing? If *Lord Weary's Castle* and *The Mills of the Kavanaughs* represent an apotheosis of modernist and New Critical methods of deploying myth, ritual, symbol, poetic form, wit, paradox, and other tropes, and *Life Studies* as well as later books express a postmodern fascination with a "demystified present," would it not be more accurate to say that Lowell's early compulsions, repressed as they were in his middle and late periods, had an uncanny way of returning in the form of a

136

postmodern sublime? Breslin would deny this, citing Lowell's avowed dissatisfaction with all sublimity after his overtly formalist phase. Others would agree. For Bloom, whatever urge "to elevate heroic wryness into a kind of sublimity" (in a poem like "Ulysses and Circe" in *Day by Day*) proves futile. "A curious flatness or deadness of tone" ("Year's Books" 24) makes bathos rather than *hypsos* the dominant emotion in the late poems. Vendler argues similarly that "Lowell refuses . . . sublimity" in his post-*Life Studies* period.

Although critics are certainly right to point out the change in the intensity of Lowell's attachment to the sublime in his middle and later periods, they are wrong to claim that he shut the door entirely on its beguiling power. Certainly in his personal conduct, which was so intimately tied to his poetry, he never quelled the seductions of sublimity. Dudley Young recounts Lowell's visit to Essex University in 1970, when he was "burning manic energy and whiskey at about twice the rate of us who were half his age. He was the large and lethal Carnival King, the Candlemas Bear come to release us from common prose; sublime, sexy, and frequently mad" (312). Like a ghost from the past, the sublime insinuated itself through cracks in Lowell's best defenses. One of the implications of his interviews with Alvarez is that the awesomeness and awfulness of the postwar era haunted even those, like Lowell, determined to repudiate it. But what is the postmodern sublime that beleaguered Lowell with such persistence? How does it figure in his poetry, and how do his shifting attitudes to it affect his stylistic shifts?

Wilson's provocative, wide-ranging study, *American Sublime: The Genealogy of a Poetic Genre*, provides clues to many of these questions. To elucidate Lowell's inconsistent appraisal of the sublime, he quotes the last stanza of "Waking Early Sunday Morning," in which those standard sites of sublimity—volcanoes and wars—and the sublime rhetoric they occasion appear hollow. Wilson explains: "Such a fall into 'the monotony of the sublime'—which Lowell early feared as a stylistic peril—is decried as one consequence of our American will-to-sublimity, now displaced from natural ('sweet volcanic cone') or human centers ('our children') to soul-dead icons such as satellites and nuclear warheads—hence comprising, in all dread and terror, '*our monotonous sublime*'" (59). Natural grandeur, military power, financial hegemony, literary prestige, romantic potency—these are only some of the sublime fruits that tantalized Lowell and that, at least after descending from his manic highs, he branded monotonous, ignominious, or both.

Wilson's disquisition on the sublime repeatedly returns to Wallace Stevens's claim in "The American Sublime": "the sublime comes down / To the spirit itself, // The spirit and space, / The empty spirit / In vacant space" (131). Lowell's "Waking Early Sunday Morning" echoes Stevens's "Sunday

Morning," and it echoes "The American Sublime" as well. As Lowell contemplates the globe as a gutted spaceship or ghostly satellite orbiting through space, his spirit empties itself of apocalyptic yearnings, at least for the moment, and confronts that other aspect of the sublime—the mesmerizing horror of the void, of infinite space. Eternal vacancy is a type of "mathematical sublime," as Kant explained. For Wilson it has emerged in recent art as a Hydra-headed monster inspiring dread and wonder: "This vastness for the nineteenth century primarily meant the counterforce of Nature-writ-large, whereas for poets of postmodernism, this newer sublime entails an experience of technological space and commodity-infinitude which ungrounds and decenters the human agent to a condition of mute subjugation and fresh wonders of accommodation" (204). In the space abandoned by the natural sublime, which was so popular for Romantics, technological and capitalist sublimes have established their ambiguous allure.

Before the immense destructiveness of nuclear warheads and the prodigious waste of capitalist overproduction Lowell articulates his postmodern protest. Wilson quotes Lowell's "Fall 1961" as an example of the sort of diminishment and despair instilled by the postmodern sublime:

> All autumn, the chafe and jar
> of nuclear war;
> We have talked our extinction to death.
> I swim like a minnow
> behind my studio window. (*FUD* ll)

Similarly, in "Waking Early Sunday Morning" the salmon leaping for the sublime will suffer tragic diminishment and death. The mushroom cloud is a postmodern analogue of the "bone-crushing waterfall" that for Romantics would have been a symbol of nature's awesome power.

Wilson contends that the invidious aspects of the postmodern sublime emanate inevitably from the origins of American culture. Lowell would certainly agree that seeds sown by America's founding fathers and cultivated by their political heirs have burgeoned into a poisonous yet seductive garden. According to Wilson: "Nuclear power . . . seems to emanate from the innermost depths of American poetics articulating self-rapture and national empowerment like a first fate, a fact of nature. Poets, too, stand implicated in this fascination with icons of national superiority, self-sublation into nature and God, the death of European history back into the primal scene of the desert—poets and scientists conjuring the technology of the Over-Soul in the sublime solitude of Los Alamos" (226). Oedipal son that he was, Lowell craved self-rapture and self-empowerment; he wanted to dethrone the American patriarchs and prove his strength was greater than theirs. If he protested against Kennedy's nuclear buildup, he also embraced Kennedy, and in his dreams even became Kennedy. If he rebuked Roosevelt for criminal war policies, he also drew attention to their similar patrician "family traditions" (*CP* 368). He liked to assume common ground with his formidable adversaries and then assume moral superiority.

Like other theorists of the postmodern sublime, Lowell interprets his aesthetic concept in ideological terms. Whether the conflict is between son and father, citizen and president, worker and executive, power is always the crucial issue. For Marx and Freud, class strife and family strife were part of a Romantic narrative whose happy conclusion depicted an empowerment of the oppressed and a reconciliation of antitheses—a classless utopia or an oedipal resolution. Lowell's response to the postmodern sublime of military and industrial power is not so simple or auspicious. It embraces antitheses while discountenancing syntheses. In his early formalist phase, Lowell attacked the excesses of American might in a style that was as imperious and impassioned as what he condemned. Devoted New Critic that he was, if he gestured toward reconciliations, he undercut them with ambiguities. In the end opposites were suspended in tension rather than happily wedded. Like Romantics before him, having given up his apocalyptic hopes for political renovation, he later retreated inward to concentrate on psychological and religious renovation, which turned out to be just as elusive. Although his forays into history and politics continued, they consistently reconnoitered figures who, for better or worse, mirrored his personal obsessions. If the postmodern sublime in its political manifestations meant Cold War power struggles, threats of nuclear Armageddon, and capitalist plunder on a massive scale, Lowell would search for a style that, like Perseus's shield, reflected and simultaneously resisted the terror, chaos, and splendor of postmodern existence.

Lowell's vision of the postmodern scene as an agon without an end recalls Jean Baudrillard's view of history's vertiginous dialectic. In the postmodern world antitheses have burned up their theses like so much fuel, according to Baudrillard, but have failed to reach a synthesis. Baudrillard's interpretation of current events recalls Yeats's grim appraisal of totalitarian movements at the beginning of the twentieth century. In "The Second Coming" everything is spiraling out of control, "the centre cannot hold," "the best lack all conviction, while the worst / Are full of passionate intensity" (187). Multitudes clamber heroically but suicidally for terrible beauties. Baudrillard proposes that the high-tech revolutions in the latter part of the twentieth century offer similar grim seductions. They have instigated a horrendous apocalypse in which the natural world has been eclipsed. Having virtually died, nature has made way for a vast array of spectacular simulations designed for transient entertainment. The sublime now emanates from commodities and ads engineered by corporate executives and advertising agencies to stimulate perpetual cycles of artificial appetite, conspicuous consumption, and stupendous waste. Baudrillard comments: "The passion of intensification, of escalation, of mounting power, of ecstasy, of whatever quality so long as, having ceased to be relative to its opposite (the true to the false, the beautiful to the ugly, the real to the imaginary), it becomes superlative, positively sublime as if it had absorbed the energy of its opposite" (186–187). The simulation of the real has created a "hyperreality," a capitalist's dream like Disneyland, a space glutted with garish fictions so captivating that they seem facts.

This postmodern sublime in which transcendence of natural exigencies is read in capitalist rather than Kantian terms is one facet of the sublime that Lowell repeatedly addresses. In a way it is at the heart of his multiperspective narrative of postmodern times. His divided attitudes toward the postmodern sublime predict those expressed by Marxist and post-Marxist critics like Jean-François Lyotard, Christopher Norris, Jameson, and Eagleton. What Jameson says about the Marxist ambivalence toward capitalism and how the sublime best captures that ambivalence rings true for Lowell. In "Postmodernism, or The Cultural Logic of Late Capitalism," Jameson notes: "Marx powerfully urges us to do the impossible, namely . . . to achieve . . . a type of thinking that would be capable of grasping the demonstrably baleful features of capitalism along with its extraordinary and liberating dynamism" (86). According to Jameson, the postmodern sublime derives from a similar contradictory sense of elation and despair over culture's glut of simulations, of depthless images and tawdry signs.

As nature dissolves into a "glossy skin, a stereoscopic illusion, a rush of filmic images without density," is the capitalist apocalypse "a terrifying or an exhilarating experience" (76–77)? Borrowing concepts from Burke and Kant to formulate what he calls "the hysterical sublime," Jameson analyzes texts that embrace the unreality of this state of affairs much as Lowell does—in psychological and political contexts. Behind the depthless images and fragmentary narratives, behind the words that seem to come from nowhere and go nowhere, he finds cultural hysteria and schizophrenia. Because the artist's imagination is structured politically, Jameson concludes morosely: "This whole global, yet American, postmodern culture is the internal and superstructural expression of a whole new wave of American military and economic domination throughout the world: in this sense, as throughout class history, the underside of culture is blood, torture, death and horror" (57).

Kant believed that sublimity arose from the imagination's confrontations with scenes so awesome or horrible that the mind at first shuddered without being able to find concepts or words to describe them; Jameson finds that same language-baffling power in high-tech culture. He suggests that "our faulty representations of some immense communicational and computer network are themselves but a distorted figuration of something even deeper, namely the whole world system of present-day multinational capitalism" (79). In contradistinction to Jameson, Kant would stipulate that the true sublime comes only when reason makes sense of overwhelming phenomena like the "immense communicational and computer network . . . of present-day multinational capitalism" and when it thereby recognizes its superior conceptual power. For Jameson the postmodern sublime inheres in a mind that merely encounters the faulty representations, schizophrenic writings, and other nonrepresentational artifacts of postmodernism, and is bemused, baffled, or horrified by them.

According to Jameson, the postmodernist's unwillingness to subdue the meteor shower of images in "mass culture" to the rational mind's intelligible order, and to locate sublimity in the mind's power to construct such an order, is due to cultural amnesia, collective irresponsibility toward the past, and breakdowns between history and its referent. "The new spatial logic of the simulacrum," he writes in his critique of avant-garde art, "can now be expected to have a momentous effect on what used to be historical time" (66). An ordinary sense of narrative time in many postmodern texts has been thrown to the winds, and what readers confront instead is a scattering of broken images—the fractured space of a collage rather than the temporal fluidity of a history. Hence we have "the randomly heterogenous and fragmentary and the aleatory . . . or schizophrenic writing" (71) of postmodern artists who blissfully ignore temporal continuity and indulge in chaotic linguistic play. In his view, texts in which signifiers float free from signifieds and from coherent narrative structures are comparable to texts written or uttered by schizophrenics and hysterics. Their expressive, chaotic bliss resembles the "pathological enthusiasms" that Lowell, too, associated with sublimity.

In the poetry written between *Land of Unlikeness* and *Near the Ocean*, Lowell generally deplores the situation in which "the retrospective dimension indispensable to any vital reorientation of our collective future has . . . become a vast collection of images, a multitudinous photographic simulacrum" (Jameson 66). He is hesitant to embrace the postmodernist's (and modernist's) narrative of spatial discontinuity and to abandon the temporal coherence of a history that points toward a definite past and future. In his late volumes of sonnets, however, Lowell edges closer to a postmodernist style of sublime disorder even while intimating his dissatisfaction with its reduction of the past to a mélange of fragmentary simulacra. Discussing Lowell's late "photographic" aesthetic, Calvin Bedient convincingly asserts: "That he was not happy with the aesthetic is plain from the poems, which sweat out their confinement to snapshot rapidity and rectilinear form" (141). History in his seemingly endless sequence of free-form, aleatory, idiosyncratic sonnets is a collage of personal obsessions from Alexander and Napoleon to Hitler and Mussolini bizarrely juxtaposed with vignettes about parents, literary mentors, lovers, and friends. *Notebook, The Dolphin, For Lizzie and Harriet,* and *History* can be read as an extended elegy for an orderly history, both ancient and recent. While these volumes reflect time's bewildering flux, they also self-reflexively diagnose, as Jameson does, the postmodern sublime as if it were symptomatic of contemporary America's pursuit of political, military, and economic hegemony. As America pursues its morally dubious goals with the cunning of a high-tech Lucifer or Ahab schooled in nuclear physics, Lowell fabricates a postmodern style that tries to mime more faithfully the frenzy and fragmentation of his and his nation's psyche. Somewhat like Eliot, who responded to his own modernist moment by offering in *The Waste Land* a diagnostic X ray of "the immense panorama of futility and anarchy which is contemporary history" (*Prose* 177), Lowell pursues a helter-skelter style to delineate personal and cultural history on the verge or in the midst of collapse.

One of Lowell's most compelling middle poems that anatomizes the postmodern condition and points toward the more discontinuous style of the later poems is "For the Union Dead." In diagnostic fashion, the poem establishes historical connections between the "multitudinous photographic simulacrum" that characterizes postmodern culture and its origins in America's industrial, military, and agrarian past. Although Lowell excoriates the savage unreality and "hysterical sublime" of the present, he also implicates himself in the milieu his conscience opposes. He, too, is "not much less abstracted from his own humanness than the wholly abstracted drivers of the driverless cars that 'nose forward like fish' and 'slide by on grease,'" and is therefore partly responsible for "the disheveled dehumanization of the city" (Bell, *Nihilist* 96). To Lowell's jaundiced eye, all parties are guilty of violating both natural productivity and civilized decorum. In an earlier Boston Civil War poem, "Chistmas Eve Under Hooker's Statue," Lowell alluded to Melville's poem "The March into Virginia," which began:

> All wars are boyish, and are fought by boys,
> The champions and enthusiasts of the State:
> Turbid ardours and vain joys

> Not barrenly abate—
> Stimulants to the power mature,
> Preparations of fate. (*Poems* 13)

In "For the Union Dead" Lowell again documents the "turbid ardours and vain joys" of political enthusiasms, which in his mind are at the poisoned root of postmodern sublimity. As Lowell finishes his stroll through Boston, he encounters increasingly subliminal simulations of historical events—not statues that represent noble sacrifice, such as Colonel Shaw's in the Civil War, but advertisements that represent holocausts and the way capitalists make even the most heinous events appealing and profitable. He declares:

> The ditch is nearer.
> There are no statues for the last war here;
> on Boylston Street, a commercial photograph
> shows Hiroshima boiling
>
> over a Mosler Safe, the "Rock of Ages"
> that survived the blast. Space is nearer.
> When I crouch to my television set,
> the drained faces of Negro school-children rise like
>   balloons. (*FUD* 72)

The ditch where Shaw's "body was thrown / and lost with his 'niggers'" (72) after the slaughter at Fort Wagner in Charleston, South Carolina, is the collective grave that is "nearer" because advancements in technology have made its opposite—space—nearer (through nuclear missiles and global telecommunications). The new collective grave *is* space. Sublimated out of existence, victims of a nuclear holocaust rise on a cloud or bubble into spacious nothingness. What Wilson has called "the nuclear sublime" has been photographed and blown up into an ad for a Mosler safe. In Lowell's poem the ad is an emblem—what Baudrillard would call a "simulacrum"—indicative of postmodern culture's flight to extremes of sublimation and savagery.

If Lowell's poems bearing witness to nuclear holocaust gesture toward a despairing silence—an end of signs—as a possible moral response (as when he writes "We have talked our extinction to death" [*FUD* ll]), his capitalist peers erect huge signs with no apparent awareness of the moral issues involved. Blind to victims of atrocity, they focus only on selling their product. The Mosler safe—a fitting icon of capitalist power and avarice— is their new church. Just as they use the holocaust for their financial gain, so they transform the name of the traditional church (the Rock of Ages) and its implicit history into a catchy slogan. All those around Lowell, including the black schoolchildren, are losing their humanity as technology (the television set in this case) mimes a nuclear explosion by "subliming" or "blowing up" everything into a spectacular spectacle of gray dots. The children are thin filmic images rising like balloons. Even "Colonel Shaw / is riding on his bubble, / he waits / for the blesséd break" (*FUD* 72). He, too, is only a representation (perhaps his statue in front of the statehouse is on television as well) and waits for some sort of apocalypse, some cataclysmic deflation so that he can return to earth, even though earth offers little consolation. Lowell expresses a "dislike of monuments [due to] the fear that abstract images will too effectively distance unpleasant realities" (*Pity* 107), as Williamson notes, and also directs his animosity at the proliferation of abstract images by unscrupulous capitalists. Surveying his Boston wasteland, Lowell implies that the postmodernist's attempt to forge a style that subverts ordinary methods of representation is an ethical alternative to the capitalist's style of sublimating everything, no matter how horrendous, into seductive images.

As in most of Lowell's poems, violent opposites collide. Here the various ascents toward sublimity lead inevitably to descents toward violence, perversion, and death. Lowell refuses to take sides by taking all sides. If he satirizes the fishlike, finned cars of the 1950s that "nose forward" with "savage servility," he reminds us that he, too, was once a savage, reptilian child fascinated by fish—his "nose crawled like a snail on the glass" (*FUD* 70) of the Boston Aquarium. A Bostonian from a prominent family that believed in the kind of political service and sacrifice articulated in Lowell's epigraph, "Relinquunt Omnia Servare Rem Publicam" ("They give up everything to serve the republic," *FUD* 70), he is also one of the "servility," a slave to ambition and career, writing a poem about a war to end institutionalized slavery in the South that has actually prolonged it or at least failed to improve the lot of many African-Americans in the North. If he commemorates Emerson's transcendentalist idealism behind Shaw's sacrifice, he denigrates the sort of "abstract" idealism and "sublime ambition" behind that other sort of sacrifice—a holocaust.

Axelrod astutely observes that Shaw is another Ahabian leaper whose devotion to sublime ideals is as uplifting as it is upsetting: "The hidden homicidal or suicidal strain that Lowell detects in Shaw . . . corresponds to the Ahab-like spirit he finds deep in the American character, a spirit of 'violence and idealism' capable in our day of producing nuclear holocaust" (170–71). Lowell worries that "the nation's ideals will collapse and the country itself fall back into its own tumultuous past" (Yenser 239), but this may not be all that bad: "On the one hand, Lowell deplores the conditions that seem to make it [global devastation] inevitable and cringes at the

horror that it must involve; but on the other hand, the conditions them-
selves are so deplorable that the thought of their destruction, even at the
expense of civilization, is not without some appeal" (239). What Lowell
particularly recoils from is *the way* such devastation is depicted and the
crass financial reasons for such depictions. Disgusted by capitalist represen-
tations and the avarice behind them, he aims his moral protest at "the
nuclear sublime," and intimates that a countersublime should be fashioned
in an art that underscores the unrepresentability of "unspeakable" horrors.

Lowell and Lyotard

Postmodern critics shed light on Lowell's political vacillations and id-
iosyncratic historiography when they adopt Kant's notion of sublime incom-
mensurability to the way contemporary reality inevitably falls short of the
ideals that try to transform it or represent it. Suffering from sensory over-
load, Kant's imagination essentially broke down. When it tried to come up
with an image for what it dimly beheld, reason had to step in to provide a
concept for the unrepresentable experience. Lowell was preoccupied from
the outset with this incommensurable gap between abstract concepts or
ideals, which for Kant were transcendent, and the recalcitrant, quixotic, and
often overwhelming world of facts that he wanted to redeem, either politi-
cally or poetically. With the collapse of Marxist regimes in Eastern Europe
and the Soviet Union, some postmodern critics have used the sublime
incommensurability of the real and the ideal to explain the difference be-
tween historical calamity and ideological goal. Marxist idealism is transcen-
dent and sublime, they argue, because thinking it gives evidence of a mental
power and moral concept that surpasses all political conditions. A Marxist
utopia is incommensurable with reality because nothing can be found out-
side its conceptualization in language to adequately represent it.

In his moving testimony "A Memorial of Marxism," which recounts two
decades of committed activity on behalf of the French Communist Party
after World War II, Lyotard offers a political explanation of Kantian sublim-
ity and enthusiasm that in several ways parallels Lowell's, and that illumi-
nates the postmodern style displayed in his sonnet sequences. Interpreting
Kant in an essay entitled "Gaps," Lyotard proposes:

> There is no sublime . . . without the development of the speculations and
> ethical capacities of the mind [which can conceive of God and the Good
> while unable to present objective correlatives for these ideals]. With the
> esthetics of the sublime it can be argued that a kind of progress in human

history is possible which would not be only the progress of technology and science . . . but of the responsibility to the Ideas of reason as they are negatively "presented" in the formlessness of such and such a situation which could occur. The French Revolution, for example, committed a monstrous amount of injustices, crimes, murders, and ended with the Terror. It nevertheless received everywhere an enthusiastic reception from a great variety of people. How was it possible? Kant's answer is that people were educated and refined enough in moral ideas to feel the presence of and respond to the attraction of the Idea of freedom within the disorders. This enthusiasm constitutes an event . . . which is the sign . . . that mankind is in progress toward the better. (*Peregrinations* 41)

In his study *The Differend,* Lyotard ponders Kant's aesthetic categories more scrupulously, and concludes that "Enthusiasm is an extreme mode of the sublime: the attempt at presentation [of an objective correlative for the Idea] not only fails, arousing the tension in question, but it reverses itself" (166), producing madness rather than a realization of divinity or virtue in the human subject. Lyotard adds: "Although ethically condemnable as pathological, aesthetically enthusiasm is sublime, because it is a tension of forces produced by Ideas, which give an impulse to the mind that operates far more powerfully and lastingly than the impulse arising from sensible representations" (166).

The French Revolution, the Communist revolutions, indeed most revolutions inspired by lofty idealism, according to Lyotard, are ethically questionable and even pathological—they are enraged outburts of repressed forces in the political unconscious—yet they also provide sublime intimations or signs of ethical progress. He argues: "Historical-political enthusiasm is . . . on the edge of dementia, it is a pathological outburst, and as such it has in itself no ethical validity. . . . In its periodic unbridling, however, enthusiastic pathos conserves an aesthetic validity, it is an energetic *sign*" (*Differend* 166–67) whose referent, albeit unrealized in actual events, is the ideal of liberation. For Lyotard, postmodern art finds its most compelling definition in "the sublime relation between the presentable and the conceivable" (*Postmodern* 79)—that is, in the difference or "gap" between object and concept, historical fact and political ideal, signifier and signified. In his evaluation of postmodernism, which differs sharply from Jameson's, he contends that the genre is not radical enough because it still hankers nostalgically after organic wholes, beautiful totalities, narrative consistencies. He calls for "the real sublime sentiment, which is in an intrinsic combination of pleasure and pain: the pleasure that reason should exceed all presentation, the pain that imagination or sensibility should not be equal to the concept" (*Postmodern* 81).

Although Lyotard praises Kant, it is a Kant made over in his own image. In the passage from Carritt's *Philosophies of Beauty* that Lowell studied under Ransom, Kant says (of the mathematical sublime): "Our imagination strives for a progress to infinity, but our reason demands a complete totality as an idea to be realized. So the very fact that our power of measuring sensible objects is inadequate to this idea, awakes the feeling of a power in us superior to sense. . . . So not the object should be called sublime, but rather the state of mind caused by an idea which excites our reflective faculty of judgement" (119). Reason's conviction that it grasps such totalities as God and the Good allows it to issue categorical imperatives. Whereas Lyotard gives enthusiasm (the "god within") an optimistic gloss as an intimation of the political Good, Kant eventually censures it as the seed of delirium and fanaticism. Whereas Lyotard wants to declare war against totality, Kant wants to make peace with it as long as it is a rational, moral idea.

Acutely aware of ideals once held with enthusiasm but now recognized as totalitarian, Lyotard finds in the concept of sublimity a way to articulate the painful contrast. In principle his Marxist ideals and enthusiasms were good. In practice they led either to noble failures or to atrocious crimes. The sublime provides a kind of refuge in which he can contemplate Marx's magnificent narrative of historical progression from oppression through dialectical struggle to utopia while despairing that the fiction never was and never can be realized. He can read history as if it were a novel or drama full of splendor and terror. Cocooned in aesthetic contemplation, he can appreciate Marx's uplifting ideals while simultaneously acknowledging their vile consequences in the actual world.

Lyotard is particularly close to Lowell not because of his consistent advocacy of Kantian sublimity and enthusiasm but because of his contradictory stances toward them. At the end of "What Is Postmodernism" it is hard to tell where he stands in his dialectical argument, just as it is hard to tell whether Lowell's subliminal ideals lead him toward the revolutionary or the totalitarian camp. Lyotard affirms: "It is our business not to supply reality but to invent allusions to the conceivable which cannot be presented" (*Postmodern* 81). Yet Lyotard repeatedly appeals to reality, especially historical reality, which has made charades of his revolutionary principles. He spurns Hegel for entertaining transcendental delusions of totality and applauds Kant because "Kant . . . knew that the price to pay for such an illusion is terror. The nineteenth and twentieth centuries have given us as much terror as we can take. We have paid a high enough price for the nostalgia of the whole and the one, for the reconciliation of the concept and the sensible" (*Postmodern* 81). Against all nostalgic backsliding toward totalitarian realism and terror, Lyotard admonishes: "Let us wage war on totality; let us be witnesses to the unpresentable; let us activate the differences and save the honor of the name" (*Postmodern* 81–82). Let us be abstract idealists, he admonishes. When Kant asserts that "our reason demands a complete totality as an idea to be realized," he is not exactly waging war on reason's totalities; reason, after all, was his totalitarian god. In his revisionary swerve from Kant, Lyotard seems to be saying: Let us be nontotalitarian intellectuals rather than totalitarian politicians; let us live in the imagination rather than in reality; let us conceive of utopias and not worry about whether they be represented historically; let us attend to good stories rather than bad histories.

Because Lowell felt the seductiveness of totalitarian regimes so strongly (at times he believed only *they* could impose a sublime ideal on a recalcitrant populace), and because his mania often convinced him he possessed the authoritarian might to enforce those ideals apocalyptically, his skepticism of idealism was more sharp-edged than Lyotard's. Nevertheless, when Lowell in his middle and later periods became increasingly self-conscious about his old ideological sublimities and enthusiasms—whether Catholic or Marxist—submitting their triumphalist teleologies to sardonic scrutiny, he resembled Lyotard in trying to win something from defeat. Realizing that the postmodern sublime of atomic bombs, multinational corporations, and Marxist hegemonies originated from one phenomenon—a massive campaign for unilateral power—he set out to erect his "autobiographical sublime" as a defensive refuge. Like other disillusioned revolutionaries and jaded Romantics, Lowell traded in one sublime for another. If sublimity could not be found in apocalyptic political events, it would have to be found in the poet's private imagination and poems. Because radical as well as reactionary ideals inevitably ended in regimes of terror when pursued with uncompromising intensity, Lowell began in his sonnet sequences to practice a "discontinuous" style that at least partly subverted the old apocalyptic narratives and rhetorics that promoted and enshrined such regimes, and that had characterized earlier books like *Lord Weary's Castle*. Of his sonnets and Berryman's *Dream Songs*, which parody as well as imitate traditional verse forms, he said:

> both [are] made of hero, event and elegy,
> the autobiographical sublime,
> both [are] discontinuous, impulsive;
> luck threw up the words, and the plot swallowed,
> beast famished for a thousand far-flung words . . . (H 2701)

Although Lowell did not collect this poem, he borrowed phrases from it in his "Afterthought" to *Notebook*. "My plot rolls with the seasons," he says, "but one year is confused with another. I have flashbacks to what I remember, and fables inspired by impulse. Accident threw up subjects, and the plot swallowed them—famished for human chances. I lean heavily to the rational, but am devoted to unrealism" (*N* 262). The "autobiographical sublime" may be Lowell's defensive answer to the disappointments with traditional political and religious sublimities. It can also be interpreted in a darker light—as another instance of his inveterate self-aggrandizement, his tendency to depose the monsters only to withdraw to the cave of his psyche where his monstrous ego dwells. If the leviathanic beast represents his poem, it also represents himself.

Although Vendler denies that Lowell pursues the sublime in these poems, she implies the opposite when she finds in them "the grand drama of the manic" (171), "Miltonic avidity for omnipotence," (127), and an egotistical story rather than a political history. "Lowell's data are not primarily historical," she says, and the "great men" he scrutinizes "all serve equally as projections of Lowell himself" (155). The sonnet sequences, however chronological, and the individual poems, however sonnetlike, are governed by chance associations and idiosyncratic patterns; they are *his story* rather than any recognizably public or "school book" history. Borrowing Foucault's vocabulary, Alex Calder calls *History* "a genealogy" in which "Lowell . . . is writing about 'great men of history' . . . [who] do not stand as monumental figures respresenting high points or low points in the onward march of civilization; rather, they tend to illustrate how closely 'instinct, passion, the inquisitor's devotion, cruel subtlety and malice' are implicated in a 'will to knowledge,' which is also a will to power" (135). The poem's lineup of "great men," Calder presciently detects, are Lowell's "ancestral types" (135)— that is, tropes for his predecessors and psyche. Narrative order is jettisoned and a chaotic leviathan—the grandiose but erratic mental and linguistic space of Lowell's historical imagination—replaces it. In his poem for Berryman, Lowell suggests the two poets are brothers in their pursuit of postmodern Moby Dicks (the "beast famished for a thousand far-flung words"). Both poets "leap for the sublime" by trying to write "the great American poem." Disillusioned with political leviathans, both navigate an inner ocean—the realm of Wordsworth's "egotistical sublime"—and as their Romantic predecessor had done in *The Prelude,* both try to write epics on the "Growth of a Poet's Mind," albeit in postmodern fashion.

For Lowell the traditional plot of an epic and even the traditional way of ending lines with rhymes are forms that give the oceanic flux of time a recognizable order. When he says in his last poem in *Day by Day,* "Those blessèd structures, plot and rhyme— / why are they no help to me now / I want to make / something imagined, not recalled?" (*DD* 127), he may be reflecting on the way his postmodern style renounced the sort of conventional narrative and prosodic patterns he once depended on to structure private and public history. His later poems favor spatial discontinuity over temporal flow, fragmentary collage over seamless history. His postmodernist arrangements of photographic simulacra, however, disturb him. Although they participate in the "death-in-life and life-in-death" nature of all artifice (as Yeats phrased it in "Byzantium" [248]), Lowell stresses their melodramatic morbidity:

> sometimes everything I write
> with the threadbare art of my eye
> seems a snapshot,
> lurid, rapid, garish, grouped,
> heightened from life,
> yet paralyzed by fact. (DD 127)

He wants to leap into imaginary spaces, into the manic play of speculation, into the sort of transcendence beyond the "dying animal" (193) that Yeats extolled in his "Byzantium" poems, but depression and conscience pull him back to temporal and spatial images in his photograph album. He ends with the assertion: "We are poor passing facts, / warned by that to give / each figure in the photograph / his living name" (DD 127). The vacillation between temporal order and spatial disorder, collective history and personal story, formalist beauty and postmodern sublimity, traditional discourse and "schizophrenic writing," the photographic fact and the unstructured image, was no doubt prompted by Lowell's manic-depressive oscillations—his desire to let his frenetic mental energies run wild and his opposite desire to rein them in.

Whereas critics of the postmodern sublime like Jameson, Baudrillard, Norris, and Wilson attack its manifestations in the paradoxically terrifying and hypnotic phenomena of high-tech culture, and apologists like Lyotard find in their versions of postmodern sublimity a refuge in which transcendental (Marxist) ideals still have an uplifting validity, Lowell tends to waver between both parties. He condemns the ideology and institutions that produce the postmodern sublime even while expressing empathy for them, and then mocks his own sublime idealism, whether liberal or conservative, as being rooted in "pathological enthusiasm." His uncertainties are embodied in the style and themes of *History*, which obsessively addresses what Lyotard called the sublime gap between apocalyptic fictions and historical realities. The "discontinuous, impulsive" syntax of individual lines and overall plot ("luck threw up the words, and the plot swallowed") as well as the sonnets that stray from the sonnet form underscore the difference between the conceivable and the unrepresentable that Lyotard praises in postmodern writing and that Jameson diagnoses as hysterical or schizophrenic. Frances Ferguson argues, "Through the poeticized personal history of the notebooks, Lowell clearly struggles to reconcile a language of representation—which represents the world of historical time—with a language of self-consciousness or spirit—which represents the eternity beyond duration" (72). Nevertheless, the final impression is of a collision between the realism of public history and the unrealism of private spirit, which leads to their ultimate split.

The title poem "History" is a kind of synecdoche of the whole *History* sonnet sequence in the way it alludes to the grand teleological narrative of the Bible—Genesis proceeding to Revelation, sin to redemption—but then undermines these masterful narratives by emphasizing the difference or gap between the closure of writing and the open-endedness of life. The very form of the poem with its contradictory juxtapositions, unexpected metaphors, and indeterminate plot embodies the incommensurability of apocalyptic ideal and political reality. If this constitutes sublimity, then Lowell indicts that sublimity. His "terrifying innocence," symbolized by "the beautiful, mist-drunken hunter's moon," is a sublime lunacy akin to the predatory hubris of Milton's Lucifer and Melville's Ahab, those twin agents typologically related to all those who foment the revolutionary upheavals of history.

The poem begins surprisingly with a personification of history as an old codger who has moved into a strange house belonging (presumably) to the poet. Alive enough to recognize the banality of death, he nevertheless has a hard time making the rubble of history cohere as an intelligible story. Like the dolphin net in "Fishnet" (*D* 15), he tries to catch and hold onto what remains, but his mind and writing let the past slip through: "History has to live with what was here, / clutching and close to fumbling all we had — / it is so dull and gruesome how we die, / unlike writing, life never finishes" (*H* 24). Lowell obsessively opens gaps between antinomies—between living history and actual death, writerly fictions and existential facts, closure and continuity. When he states, "Abel was finished; death is not remote, / a flash-in-the-pan electrifies the skeptic, / his cows crowding like skulls against high-voltage wire, / his baby crying all night like a new machine" (*H* 24), he imagines Abel's death as the beginning of history, as the origin of atrocities, as well as something "finished" like a remote fiction (the story of Cain and Abel preserved in the Bible). If the farmer is Cain, he is also the poet electrified, like the soldier in Stevens's "Esthetique du Mal," by the nearness and brute power of death. His belligerent enthusiasm implicates him in history's atrocities and threatens to repeat them, at least in his imagination. At the end of the poem he merges with the innocent moon goddess, the huntress Artemis, as Lowell accentuates the horrors that childlike innocence and simpleminded idealism can instigate when pursued with a lunatic hunter's passion:

> As in our bibles, white-faced, predatory,
> the beautiful, mist-drunken hunter's moon ascends—
> a child could give it a face: two holes, two holes,
> my eyes, my mouth, between them a skull's no-nose—
> O there's a terrifying innocence in my face
> drenched with the silver salvage of the mornfrost. (H 24)

Cold and passionate as the dawn, Lowell portrays himself as a child might— as a cartoon figure in a simplistic drawing composed of vacant holes. Although a child *could* give him a face, he remains unrepresented. He seems inhuman, lunar, and sublime in his godlike power and vague otherworldliness—quite different from Lyotard's virtuous idealist.

Coming at the beginning of *History*, the poem suggests that the unrepresentable looms over the nightmare of history like a lunar or lunatic deity—a kind of daemonic white goddess. Lowell's postmodern task, in Lyotard's Kantian words, is to "put forward the unpresentable in presentation itself" (*Postmodern* 81), but Lowell delivers his presentation with a self-lacerating candor that might strike Lyotard as offensive. Lowell's historical ideal is not moral, as in Lyotard's case, so much as maniacal. All too familiar with the destructive consequences of unpresentable ideals, Lowell mocks them in himself and in history. Although the childlike aspirations that motivate Lowell's as well as history's enthusiasms may ultimately be transcendent, irrational, ineffable, and, when framed by the "blessèd structures" of grammar, meter, plot, and rhyme, severely distorted, Lowell nevertheless gives them a shape, albeit an unconventional one. In the end, the "unpresentable" childlike face he superimposes on history is his own, and one he disfigures because he knows how easily its faceless ideals can disfigure others.

Although Lowell's shifting attitudes toward the postmodern sublime create dramatic tension and pathos in his poetry, and provoke corresponding stylistic shifts to accommodate them, he can also fall into the kind of complacent, resigned mood that some critics have found in a disillusioned idealist like Lyotard. In discussing Lyotard's political disenchantment, Christopher Norris could be criticizing a tendency in Lowell as well, at least the Lowell of the last poems in *Day by Day*. Norris complains that Lyotard

gave up hope in capitalism, Marxism, and even "a politics of genuine social-
ist democracy" because:

> From Lyotard's standpoint this could only be another unfortunate ex-
> ample of the confusion between "cognitive" and "speculative" language-
> games, or the specific form of "transcendental illusion" that impels us to
> read the "signs" of history as if they belonged on the side of actual
> events, rather than on the side of the enthusiast-spectator whose re-
> sponse—as with the sublime—can never find an adequate or commen-
> surable object in the procession of real-world historical developments.
> So at the end of all Lyotard's immensely subtle and ingenious argumen-
> tation we are left with the message—to put it very simply—that political
> theory is one thing and practical politics quite another, since any passage
> between these strictly disparate phrase-regimes will give rise either to
> vain utopian hopes or to a mood of cynical post-revolutionary despair.
> (14–15)

For Lowell the sublime can also become a kind of aesthetic cop-out, a
transcendent refuge from political and personal despair, in which the arm-
chair idealist blissfully contemplates utopias that might have been but never
were. The poem *"Milgate,"* for instance, discovers the sublime in his third
wife's aristocratic mansion in Ireland, with its aesthetic "uselessness . . . /
splendor, extravagance" (*DD* 64). He could be Yeats extolling Lady Gregory's
"great house" of ceremony, ritual, and poetry, and the utopian Ireland where
such activities would be sanctified, when he praises his own Irish Lady,
Caroline Blackwood, for preserving:

> *Milgate*
> enclosures to sun and space to cool,
> one mural varied in fifty windows,
> sublime and cozy, stripped of creeper,
> its severity a blaze of salmon-pink,
> its long year altered by our small. . . . (*DD* 64)

In his sublime nest above the real world's hardships, however, he continues
to measure the difference, the depressing abyss, between the enthusiast's
ideal and its tragic result, between "something imagined, not recalled," as
he says in "Epilogue," and the collective photograph of "what happened,"
the "poor passing facts" (*DD* 127) of history. Nevertheless, the tone of the
poem as well as of many other poems in *Day by Day* suggests that Lowell
has given up his rebellious confrontation with his aristocratic background
and closed ranks with former adversaries.

• • •

His best later poems depict in visceral detail the various incarnations of the postmodern sublime—especially as it relates to the military-industrial complex—and offer a dynamic response that oscillates between furious denunciation and guilty identification. When the poems map the quests for sublime ideals that, like Lucifer's battle for godhood and Ahab's hunt for Moby Dick, come to tragic ends, his pathos is stirring. On the other hand, when Lowell retreats to his cozy mansion to contemplate aesthetic ideals cut off from their ideological origins and political consequences, he slips from the energizing heights of *hypsos* to the static plains of bathos. As critics of his later work complain, his language often slackens into cliché. His subjects become monotonously sublime as well as monotonously banal. *Notebook* "does not so much 'roll with the seasons' as resemble a circular clothesline on which Lowell has continued to pin laundry" (134), as Calder wittily protests. Another dissenter charges that the multitudinous sonnets come across as "simply chatter, though often of a literary sort . . . lying somewhere between entries in a personal diary and notes toward the making of a real, fully orchestrated series of poems" (Bromwich 37, 39). His art, as Lowell himself sadly admits, becomes "threadbare," a patchwork of slapdash, throwaway lines. Although the agon of sublimity took its toll on Lowell and on those close to him, he needed it, almost like a drug or the memory of a drug, to inspire his best work. His frenzied sparring with figurative and literal fathers was hellish, but, as Blake would say, heavenly, too. His poems of "battle and progress" were his strongest, even though the experiences behind them sapped his poetic gifts. His allegorical "one story" is a record of sublime triumphs—whether classical or Romantic, whether political, psychological, or religious—won in trials that proved to be defeating in the end.

Works Cited

Index

Works Cited

Many quotations come from uncollected material kept at the Robert Lowell archive at Harvard's Houghton Library. Because much of it is not dated and not paginated, I have given the file number of the folder or notebook in which the material appears and indicated with an "H" that the material comes from the Houghton Library. The abbreviations used to indicate Robert Lowell's works appear in the citations.

Allen, Gay Wilson. *Waldo Emerson*. New York: Viking, 1981.

Altieri, Charles. "Poetry in a Prose World." In *Profile of Robert Lowell*, edited by Jerome Mazzaro, 19–31. Columbus, Ohio: Charles E. Merrill, 1971.

Alvarez, A. "Robert Lowell in Conversation." In *Profile of Robert Lowell*, edited by Jerome Mazzaro, 32–40. Columbus, Ohio: Charles E. Merrill, 1971.

———. "A Talk with Robert Lowell." *Encounter* 24 (Feb. 1965): 39–43.

Arensberg, Mary, ed. *The American Sublime*. Albany: State Univ. of New York Press, 1986.

Axelrod, Steven Gould. *Robert Lowell, Life and Art*. Princeton: Princeton Univ. Press, 1978.

Barish, Evelyn. *Emerson, The Roots of Prophecy*. Princeton: Princeton Univ. Press, 1989.

Baudrillard, Jean. *Selected Writings*, edited by Mark Poster. Stanford: Stanford Univ. Press, 1988.

Bedient, Calvin. "Illegible Lowell (The Late Volumes)." In *Robert Lowell*, edited by Steven Gould Axelrod and Helen Deese, 139–55. Cambridge: Cambridge Univ. Press, 1968.

Bell, Vereen. *Robert Lowell, Nihilist as Hero*. Cambridge, Mass.: Harvard Univ. Press, 1983.

———. "Robert Lowell, 1917–1977." In *Robert Lowell*, edited by Jeffrey Meyers, 240–43. Ann Arbor: Univ. of Michigan Press, 1988.

Berryman, John. *The Freedom of the Poet*. New York: Farrar, Straus & Giroux, 1972.

Blake, William. *Complete Writings*, edited by Geoffrey Keynes. Oxford: Oxford Univ. Press, 1976.

Bloom, Harold. *A Map of Misreading*. New York: Oxford Univ. Press, 1975.

———. "The Year's Books." *The New Republic* 177 (Nov. 26, 1977): 24–26.

———. *Agon*. New York: Oxford Univ. Press, 1982.

———. *The American Religion*. New York: Simon & Schuster, 1992.

Bly, Robert. "Robert Lowell's *For the Union Dead*." In *Robert Lowell: A Portrait of the Artist in His Time*, edited by Michael London and Robert Boyers, 73–76. New York: David Lewis, 1970.

Bishop, Elizabeth. *The Complete Poems*. London: Chatto & Windus, 1970.

Breslin, James. *From Modern to Contemporary*. Chicago: Univ. of Chicago Press, 1984.

Bromwich, David. "Notebook." In *Robert Lowell*, edited by Harold Bloom, 35–40. New York: Chelsea House, 1987.

Brooks, Esther. "Remembering Cal." In *Robert Lowell*, edited by Jeffrey Meyers, 281–87. Ann Arbor: Univ. of Michigan Press, 1988.

Brown, Ashley. Letter to Henry Hart. Sept. 26, 1990.

Bunyan, John. *The Pilgrim's Progress*, edited by Roger Sharrock. Harmondsworth: Penguin, 1965.

Burke, Edmund. *A Philosophical Enquiry into the Origin of our Ideas of the Sublime and Beautiful*, edited by James T. Boulton. Notre Dame, Ind.: Notre Dame Univ. Press, 1968.

Calder, Alex. "*Notebook 1967–68:* Writing the Process Poem." In *Robert Lowell*, edited by Steven Gould Axelrod and Helen Deese, 117–38. Cambridge: Cambridge Univ. Press, 1986.

Carritt, E. F. *Philosophies of Beauty*. Oxford: Clarendon, 1931.

Chauncey, Charles. "Enthusiasm Described and Caution'd Against." In *Puritan Rhetoric: The Issue of Emotion in Religion*, by Eugene E. White, 103–16. Carbondale: Southern Illinois Univ. Press, 1972.

Clark, Blair. "On Robert Lowell." In *Robert Lowell*, edited by Jeffrey Meyers, 254–58. Ann Arbor: Univ. of Michigan Press, 1988.

Cosgrave, Patrick. *The Public Poetry of Robert Lowell*. London: Victor Gollancz, 1970.

Costello, Bonnie. *Elizabeth Bishop: Questions of Mastery*. Cambridge, Mass.: Harvard Univ. Press, 1991.

Diehl, Joanne Feit. "In the Twilight of the Gods: Woman Poets and the American Sublime." *The American Sublime*, edited by Mary Arensberg, 173–214. Albany: State Univ. of New York Press, 1986.

Eagleton, Terry. *The Ideology of the Aesthetic*. Oxford: Basil Blackwell, 1990.

———, "Vulgar, Vain and Venal." *TLS* 28 (1993): 7–8.

Ehrenpreis, Irvin. "The Age of Lowell." In *Robert Lowell: A Portrait of the Artist in His Time*, edited by Michael London and Robert Boyers, 155–86. New York: David Lewis, 1970.

Eliot, T. S. *Selected Poems*. New York: Harcourt, Brace & World, 1930.

———. *Four Quartets*. New York: Harcourt, Brace & World, 1943.

——. *Selected Prose*, edited by Frank Kermode. London: Faber, 1975.

Emerson, Ralph Waldo. *The Complete Works of Ralph Waldo Emerson*, edited by Edward Waldo Emerson. 12 vols. Boston: Houghton Mifflin, 1903–1904.

——. *The Collected Works of Ralph Waldo Emerson*. [*CW*], edited by Alfred R. Ferguson and Joseph Slater et al. 4 vols. to date. Cambridge, Mass.: Harvard Univ. Press, Belknap Press, 1971–.

Ferguson, Frances. "Appointments with Time." In *Robert Lowell*, edited by Harold Bloom, 59–72. New York: Chelsea House, 1987.

Fletcher, Angus. *Allegory*. Ithaca, N.Y.: Cornell Univ. Press, 1964.

Freeman, Barbara. "The Rise of the Sublime: Sacrifice and Misogyny in Eighteenth Century Aesthetics." *Yale Journal of Criticism* 5 (1992): 81–99.

Freud, Sigmund. *Totem and Taboo*. New York: Vintage, 1918.

——. "The Future of an Illusion." In *Standard Edition of Complete Psychological Works of Sigmund Freud*, vol. 11. London: Hogarth, 1961.

——. *A General Introduction to Psychoanalysis*. New York: Washington Square, 1961.

Frye, Northrop. *Anatomy of Criticism*. Princeton: Princeton Univ. Press, 1957.

——. *The Great Code*. New York: Harcourt, Brace, Jovanovich, 1982.

Gelpi, Albert. "The Reign of the Kingfisher." In *Robert Lowell*, edited by Steven Gould Axelrod and Helen Deese, 51–69. Cambridge: Cambridge Univ. Press, 1986.

Gilbert, Sandra. "Mephistophilis in Maine: Rereading 'Skunk Hour.'" In *Robert Lowell*, edited by Steven Gould Axelrod and Helen Deese, 70–79. Cambridge: Cambridge Univ. Press, 1986.

Gilson, Etienne. *The Spirit of Mediaeval Philosophy*, translated by A. H. C. Downes. New York: Charles Scribner's Sons, 1936.

——. *The Mystical Theology of Saint Bernard*. New York: Sheed & Ward, 1940.

Hamilton, Ian. *Robert Lowell*. London: Faber, 1982.

Hall, Donald. *The Weather of Poetry*. Ann Arbor: Univ. of Michigan Press, 1982.

Hardwick, Elizabeth. *Sleepless Nights*. New York: Random House, 1979.

Hecht, Anthony. *Obbligati*. New York: Atheneum, 1986.

——. "On Robert Lowell." Interview with Nancy Schoenberger. New York: New York Center for Visual History, 1987.

Hill, Geoffrey. *The Lords of Limit*. London: André Deutsch, 1984.

Hulme, T. E. *Speculations*. London: Routledge & Kegan Paul, 1924.

Jameson, Fredric. "Postmodernism, or The Cultural Logic of Late Capitalism." *New Left Review* 146 (1984): 53–92.

Jamison, Kay Redfield. *Touched with Fire*. New York: Free Press, 1993.

Jarrell, Randall. "From the Kingdom of Necessity." In *Robert Lowell: A Portrait of the Artist in His Time*, edited by Michael London and Robert Boyers, 19–27. New York: David Lewis, 1970.

——. "The Mills of the Kavanaughs." In *Robert Lowell: A Portrait of the Artist in His Time*, edited by Michael London and Robert Boyers, 38–43. New York, David Lewis: 1970.

Kalstone, David. *Becoming a Poet*. New York: Farrar, Straus & Giroux, 1989.

Kant, Immanuel. *The Critique of Judgement*, translated by James Creed Meredith. Oxford: Clarendon, 1952.

Kazin, Alfred. "From *New York Jew*." In *Robert Lowell*, edited by Jeffrey Meyers, 250–51. Ann Arbor: Univ. of Michigan Press, 1988.

Keats, John. *John Keats*, edited by Elizabeth Cook. New York: Oxford Univ. Press, 1990.

Knox, Ronald A. *Enthusiasm*. Oxford: Oxford Univ. Press, 1950.

Kramer, Lawrence. "Freud and the Skunks: Genre and Language in *Life Studies*." In *Robert Lowell*, edited by Steven Gould Axelrod and Helen Deese, 80–98. Cambridge: Cambridge Univ. Press, 1986.

Kronick, Joseph. "On the Border of History: Whitman and the American Sublime." In *The American Sublime*, edited by Mary Arensberg, 51–82. Albany: State Univ. of New York Press, 1986.

Kunitz, Stanley. "Talk with Robert Lowell." In *Profile of Robert Lowell*, edited by Jerome Mazzaro, 53–59. Columbus, Ohio: Charles E. Merrill, 1971.

———. "The Sense of a Life." In *Robert Lowell*, edited by Jeffrey Meyers, 230–35. Ann Arbor: Univ. of Michigan Press, 1988.

Larkin, Philip. *The Less Deceived*. London: Marvell, 1955.

Longinus. *On the Sublime*, translated by W. Hamilton Fyfe. Cambridge, Mass.: Harvard Univ. Press, 1932.

Lowell, Robert. "Dante's Inferno." *The Vindex* 59 (1935): 130–31.

———. "The True Light." *The Vindex* 59 (1935): 129–30.

———. "War: A Justification." *The Vindex* 59 (1935): 156–58.

———. "A Suicidal Fantasy." *Hika* (March 1939): 19.

———. "Maule's Curse." *Hika* (April 1939): 17–21.

———. "Sublime Feriam Sidera Vertice." *Hika* (Feb. 1940): 17.

———. "Moulding the Golden Spoon." *Hika* (June 1940): 8–35.

———. *Land of Unlikeness* [*LU*]. Cummington, Mass.: Cummington Press, 1944.

———. *Lord Weary's Castle and The Mills of the Kavanaughs* [*LWC; MK*]. New York: Harcourt, Brace & World, 1951.

———. *Life Studies and For the Union Dead* [*LS; FUD*]. New York: Farrar, Straus & Giroux, 1964.

———. "Visiting the Tates." *Sewanee Review* 68 (1965): 556–59.

———. *Near the Ocean* [*NO*]. New York: Farrar, Straus & Giroux, 1967.

———. *Notebook* [*N*]. New York: Farrar, Straus & Giroux, 1967.

———. *Prometheus Bound* [*PB*]. New York: Farrar, Straus & Giroux, 1969.

———. *The Dolphin* [*D*]. New York: Farrar, Straus & Giroux, 1973.

———. *For Lizzie and Harriet* [*FL&H*]. New York: Farrar, Straus & Giroux, 1973.

———. *History* [*H*]. New York: Farrar, Straus & Giroux, 1973.

———. *Day by Day* [*DD*]. New York: Farrar, Straus & Giroux, 1977.

———. *Collected Prose* [*CP*], edited by Robert Giroux. New York: Farrar, Straus & Giroux, 1987.

Lyotard, Jean-François. *The Postmodern Condition*. Minneapolis: Univ. of Minnesota Press, 1984.

———. *The Differend*. Minneapolis: Univ. of Minnesota Press, 1988.

———. *Peregrinations*. New York: Columbia Univ. Press, 1988.

Mailer, Norman. *The Armies of the Night*. New York: Signet, 1968.

Martin, Jay. "Grief and Nothingness: Loss and Mourning in Lowell's Poetry." In *Robert Lowell*, edited by Steven Gould Axelrod and Helen Deese, 26–50. Cambridge: Cambridge Univ. Press, 1986.

Mazzaro, Jerome. *The Poetic Themes of Robert Lowell*. Ann Arbor: Univ. of Michigan Press, 1965.

Melville, Herman. *Moby Dick*, edited by Alfred Kazin. Boston: Houghton Miflin, 1956.

———. *Poems. The Works of Herman Melville, Standard Edition*, vol. 16. New York: Russell & Russell, 1963.

Michelson, Bruce. "Randall Jarrell and Robert Lowell." In *Robert Lowell*, edited by Harold Bloom, 139–61. New York: Chelsea House, 1987.

Miller, Perry. *Jonathan Edwards*. New York: William Sloane, 1949.

Monk, Samuel. *The Sublime*. New York: MLA, 1935.

Morris, David. *The Religious Sublime*. Lexington: Univ. Press of Kentucky, 1972.

Norris, Christopher. *What's Wrong with Postmodernism*. Baltimore: Johns Hopkins Univ. Press, 1990.

Parker, Francis. "Brantwood Camp." In *Robert Lowell*, edited by Jeffrey Meyers, 252–53. Ann Arbor: Univ. of Michigan Press, 1988.

Pease, Donald. "Sublime Politics." In *The American Sublime*, edited by Mary Arensberg, 21–50. Albany: State Univ. of New York Press, 1986.

———. *Visionary Compacts*. Madison: Univ. of Wisconsin Press, 1987.

Perloff, Marjorie. "*Poètes Maudits* of the Genteel Tradition." In *Robert Lowell*, edited by Steven Gould Axelrod and Helen Deese, 99–116. Cambridge: Cambridge Univ. Press, 1986.

Plath, Sylvia. *Ariel*. New York: Harper & Row, 1965.

———. *Collected Poems*, edited by Ted Hughes. London: Faber, 1981.

Pound, Ezra. *Selected Poems*. New York: New Directions, 1926.

Quilligan, Maureen. *The Language of Allegory*. Ithaca, N.Y.: Cornell Univ. Press, 1979.

Ramazani, Jahan. "Yeats: Tragic Joy and the Sublime." *PMLA* 104 (1989): 163–77.

Ransom, John Crowe. *World's Body*. New York: Charles Scribner's Sons, 1938.

———. "Artists, Soldiers, Positivists." *Kenyon Review* 6 (1944): 276–81.

———. *Beating the Bushes*. New York: New Directions, 1972.

Roberts, David. *Jean Stafford*. Boston: Little, Brown, 1988.

Schou, Mogens. "Special Review of Lithium in Psychiatric Therapy and Prophylaxis." In *Manic-Depressive Illness*, edited by Edward A. Wolpert, 357–96. New York: International Universities Press, 1977.

Seidel, Frederick. "The Art of Poetry." In *Robert Lowell*, edited by Jeffrey Meyers, 48–73. Ann Arbor: Univ. of Michigan Press, 1988.

Shaftesbury, Earl of. "A Letter Concerning Enthusiasm." In *Characteristics of Men, Manners, Opinions, Times, etc*, edited by John Robertson, vol. 1. Gloucester: Peter Smith, 1963.

Shapiro, Gary. "From the Sublime to the Political." *New Literary History* 2 (1985): 213–36.

Standerwick, DeSales. "Notes on Robert Lowell." In *Profile of Robert Lowell*, edited by Jerome Mazzaro, 3–12. Columbus, Ohio: Charles E. Merrill, 1971.

Staples, Hugh. *Robert Lowell, The First Twenty Years*. London: Faber, 1962.

Stevens, Wallace. *Letters of Wallace Stevens*, edited by Holly Stevens. New York: Knopf, 1972.

———. *The Collected Poems*. [*CP*]. New York: Vintage, 1982.

Tate, Allen. *Collected Essays*. Denver: Alan Swallow, 1959.

Taylor, Peter. Letter to Henry Hart. Dec. 12, 1990.

Thompson, John. "On Robert Lowell." Interview with Nancy Schoenberger. New York: New York Center for Visual History, 1986.

Tillinghast, Richard. "Robert Lowell in the Sixties." In *Robert Lowell*, edited by Jeffrey Meyers, 261–65. Ann Arbor: Univ. of Michigan Press, 1988.

Veitch, Jonathan. "'Moonlight in the Prowling Eye': The *History* Poems of Robert Lowell." *Contemporary Literature* 33 (1992): 458–79.

Vendler, Helen. *Part of Nature, Part of Us*. Cambridge, Mass.: Harvard Univ. Press, 1980.

Wallingford, Katherine. *Robert Lowell's Language of the Self*. Chapel Hill: Univ. of North Carolina Press, 1988.

Warren, Robert Penn. *Selected Poems, 1923–1975*. London: Secker & Warburg, 1976.

Weiskel, Thomas. *The Romantic Sublime*. Baltimore: Johns Hopkins Univ. Press, 1986.

Williamson, Alan. *Pity the Monsters*. New Haven: Yale Univ. Press, 1974.

———. "The Reshaping of 'Waking Early Sunday Morning.'" *Agenda* 3 (1980): 47–62.

———. "Robert Lowell: A Reminiscence." In *Robert Lowell*, edited by Jeffrey Meyers, 266–73. Ann Arbor: Univ. of Michigan Press, 1988.

Wilson, Rob. *American Sublime: The Genealogy of a Poetic Genre*. Madison: Univ. of Wisconsin Press, 1991.

Winters, Yvor. *Maule's Curse*. Norfolk, Va.: New Directions, 1938.

Wordsworth, William. *Selected Poems and Prefaces*, edited by Jack Stillinger. Boston: Houghton Mifflin, 1965.

Yeats, William Butler. *The Poems*, edited by Richard J. Finneran. New York: Macmillan, 1983.

Yenser, Stephen. *Circle to Circle*. Berkeley: Univ. of California Press, 1975.

Young, Dudley. "Life with Lord Lowell at Essex U." In *Robert Lowell*, edited by Jeffrey Meyers, 312–17. Ann Arbor: Univ. of Michigan Press, 1988.

Index